CU00778984

Tomorrow's Transaction
The 2012 Reader

A selection of posts from the
Tomorrow's Transactions Blog from 2011/2012

By David G.W. Birch
Edited by Angela Doyle

Published in the United Kingdom in 2012 by:

Mastodon Press
Tweed House,
12 The Mount,
Guildford,
Surrey,
GU2 4HN.
England.
http://www.mastodonpress.com/

ISBN
Paperback: 978-0-9569236-0-8
Kindle: 978-0-9569236-1-5

Printed in Great Britain by CPI Group (UK) Ltd, Croydon, CR0 4YY

You can contact Consult Hyperion at:
Consult Hyperion
Tweed House,
12 The Mount,
Guildford,
Surrey, GU2 4HN,
England.
Telephone: +44 (0) 1483 301 793
Fax: +44 (0) 1483 561 657
info@chyp.com
http://www.chyp.com

Contents

PREFACE 4

PART 1 – PEOPLE 6

CHAPTER 1: IDENTIFICATION AND AUTHENTICATION 7
CHAPTER 2: SOCIAL MEDIA AND ORGANISATIONS 33
CHAPTER 3: POLITICAL, LEGAL AND REGULATORY 48

PART 2 – NETWORKS 57

CHAPTER 4: FINANCE AND BANKING 58
CHAPTER 5: RETAIL AND TRANSPORT.. 124
CHAPTER 6: PUBLIC SECTOR AND NGOS 171
CHAPTER 7: TELECOMS AND MEDIA 179

PART 3 – MONEY 197

CHAPTER 8: HISTORY AND FUTURE 198
CHAPTER 9: PAYMENT SYSTEMS.. 213
CHAPTER 10: CASH REPLACEMENT 268

GLOSSARY 282

INDEX 285

Preface

There is a real challenge confronting any consultancy that wants a blog. How do you talk about cool stuff without giving up your customer's secrets? In our case, because Consult Hyperion's position is based on thought leadership, it is doubly problematic. We want to be seen as being at the forefront of the secure electronic transaction space (everywhere from mobile payments to contactless ticketing to virtual identity to electronic government) but we cannot talk about any of the projects that we are working on and excited about until they are announced to the public, at which point everyone will know about them!

These constraints do tend make writing the blog (on occasion!) a tightrope walk balancing legal (and moral!) responsibilities on one hand and the need to produce posts that people actually want to read on the other. I hope I have managed to do that in the posts selected for this blook as well as for the blog as a whole. I also hope I am right in judging that integrity is the key to the blog's "voice". When I am critical of products or services I am honestly and openly and constructively critical. Conversely, praise is similarly genuine and not PR.

With all that said, I trust you will enjoy the latest collection. In response to comments received over the last couple of years, we have decided to bring together the *Digital Money Reader* and the *Digital Identity Reader* into this single *Tomorrow's Transactions Reader*. It no longer made sense to produce the two separate volumes when so many of the issues discussed span the two topics and are of interest to people looking from either perspective. Integrating this content has necessitated restructuring the blog categories (which in turn form the Chapter breakdown for this Reader). I've chosen a breakdown that focuses on the interaction between people, technology and money. More specifically, a breakdown that explores Consult Hyperion's long held vision of the future of transactions at the intersection of people, networks and money. Or, to put it another way, digital identity, digital networks and digital money.

Digital **networks**, the exploitation of new information and communications technologies, cover a very wide field indeed. We are only interested in digital networks when they are put to use in the four particular areas (finance, communications, retail and transport, public sector and NGOs) where the nature of transactions is being changed at an amazing rate and where Consult Hyperion's experiences from around the world might be useful, and where they interact with **people** and **money** to create the new fields of digital money and digital identity, the fields where Consult Hyperion's goal is thought leadership.

About the author:

David G.W. Birch is a Director of Consult Hyperion, the IT management consultancy that specialises in electronic transactions. Here he provides specialist consultancy support to clients around the world, including all of the leading payment brands, major telecommunications providers, government bodies and international organisations including the OECD. Before helping to found Consult Hyperion in 1986, he spent several years working as a consultant in Europe, the Far East and North America. He graduated from the University of Southampton with a B.Sc (Hons.) in Physics.

Described at the Oxford Internet Institute as "one of Britain's most acute observers of the internet and social networks", in The Telegraph as "one of the world's leading experts on digital money", in The Independent as a "grade-A geek", by the Centre for the Study of Financial Innovation as "one of the most user-friendly of the UK's uber-techies" and in Financial World as "mad", Dave is a member of the editorial board of the E-Finance & Payments Law and Policy, a columnist for SPEED and well-known for his thought leadership blogging and podcasting at *Tomorrow's Transactions*.

He has lectured to MBA level on the impact of new information and communications technologies, contributed to publications ranging from the Parliamentary IT Review to Prospect and Financial World. He wrote a Guardian column for many years. He is a media commentator on electronic business issues and has appeared on BBC television and radio, Sky and other channels around the world.

Acknowledgement:

This blook was only made possible by the hard work of Angela Doyle at Consult Hyperion. All I did was to suggest the posts to be included: everything else is down to her and I can't thank her enough. Dave Birch, February 2012.

Part 1 – People

Chapter 1: Identification and Authentication

It's really hard to work out what to do about digital identity. Should people be forced to use one digital identity, or should they be allowed many? Should that one be in their "real" identity or not? Instead of deal with a complex topic properly, we seem to be switching between being paralyzed on one hand and panicked into making bad decisions on the other. One of the reasons for the complexity of the topic, I am sure, is that identity doesn't mean the same thing in the virtual world as in the mundane. Online identity is richer, more complex and more sophisticated than mundane identity. Unfortunately, both governments and businesses have yet to make the paradigm shift (I'm using the phrase in its genuine sense here, in the sense of a model of reality) and remain trapped in computer age implementation of cardboard age concepts when there is a desperate need for a communications age vision. I hope some of these posts will help to explain why and provide some of that vision.

Do we really want a panic button? - 02/04/2011

The relationship between identity and privacy is deep: privacy (in the sense of control over data associated with an identity) ought to be facilitated by the identity infrastructure. But that control cannot be absolute: society needs a balance in order to function, so the infrastructure ought to include a mechanism for making that balance explicit. It is very easy to set the balance in the wrong place even with the best of intentions. And once the balance is set in the wrong place, it may have most undesirable consequences.

> *An obsession with child protection in the UK and throughout the EU is encouraging a cavalier approach to law-making, which less democratic regimes are using to justify much broader repression on any speech seen as extreme or dangerous...*
>
> *[From Net censors use UK's kid-safety frenzy to justify clampdown • The Register]*

So a politician in one country decides, say, that we should all be able to read out neighbour's emails just in case our neighbour is a pervert or serial killer and the next thing we know is that Iranian government supporters in the UK are reading their neighbours emails and passing on their details to a hit squad if the emails contain any anti-regime comments.

> *By requiring law enforcement backdoors, we open ourselves to*
> *surveillance by hackers and foreign intelligence agencies*

[From slight paranoia: Web 2.0 FBI]

This is, of course, absolutely correct, and it was shown in relief today
when I read that…

> *Someday soon, when pro-democracy campaigners have their*
> *cellphones confiscated by police, they'll be able to hit the "panic*
> *button"—a special app that will both wipe out the phone's*
> *address book and emit emergency alerts to other activists… one*
> *of the new technologies the U.S. State Department is promoting*
> *to equip pro-democracy activists in countries ranging from the*
> *Middle East to China with the tools to fight back against*
> *repressive governments.*

[From U.S. develops panic button for democracy activists |
Reuters]

Surely this also means that terrorists about to execute a dastardly plot in
the US will be able to wipe their mobile phones and alert their co-
conspirators when the FBI knock on the door and, to use the emotive
example, that child pornographers will be able to wipe their phones and
alert fellow abusers when the police come calling. Tough choices indeed.
We want to protect individual freedom so we must create private space.
And yet we still need some kind of "smash the glass" option, because
criminals do use the interweb tubes and there are legitimate law
enforcement and national security interests here. Perhaps, however, the
way forward to move away from the idea of balance completely.

> *In my own area of study, the familiar trope of "balancing privacy*
> *and security" is a source of constant frustration to privacy*
> *advocates, because while there are clearly sometimes tradeoffs*
> *between the two, it often seems that the zero-sum rhetoric of*
> *"balancing" leads people to view them as always in conflict. This*
> *is, I suspect, the source of much of the psychological appeal of*
> *"security theatre".*

[From The Trouble With "Balance" Metaphors]

This is a great point, and when I read it it immediately helped me to think
more clearly. There is no evidence that taking away privacy improves
security, so it's purely a matter of security theatre.

> *Retaining telecommunications data is no help in fighting crime,*
> *according to a study of German police statistics, released*

Thursday. Indeed, it could even make matters worse... This is because users began to employ avoidance techniques, says AK Vorrat.

[*From Retaining Data Does Not Help Fight Crime, Says Group - PCWorld*]

This is precisely the trajectory that we will all be following. The twin pressures from Big Content and law enforcement mean that the monitoring, recording and analysis of internet traffic is inevitable. But it will also be largely pointless, as my own recent experiences have proven. When I was in China, I wanted to use Twitter but it was blocked. So I logged in to a VPN back in the UK and twittered away. When I wanted to listen to the football on Radio 5 while in Spain, the BBC told me that I couldn't, so I logged back in to my VPN and cheered the Blues. When I want to watch "The Daily Show" from the UK or when I want to watch "The Killing" via iPlayer in the US, I just go via VPN.

I'm surprised more ISPs don't offer this as value-added service themselves. I already pay £100 per month for my Virgin triple-play (50Mb/s broadband, digital TV and telephone, so another £5 per month for OpenVPN would suit me fine).

Wallets, brokers and auctions - 05/04/2011

There was an involved discussion about convergence of transaction platforms on a project that I am involved with and it set me thinking about what convergence actually means in this space and what the impact of that convergence might be. I started by remembering something that I'd read at Payments Views.

A couple of weeks ago, eBay held an Analyst Day where eBay senior management shared their thinking about the future of the changing commerce landscape – and how they're thinking about taking the "e" out of eCommerce... What's this taking out the "e" business all about? It's about the influence of mobile on integrating online and offline commerce together.

[*From The PayPal*]

Scott is typically accurate with his comments hereafter. The strategic direction is convergence. Not the simplistic kind of convergence, where our mobile phones become watches, cameras, wallets and devices for getting stones out of horses hooves. This simply hasn't happened. Sometimes I use my iPhone, sometime my iPhone, sometimes my MacBook Pro, sometimes my MacBook Air, sometimes my Apple TV (spot a bit of a theme here?) and sometimes I still walk into a store to buy things. The point is that the strategic direction of transactions is convergence so that whichever of these channels I use, I use the same digital money and digital identity infrastructure. It's the transactions that become integrated, not the devices. And by integrating across channels, the transaction systems give me a better service, whether in terms of loyalty, fraud protection, price or whatever. I then continued by remembering a good report on e-payments that I'd read a couple of months ago.

> A new O'Reilly/PayPal report on web-native payment platforms, *"ePayments: Emerging Platforms, Embracing Mobile and Confronting Identity,"* is now available for download. Among the topics covered in the report are the rise of payment platforms, the mobilization of money, and the advent of contactless payment in mobile commerce.

> *[From 3 mobile payment products hint at the future - O'Reilly Radar]*

The thought experiment in the O'Reilly Radar "report about auctioning payments set me thinking. The idea is that, rather as advertising networks such as DoubleClick auction page impressions to advertisers in real-time (when you click on a page, the advertising network sends the details to advertisers who get 20 milliseconds to respond with a bid, and then the advertisement from the highest bidder is displayed) so when you click on "pay", the payment platform might bundle together some facts about the transaction and auction them to processors. Presumably, one of the key elements in the bid decision would be related to fraud, especially if the pricing for the fraud management is unbundled from the pricing for the transaction itself and any other value-added services.

If this analysis is correct, then there will be a premium on identity and authentication because the higher the standard of identification that can be provided to the processors, the lower the bid! This would mean - to continue the thought experiment - that we would have a very accurate means of pricing identities. I imagine that this accurate pricing would reveal at least two interesting things. First of all, whether an identity is "real" or not is immaterial to the price, because the price will be based mainly on reputation (ie, transaction history). Secondly, the strength of the authentication will be directly reflected in price but for smaller transactions the price increments from 2FA to 3FA will be minimal. Thus, pricing will point towards pseudonymous 2FA as the "sweet spot" for transactional identities. So far, so good. Can we use this analysis to make some predictions about who might be best-placed to take advantage of this converged platform then? Well, last year I read that (all other things being equal) then it really should be the mobile operators. Qualcomm call these "horizontal models" for mobile operator value-added services - what I would call the "smart pipe" future of the mobile operator - and say that if operators do make a play in delivering intelligent services now, the potential upsides are great because...

> They will strategically position themselves as a valued service provider to their subscribers - getting the retail experience right on mobile will be critical to capturing value;
>
> They can act as an honest broker - trusted, secure, in their interests to protect and cater to their users' needs;
>
> They stand to gain from the uptick in usage as well as providing services using their billing platforms and the knowledge of their subscribers;
>
> The potential of data analytics to turn digital footprints into value for consumers, MNOs and other players that have been cited in the two sided business model begins to emerge.
>
> [From Mobile]

I think this is broadly correct—especially the part about the honest broker, protecting the "real" identity of the consumers—and I think it means that operators must be more aggressive about their digital identity infrastructure as well as their digital money infrastructure. After all, who has this "retailing experience that is not tied to any one operating system"? The mobile operators do, but so does Apple. On the other hand, the mobile operators have a direct billing relationship with customers (and they know where they are). It's time for the operators to start talking to processors about creating the mobile transaction auction house.

Reputation does not depend on "real" identity - 12/04/2011

OK, at the extreme risk of boring everyone to tears, let's ask the same old question again: should you be allowed to do things on the Internet without giving away your "real" identity? Remember this was something that was discussed here a little while back, using the simple case of newspaper comments as an example. Someone has come up with an interesting way of solving for two problems simultaneously: paying for news online and making people responsible for their comments...

> However, he recently went back and was surprised that, in order to comment you need to hand over your credit card, and the paper will charge you $0.99. Obviously, this is more to prove that you are who you say you are, but it does seem a bit distorted

when the newspaper wants to charge people just to comment. Also, once charged, your name and hometown are automatically associated with your comments.

[From <u>Newspaper Wants You To Pay To Comment | Techdirt</u>]

Interesting. I think the idea of paying to comment is very interesting. I might be tempted to do that in some cases. But paying to give up your real name? I'm not so sure. I might well want to comment on something without that kind of disclosure. Back to "real names" again. The discussion goes on and on.

Why does a comment with a real name have so much more value?

[From <u>The Real "Authenticity Killer" (and an aside about how bad the Yahoo brand has gotten) — Scobleizer</u>]

This isn't always true. A nurse at a hospital, forced to comment with her real name, is highly unlikely to post anything critical of a doctor. There's a difference between an authenticated persona (so that the web site can be sure she really is a nurse at the hospital) that may be based on a pseduonym (or even a cryptographically strong unconditionally unlinkable anonym) and an authenticated identity. There may be many reasons why the latter is undesirable.

Mexico announced a plan Monday to reward people who report suspected money laundering, under a program that will allow them to get up to one-quarter of any illicit funds or property seized. Under the new plan, people can file reports in person, by telephone or by e-mail. The exact percentage of individual rewards will be determined case by case by a special committee.

[From <u>Mexico sets rewards for reporting money laundering | ajc.com</u>]

Would you e-mail in a tip about a suspected money launderer and expect to pick up the reward? It seems to me that this is a good example of system that demands real names for integrity but real names mean it can never work. (Although, and it's outside the scope of this piece, it is entirely cryptographically possible to enable the payment of rewards to anonymous people).

Public servants, law enforcement and banking system employees will not be eligible for the rewards, in part because it is already their duty to report suspicious transactions.

[From Mexico sets rewards for reporting money laundering | ajc.com]

Good luck to anyone who decides to report in person, or by telephone. SIM registration is mandatory in Mexico, which means that the money launderers will find you before the police do—don't forget, they have more money than the police do. Come to that, they have more money than anyone does.

> *More shocking, and more important, the bank was sanctioned for failing to apply the proper anti-laundering strictures to the transfer of $378.4bn – a sum equivalent to one-third of Mexico's gross national product – into dollar accounts from so-called casas de cambio (CDCs) in Mexico, currency exchange houses with which the bank did business.*
>
> *[From How a big US bank laundered billions from Mexico's murderous drug gangs | World news | The Observer]*

Given the stringent anti-money laundering (AML) regulations in place around the globe—which meant it took me 15 minutes to put a few quid on my Travelex prepaid card at Heathrow, something I will never do again—I'm surprised that this could have happened, but there you go. Perhaps instead of hassling people trying to load low-value prepaid payment accounts, the authorities could focus on the counterparties in larger electronic transfers. Hence the discussions about Legal Entity Identifiers (LEIs) that have been going on recently. Many interbank payment messages have account identifiers only—you could send money to my account with the name Carlos Tevez and it would still get to me because it's only the account stuff that matters—and the some law enforcement agencies want to stop this and have banks validate the names as well (it will help to track funds to and from suspects I guess).

> *LEI will be assigned at the over all corporate entity level and also at subsidiary levels. Its usage will be standardized Internationally. My immediate thought was, never mind systemic risk, this is the perfect means to route B2B transactions across a myriad of financial systems and payment schemes worldwide!*
>
> *[From Reflections on NACHA Payments 2011 — Payments Views from Glenbrook Partners]*

I'm sure I'd heard somewhere before, possibly at IPS 2010, that the plan was to use the SWIFT business identifier codes (BICs), but apparently that's no longer the case.

Vandenreydt said SWIFT is changing its tune due to a recent meeting of the International Standardization Organization's Technical Committee 68, where SWIFT has a seat. At the meeting, participants concluded that developing a new code would help avoid ambiguities that might be involved if existing codes are used. "[The committee] wants a pure number without country or other information," Vandenreydt added. The BIC is made up of eight to 11 alphanumeric characters with four letters for the bank, two letters for the country, two digits for the location, and three digits for the specific branch.

The utility is still working with ISO on what the identifier would look like. Vandenreydt said that process could take up to three months, though he expects a decision to be made sooner. He noted the proposal also depends on other details about the initiative that haven't been specified by OFR, such as how long the registration authority would have to ramp up the system, whether IDs will be assigned or requested, and how many codes are expected.

[From SWIFT]

So here's a positive suggestion. Forget about the 1960s notion of an identifier as a unique alphanumeric code and instead make the identifier a pseudonym attested by a bank. So we become consult.hyperion!barclays.co.uk or something similar. It doesn't matter whether the sender, or anyone else, knows who Consult Hyperon is, because the identifier tells them that Barclays does. And for 99% of real-world transactions, that's enough. What's important is that we are always consult.hyperion!barclays.co.uk in all relevant linked transactions. Then, if consult.hyperion!barclays.co.uk is found to be sending money to Osama bin Laden on a regular basis, the appropriate law enforcement agencies can provide Barclays with a warrant and Barclays will disclose. For general commerce, the persistence is the critical foundation. The always-accurate Eve Maler pointed this out a while back:

The neat thing is, we do this all the time already. When you meet someone face-to-face and they say their Skype handle is KoolDood, and later a KoolDood asks to connect with you on Skype and describes the circumstances of your meeting, you have a reasonable expectation it's the right guy ever after. And it's precisely the way persistent pseudonyms work in federated identity: as I've pointed out before, a relying-party website might not know you're a dog, but it usually needs to know you're the same dog as last time.

[From Tofu, online trust, and spiritual wisdom | Pushing String]

Quite. But there's another point. You don't need to be a "real" persistent identity to have a reputation, as should be obvious. A useful reminder of this came at the end of 2010, when an anonymous critic was named the Village Voice's "Music Critic of the Year".

> *Twitter spokesperson Matt Graves called it a "milestone"; whether he's serious or not, ("dead serious," he later said) @discographies certainly carries a certain seriousness throughout today's interview in the Village Voice.*

[From Anonymous Twitter]

I'm not sure that meritocracy is the right word, but I think the sentiment is accurate: you have to earn reputation to attach to your identifier, and once it's been earned it's hard to replicate (unlike intellectual property). So I might want to send money to @discographies without knowing or caring whether @discographies is a roomful of students or an internationally-known music critic. (And, over on Digital Money, I will point out that I want to send money to @dgwbirch—which is an entirely unique Twitter identifier—by MasterCard, PayPal, WebMoney, M-PESA or anything else, but that's another point entirely.) Why can't @discographies be mutated into discographics!wellsfargo.com or whatever?

It's an entirely plausible model: banks managing reputation, because it's more important than money. The presence of banks legitimises the market, so knowing that a bank has carried out some KYC on @discographies means that other players can treat the reputation attached to it seriously without being concerned about the "real" identity.

Should we identifty prepaid product users? - 20/04/2011

At last year's conference on *The Macroeconomics of Mobile* held at Columbia University in April 2010, Carol van Cleef (a partner at Paton Boggs LLP in Washington) gave a presentation on the "Opportunities and Dangers of E-Payments", in which she noted that the Mumbai terrorists used mobile phones and "showed themselves to be part of the mobile phone generation" (as, I imagine, they showed themselves to be part of the mass transit generation and the automatic weapons generation). She notes that the attackers were using their own phones (so the IMEIs could be tracked, making the life of law enforcement easier) and that they had purchased more than 37 SIMs in different names using false identification (so the compulsory SIM registration was shown to be pointless—although some of the SIM card sellers were arrested). She also says that the most critical tool for drug traffickers in Canada is the prepaid phone (I'm sure she's wrong: I'll bet its either cash or cars).

I remember thinking when I read this at the time that this continued law enforcement focus on the prepaid phone and the prepaid card, both of which are critical tools for financial inclusion, would end up with restrictions on both that would make no difference to criminals but would make life much harder for the financially excluded, because of the strong link between identity and money.

Why do I think that? Well it is just not clear to me that demanding strong proof of identity for prepaid products will help. In Mexico there is a national registry for prepaid phones and all purchasers are recorded and fingerprinted, the operators keep calls logs, texts and voice mail for a year (in a database only accessible with a court order—or by criminals, I'd wager). All prepaid phones not in the registry were supposed to be turned off this month, although a quick round of googling and searching couldn't tell me whether this is actually happening or not. As I wrote a couple of weeks ago, in the context of the Mexican government's reward scheme for people who call in reports of money laundering:

> *Good luck to anyone who decides to report in person, or by telephone. SIM registration is mandatory in Mexico, which means that the money launderers will find you before the police do*

[From Reputation does not depend on "real" identity]

If we focus on phones, for a moment, is it reasonable to assume that demanding identity in the purchase of phones (prepaid or otherwise) will do anything to reduce crime (or will it simply shift the crime to acquiring identities and actually raise the criminal premium on those identities?).

> *Eight men and one woman have been arrested on suspicion of conspiracy to defraud... calling expensive premium-rate numbers owned by the fraudsters that charge up to £10 a minute... O2 had a total of £1.2m stolen through premium phone lines throughout July, with police claiming that a West African gang bought the phones from high street stores using false identities.*

[From British police arrest iPhone]

Like many similar scams, this isn't a mobile fraud or a payment fraud or any other kind of fraud: it's basic identity fraud, yet again. To some extent, therefore, one has to be a tiny bit unsympathetic to O2. Clearly, if they make everyone jump through hoops to get an iPhone then they won't sell very many of them. On the other hand, allowing people to take out contracts without really proving who they are or (and this is the commercial arrangement that is lacking) providing an identity that is underwritten by someone who will take liability for it being wrong, means accepting risk. Remember, it's not the mobile operators, handset manufacturers or criminals who pay for the police raids, the court system, and the prison time: it's us, the taxpayer. So the distribution of risks is not aligned with the distribution of liabilities, as is so often the case in the world of identity fraud. This isn't a UK-only problem. It is very clear that in countries without secure national identity registers (ie, almost all countries), requiring mobile operators to determine the identity of subscribers (contract or prepaid) will solve nothing. This does not, by the way, mean that it is impossible to catch criminals. Far from it.

> *Deputy District Attorney Mena Guirguis said that after Manunga and her former boyfriend stopped dating in 2008, she took out a pre-paid cell phone in his sister-in-law's name, and started sending the threatening text messages to her regular cell phone… Her scheme was uncovered when the victims went to the phone store, talked with the salesman and learned that Manunga had bought the pre-paid phone under the sister-in-law's name, Guirguis said.*

> *[From <u>Woman jailed for making threats – to herself | sister, law, manunga - News - The Orange</u>]*

What this story shows is that actual police work is helped by the perps using mobile phones, even if you don't know the identity of the person using the phone, because phones mean tracking and tracing and location. We read today that iPhones keep a complete record of everywhere they've been…

> *Apple iPhone users' movements are being tracked and stored without their knowledge in a file that could easily be accessed by a snooping employer or jealous spouse.*

> *[From <u>Apple</u>]*

Surely it would be better to have criminals running around with iPhones, sending money to each other using mobile networks and generally becoming data points in the internet of things than to set rigorous, quite pointless identity barriers to keep them hidden.

Let's not panic about online identity – 29/07/2011

There's an increasing moral panic about online identity underway, and it's resulting in some very strange proposals for unenforceable legislation. I've been reading about one such example in the UK called "Clare's Law".

According to the Mail on Sunday, Theresa May, the Home Secretary, has indicated in a letter that she is considering the idea.

[From Government considers 'Clare's Law' - Telegraph]

I didn't really read the rest of it, but I assume the idea is that when you click on an online newspaper article at, let's say, the Daily Mirror or the Daily Mail, then you are automatically connected to some kind of police database that will tell you whether the reporter has been arrested or imprisoned for phone hacking or whether, let's say, Trinity Mirror or Associated Newspapers have been involved in any underhand news-gathering techniques. If I thought for one moment that implementing laws like this would actually stop women being murdered or children being bullied to death, then I would support it wholeheartedly. But they won't. In fact, as far as I can tell from the statistics, widespread internet use in the UK has led to a reduction in the number of murders. Pointless knee-jerk legislation around poorly-understood technologically-uninformed debate is not solely a British phenomenon.

He recommended the introduction of an "Internet Driving License" in schools that would explain the dangers of Facebook

[From Germany considers banning wild Facebook]

Now it's a bit harsh to pick on Facebook, but the truth is that teenagers (from my personal experience) understand perfectly well how Facebook works, so this is almost certainly unnecessary. But if there was an Internet Driving License that you had to use to log in to web sites, that would almost certainly make the situation far worse, since this website would now know exactly who you are, and this information would then be freely obtained by perverts, the secret police, News International or whoever else wants to pry. Why is this better than anonymity (which doesn't exist anyway - look what happened to the not-Anonymous-at-all hackers). As I have posted at boring length and with tedious repetition, this is the wrong way to go.

Most websites don't need or even want or need to manage the identities of their users—they simply want a way to reliably identify their users over time.

[From Facebook]

Indeed. So I could use my Facebook identity "Dixie Flatline" to do all the sorts of things I need to do online, and everything would work fine. Google could show me the right search results, The Telegraph could show me the right adverts. But wait...

He also talks about his decision to become the first outside investor in Facebook. The two things that stuck out for him about Facebook were: a) the fact that this was the first site where people logged in with their real identities, and so it had the potential to be an identity layer for the web

[From Peter Thiel: If I'd Known, I Would Never Have Started PayPal]

None of my Facebook identities are in my real name, so I'm not sure about this. And I'm absolutely not sure about the implicit judgement that only my "real" identity should be allowed or valued.

I remembered Gresham's Law from my business school days explaining why 'bad' money drives out good money... It seems bad identity, like bad money, drives out good identity.

[From Why bad Identity drives out good identity]

Well, I'm not sure about this analysis either. They're talking about using Facebook Connect to make it easy to log in to comment on various newspaper sites. I wanted to take advantage of the convenience of using Facebook to log in and comment in various places, so naturally I did what any normal person would do and I created a synthetic person. I made up a name, got an e-mail address, made up a few details—schools attended, that kind of thing—and hit OK. My synthetic person has, at the time of writing, got two friends already (I sent friend requests to everyone who attended the university that my imaginary person had pretended to go to, and two of them accepted, so I sent requests to their friends and now my entirely synthetic persona has five friends!).

Anyway, I'm quite happy having my "business" persona for commenting on things to do with work and a quite separate "citizen" persona for taking part in political debates, being rude about celebrities and asking questions on technical issues where I don't want to reveal who I am. I'm not pretending to be someone else, which is a different issue entirely (and, of course, wrong).

Fouad Mourtada was arrested on 5 February on suspicion of stealing the identity of Prince Moulay Rachid, younger brother of King Mohammed VI... Mr Mourtada was convicted of "villainous practices linked to the alleged theft of the [prince's] identity".

[From BBC NEWS | World | Africa | Jail for Facebook]

My synthetic identity isn't really anonymous. If I used that identity to bully a schoolgirl to death, then I would hope that it wouldn't take the police more than five minutes to get a warrant to find out from Facebook what e-mail address is used, which IP addresses I've logged in from, and so forth. In an hour or two they would be knocking on the door to arrest me.

> *Randi Zuckerberg wants to eliminate the freedom to post anonymously online. "I think people hide behind anonymity and they feel like they can say whatever they want behind closed doors," Randi said.*

> *[From Facebook]*

Either Peter or Rachel must be wrong, but whatever. Either Facebook uses real names as Peter says, or it doesn't, as Rachel says. But "real names" in any case are a useless "pointer" to a real person.

> *Mark S. Zuckerberg, an Indianapolis bankruptcy attorney, might not consider Facebook founder Mark Zuckerberg to be a friend. That's because the world's largest social networking website has shut down the lawyer's personal Facebook account... "I was originally denied an account with Facebook two years ago because of my name, and I had to send them copies of my driver's license, birth certificate and Indianapolis Bar Assn. license just to get them to believe that I exist and to allow me to set up my page".*

> *[From Facebook]*

That doesn't sound like a terribly cost-effective identity management system to me, so I don't know that an Internet Drivers License based on Facebook will necessarily sweep the web (although that's not to say that Facebook couldn't be a useful Identity Providers in an NSTIC structure). So what's the deal with the "anonymity" that doesn't actually exist? You'd have to be a pretty stupid criminal to use Facebook to commit a crime.

> *Ashley Mitchell, 29, broke into the Zynga mainframe, stole the identity of two employees and transferred chips said to be worth more than £7m to him... the company became aware in August 2009 that large amounts of chips were vanishing and suspected the two employees whose identities Mitchell had adopted. However, investigators then realised the system had been hacked and narrowed the search to Paignton. Mitchell's neighbours had their computers seized because he was "piggy-backing" on their unsecured Wi-Fi connections.*

> *[From British hacker jailed over £7m virtual gaming chips scam | Technology | The Guardian]*

Tomorrow's Transactions—The 2012 Reader

This is part of the plot of a novel that I'm writing that involves a guy taking revenge on a love rival by downloading child porn to the rival's laptop. It's the perfect crime, because the love rival gets arrested and his life is ruined even though he is never charged with anything. In my novel, the protagonist gets away with it, but in real life...

> *Mitchell was eventually identified because he used his own Facebook profile during one of his attempts to hack into the system.*
>
> *[From British hacker jailed over £7m virtual gaming chips scam | Technology | The Guardian]*

Doh! You'd get caught whether you used your real name or not, but even so it's pretty dumb to use your real name. Perhaps Facebook's addictive qualities will turn out to be a net benefit to law enforcement.

> *The victim later noticed that the intruder also used her computer to check his Facebook status, and his account was still open when she checked the computer.*
>
> *[From Burglar leaves his Facebook]*

For all sorts of reasons, then, it doesn't make any difference whether you use your real name or not, and the whole discussion about real names on Facebook and the connection between real names and crime and other unwanted behaviour is, to my mind, limited.

> *A Facebook spokesperson said the website does not comment on individual accounts, but said it believes a "real name culture" creates more accountability and a safer and more trusted environment.*
>
> *[From Facebook]*

So is it good or bad that people can say whatever they want online? If you want to complain about Big Brother (or indeed her little brother, Mark Zuckerberg of Facebook fame) should you be able to do so anonymously? In George Orwell's 1984, the state had a two-way TV screen installed in all homes so that it could both control the discourse, and thus shape people's opinions—Goebbels said that successful propaganda was that that left people unaware of the source of their convictions—and spy on everyone at the same time. When he was writing, in the 1940s, he could never have imagined that not only would we buy Big Brother's screens and carry them around with us at all times but that we would voluntarily sign up to be monitored! We've already seen how government agencies from despicable regimes use social media to spy on dissidents:

forcing everyone to use their real name would make it so much easier for them.

> *We are all being tracked in ways we probably won't like, not only by commercial concerns but by Governments and other political interests. Web 2.0 and its social networks makes this scarily easy*

[From Why the world's secret police want you to join Facebook]

There are genuine issues to be dealt with here. Bad things do happen, and the public and politicians want something to be done. By all means go ahead and send me abusive Facebook messages in bogus names - I will just block them and move on. And to be honest, if someone is going to send me death threats, I'd rather it was via Facebook so that they can be tracked down and caught.

> *So many high-profile incidents in such a short time has sparked a storm of public outrage, with Premier Anna Bligh personally penning a letter to Facebook founder Mark Zuckerberg, while Prime Minister Kevin Rudd said he would consider appointing an online ombudsman, describing cyber crime and internet bullying as "frankly frightening".*

[From Dealing with the dark side of Facebook]

Whether Facebook bullying is more or less of a problem than regular bullying, I couldn't say as I don't have the expertise. But then, nor do any of the people in government who are dreaming up legislation on the topic. In fact, I don't know what the government, regulators, legislators, lobbyists actually want since as a society we don't have a coherent strategy for identity in the online world.

> *I won't dwell on the irony that the government that's keen to protect you from privacy-violating Web trolls also wants the Web's plumbing retrofitted to make wiretapping easier. But the last organization I want designing my Web browser is the federal government.*

[From If you want Web privacy]

I don't think they're quite suggesting that just yet, but I understand the sentiment.

> *Slate technology columnist Farhad Manjoo likes my argument but says: "I doubt there's a market for such a browser. People don't care about privacy. They just say they do. If they did, they wouldn't use Facebook."*

[From If you want Web privacy]

I feel this is too simplistic. It's like saying that people don't care about road safety because some of them get run over. But hey, I'm a parent as well as a consultant so if someone offered me a magic wand that would stop kids from getting run over, it would be very tempting to take it. Since there isn't a magic wand to stop people from being horrible to each other on the Internet, and forcing people to give their real names will not only not stop the problem but will also be dangerous, we have to go down another path involving trusted intermediaries.

Some day, not so far out in the future, there will be a parallel web that you can only enter by signing up with some form of id, a credit card for example, a verified by Visa web.

[From Editorial: Facebook]

I don't doubt that this is true, although I think a Virgin Media web and a Sky web and a TalkTalk web are more likely than a Visa web. This is, in essence, the same idea that I wrote about last year.

On the red, open, internet people and organisations will exchange encrypted data across an untrusted network. Some people may choose not to connect to the red internet at all and only crazy people (and organisations) will send unencrypted data to unauthenticated counterparties.

On the blue, closed, internet you will need to authenticate yourself before you are allowed to access anything and a digital identity infrastructure will deliver privacy (and in some cases anonymity) through cryptography, not through data protection registrars or privacy ombudsmen.

[From Digital Identity: Red army]

Now, I would ague that the with proper technology, implemented in privacy-enhacing ways to support sensible business models, then as an individual I will have more privacy using a bank-provided pseudonym across an encrypted VPN (the blue Net) than I will have using the red Net. In other words, privacy and anonymity are not the same thing at all. Get rid of anonymity wouldn't necessarily end privacy and more privacy doesn't necessarily mean more anonymity.

Who you are, though, is just one aspect of the overall conversation about the future of privacy. At a public hearing organised by the FCC and the FTC.

The industry participants by and large thought privacy concerns about location services were overblown. Consultant Brandt Squires went so far as to say, "I'd like to think privacy is a thing of the past, but it's not necessarily so."

[From Mayor of Starbucks Today, Local Hero Tomorrow: The Power and Privacy Pitfalls of Location Sharing | Center for Democracy & Technology]

I wouldn't like to think that at all. I'd like to think that it's a matter of control. If I'm posting comments that are against, say, the Syrian government under the nom de plume John Doe, then I still don't want Syrian government secret service agents to track me down and blow me up, even if they don't know my real name. Piecemeal panic about anonymity isn't going to get us anywhere. We need to develop a proper policy toward privacy and then use that policy to set strategies for commerce, crime and chat. Let's not put the cart before the horse no matter how great the panic.

We don't know whether we want real names or not – 08/09/2011

There's an ongoing, and familiar, debate in progress about people calling each other—and themselves—names online. You only have to spend a few minutes looking at the comments on *The Daily Mail* or in the *Guardian's Comment is Free* to see that people can be very mean to each other online where there identities are hidden. Not as mean to each other as they are offline, where identities are known, but mean nonetheless.

Psychological research has proven again and again that anonymity increases unethical behavior. Road rage bubbles up in the relative anonymity of one's car. And in the online world, which can offer total anonymity, the effect is even more pronounced.

[From Online, Anonymity Breeds Contempt - NYTimes.com]

I'm sure this is true. But I'm also sure that in some cases you need sort-of-anonymity in order to get valuable input.

People's faces, real names and brief biographies ("John Doe from Lexington") are placed next to their public comments, to establish a baseline of responsibility.

[From Online, Anonymity Breeds Contempt - NYTimes.com]

Posting the real name and face of a nurse next to her comment about poor hygiene standards in a hospital, for example, is hardly likely to make the discourse better. I think we shouldn't confuse the issue about strategies to improve the quality of online comment and debate on newspaper websites (always going to be an uphill struggle, frankly, if you are going to allow the public access to them) with the bigger picture about online anonymity. This has hit the headlines again because of the fuss about Google+'s "real names" policy and Eric Schimidt's comments about. Even the FT has been discussing it.

> *The web equivalent of anonymous pamphlets – taking to Twitter or to microblogs in China and in Arab countries to demand accountability or freedom from undemocratic governments – is a vital use of the internet. If everyone not only had to be identified but could be traced by security services, freedom of expression would suffer.*

[From It is right to curtail web]

Well… yes. But that's an argument that proves that it isn't right to curtail web anonymity. And in any case, this is nothing to do with Eric Schmidt's comments on the subject. He was arguing that Google wants to know your real name so that it can market to you, sell your details to advertisers and so forth. Right now, when I have to log in to a double-glazing company web site to get a quote, I always give a made-up name, made-up date of birth and so forth. I don't want someone from the double-glazing company website on my doorstep when I get home. But under Eric's plan, there would be no hiding from the marketeers.

> *There are people who do really evil and wrong things on the Internet, and it would be useful if we had strong identity so we could weed them out*

[From Google]

I don't think he means double-glazing salesmen, but people who won't reveal personal data.

> *So if we knew that it was a real person, then we could sort of hold them accountable, we could check them, we could give them things, we could you know bill them, you know we could have credit cards and so forth and so on*

[From Andy Carvin - Google]

Quite. He is admirably, and commendably, honest and transparent. This isn't about politics, or rights, or freedom. It's about advertising. Now, let's be clear. I am not anti-commercial. Far from it. I understand that people need to sell me stuff. In fact, more than that, I want people to sell me stuff. I like it when people sell me stuff I want. When Amazon recommends a great book to me, I love them for it. But, in the general case, does Amazon need to know whether I am real person, one persona of a real person, a dorm room or a small business or a married couple? It doesn't: it looks at what JohnDoe1776 buys and makes recommendations. That's it.

> *Saying that he's been thinking about identity for 20 years, Schmidt calls it a "hard problem": "The Internet would be better if we had an accurate notion that you were a real person", he says.*

[From Google]

Yes, it would. But that's not an argument for anonymity or not-anonymity. As I have posted repeatedly over several years, it is better understood as an argument about credentials, authenticated attributes and the separate-but-related binding of virtual identities to digital identities and digital identities to RWLEs (Real World Legal Entities—I wish I could think of another, better title).

> *An anonymous virtual identity with the credentials IS_A_PERSON and IS_OVER_18 would serve most people for most purposes most of the time*

[From Digital Identity: IS_A_PERSON]

It would also make identity theft much harder: every time Google or Facebook force you to use your real name, that makes it more likely that your real name will be stolen or used inappropriately. It's the same argument I always use about putting names on chip and PIN cards - the only people who benefit from this are thieves who steal the cards. Eric is certainly correct when says it's a hard problem though.

> *The goal to "protect anonymity of good people, but not allow anonymity of bad people" sounds really hard to implement: How do you separate "good" from "bad" people?*

[From A CTO analysis: Hillary Clinton's speech on Internet freedom | 1 of 45]

Well put. We (the public) have no idea what we want. We want anonymity for Syrian dissidents but not for pedophiles. We want anonymity for hospital nurses blowing the whistle on incompetent surgeons but not for looters. We want anonymity for celebrities in some circumstances but not others. Most of all, and most paradoxically, we want the authorities to spy on other people but not on us. Once you create the ability to simply, easily and inexpensively track people, then I'm afraid the genie is out of the bottle.

> *But if there was an Internet Driving License that you had to use to log in to web sites, that would almost certainly make the situation far worse, since these websites would now know exactly who you are, and this information would then be freely obtained by perverts, the secret police, News International or whoever else wants to pry.*

[From Let's not panic about online identity]

I don't know what the answer is. I take part in activities such as the Cabinet Office's Identity Assurance Privacy and Consumer Group and the Centre for the Study of Financial Innovation's Research Fellowshop to try and learn as much as possible about the issues and to try to help our clients make informed decision about identity strategy, but I can't help but feel we are some way from a solution. What I am certain of, though, is that we should be formulating national policy and not allowing corporates to bypass proper public debate and discussion on the topic.

Pseudos corner – 16/11/2011

There was an interesting twittervation going on about pseudonyms, stimulated by this post

> *I do want to talk about what the "no pseudonyms" policy adopted at G+ means for women, LGBT folk, and civil servants.*

[From Why Google]

Hey! What about me! I want pseudonymity too! It isn't about people being able to "hide", it's about given people choices about how they interact and the ability to interact in different ways via different persona. I don't think this in conflict with having an identity infrastructure, I think it should be part of that infrastructure. As far as I'm concerned we need an infrastructure more than ever, which is why I find this kind of comment puzzling.

> *It won't work; and if it did, you would have to trust big government to stay benign as it tracks your every online step. As for the latter, ask the citizens of Egypt, Tunisia, China, Iran, and other countries that closely monitor their citizens' Internet usage (or block it in whole or part).*

[From Internet Evolution - Robert McGarvey - Why an Internet 'Driver's License' Won't Work]

Let's put to one side the question of whether the US wants to monitor or block citizen's internet usage (although generally on behalf of Disney rather than democracy) and address the central point. What has NSTIC got to do with trusting the government? Most people will use IDs provided by their bank, mobile operator, sports team or favourite pop group. I really, really doubt that the DMV will be able to compete for the business.

> *Olden suggests building a single sign-on from a handful of IDs that are in wide use. Think Facebook, Gmail, perhaps Yahoo. Facebook alone is emerging as a kind of de facto single sign-on with 500 million users... So scratch Commerce's NSTIC, and find ways to lace together the passwords we already use.*
>
> *[From Internet Evolution - Robert McGarvey - Why an Internet 'Driver's License' Won't Work]*

This is confusing two entirely different issues. Issue no.1 is what framework we use for identity, and NSTIC seems to me to be as good as any other (although, as I have often written, I would have liked to have seen an emphasis on pseduonymity as the norm). Issue no.2 is which identities we use. If we only use the same, single identity everywhere that we go through the interweb tubes, then the "owner" of that identity will indeed be able to monitor our journey. I don't care whether that owner is the Feds or Facebook, I don't want it to happen.

Personally, I would want a pseudonymous identity from someone like my bank. That why I could do stuff online, and people online could interact with me knowing that the bank knows who I am, if you see what I mean. I don't think that managing a few identities will be at all different, thanks to the magic of the mobile phone. I spotted an interesting comment on this mobile future in a very positive review of Google Wallet in the Wall Street Journal.

> *Google Wallet can't hold your driver's license or other official forms of identification, so even if it takes off and works everywhere, you'll still have to carry your license with you.*
>
> *[From The Digital Solution: Google]*

In the long run, as we all know, it's the digitisation of identity that will have the biggest impact on society and it's very interesting to me that the arrival of mobile wallets has stimulated these thoughts.

It would be easy to carry an MIC, or "Mobile Identification Card" on my phone, instead of a physical card in my leather wallet (Google, are you listening?)

[From Invasion of the Invisible Wallet]

So what would it take to get my bank pseudonym and (in the US example) the driver's license into the Google Wallet? We have the technology and we have a framework—NSTIC in the USA and Identity Assurance in the UK—but we need some thing to kick-start and coagulate the swirling possibilities. If we're all agreeing that government identities are going to do it, then perhaps we should focus on something else.

Government agencies could (and should, in my opinion) become attribute providers, so there's no reason why they couldn't issue an electronic drivers license in the NSTIC framework. You provide your proof of identity to the DMV along with a digital identity (in essence a public key from a key pair held in the secure element of the Google phone and accessible from the Google Wallet) and the DMV sends you back a public key certificate (your public key together with the relevant attributes signed by a DMV private key). This would combine my private sector identity and my public sector attribute to deliver the Google Wallet fantasy mentioned above.

Federal Chief Information Officer Steven VanRoekel last week released a long-awaited memorandum requiring that, over the next three years, agencies launching or upgrading sites that prompt people to obtain a username and password also must be compatible with logon services handled by certified third-party vendors.

[From White House may cut purse strings to enforce online credentialing | Ready-Sourcing.com - World Industrial Sourcing News covering national and international Trading affairs.]

It's a small step, but requiring government sites to offer (in essence) NSTIC-compatible access alongside usernames and passwords will help to get things moving: companies will begin to develop software that offers this possibility. Yes there's a long way to go, but I think both public and private sector organisations can at least begin to formulate strategy bounds and think about the strategic role of identity in their futures.

Say aaarrggh! – 12/01/2012

There's a clearly a desperate need for a 21st-century trust infrastructure for both people and things in Italy. Here's some news from the Internet of Things.

Work by the University of Turin's mountain pastoral department has given consumers the ability to check individual cheeses, wheel by wheel, and get a large dollop of information to back up the evidence of their taste buds... The University of Turin's Giampiero Lombardi said the consumer accesses the information through QR codes and an RFID tag printed onto the cheese wheel wrapper... For individual farmers, setting up the database and ability to use QR codes and RFID tags cost between 700-2000 Euros, but the researchers are hoping that farmers from each Alps grazing zone will collaborate on the equipment to lower the individual price.

> *[From Italian cheese puts traceability to the test - National Rural News - Agribusiness and General - General - Stock & Land]*

Since QR codes are trivial to copy, and cheap RFID tags not much better, the security of this system rests on the integrity of the database, and maintaining that is expensive, hence the price tag. But nevertheless good luck to them, because there are undoubtedly parts of Italy where the reporting of cheese origin falls below the high standards that consumers might expect. I wonder if the crackdown on bogus cheese is part of the Italian government's renewed interest in shrinking less-regulated parts of the economy.

> *Under the new rules all payments in cash will be forbidden above a €1,000 threshold. The threshold was previously fixed at €2,500, surely a bit too high for a country struggling with endemic tax evasion like Italy;*

> *[From Open Europe Blog]*

Hurrah! Go for the belly of the beast, that's what I say. Anyway, what I wanted to say was that the apparent existence of black-market illegally labelled cheese does not put me off of visiting Italy (I shall be in Rome in April for the EPCA). But this does.

One in five Italian dentists is unqualified, along with an estimated 10,000-15,000 doctors, it was reported today.

More than a thousand people were charged in Italy last year with unauthorised exercise of a medical profession. They included fake doctors, spurious dentists and even a few sham nurses.

In an average year, according to police figures, about 1,000 people have been convicted of the offence. But the penalty is only a fine of up to €516 (£440).

> *"We catch phoney dentists who laugh in our face," Captain Marco Datti of the carabinieri told the daily La Repubblica. "They say: 'I'll just pay €500, change premises and start again'."*
>
> *[From Health warning over Italy's fake dentists and phoney doctors | World news | The Guardian]*

I'm sick of the sight of that diploma, as anyone in our office will tell you! In the last couple of months I've been there half a dozen times to get a new crown, fix a broken tooth, get a filling. I hate going to the dentist. (My present dentist excepted, naturally.) Still, at least here in Britain we can sure that we are visiting a real dentist. Oh, wait...

> *The UK's dental regulator, the General Dental Council (GDC), has successfully prosecuted two individuals for practising dentistry illegally.*
>
> *The cases bring the total number of successful prosecutions by the GDC to five in the last six months.*
>
> *[From Dentistry.co.uk | News | Two fake 'dentists' fined]*

How much effort is it to print out a fake diploma and stick it on a wall? The one of the wall of my dentist's office looks very impressive, but I haven't the slightest idea how to verify it. There's no chip, no digitally-signature, no biometric link to the dentist. I can't even read what it says because it's in Latin.

If I seem obsessed with the dental example, it's because I am a total baby at the dentist. So these kinds of stories literally make me sick. My hands are shaking as I type this...

> *A bogus dentist is facing court in the US after detectives discovered his makeshift surgery - stocked with DIY rather than dental tools. And officials in Palm Beach, Florida, believe that there may be as many as 300 unlicensed dentists in the city and surrounding counties.*
>
> *[From BBC News | Health | Fake dentist 'pulled teeth with pliers']*

Now I don't want to go to Florida either! What if I get toothache? What if I'm rushed to a dental survey only to be operated on a by a boy from (very probably) Brazil? From now on, I'm going to use this as the very real test case for any proposed mass-market trust infrastructure. When I break a tooth in Boca Raton, how is the infrastructure going to tell me whether the man in the white coat is actually dentist?

Seriously. How?

Never mind the boring, standard, examples and use cases for (e.g.) NSTIC. How will NSTIC help me to know that I have booked an appointment with a big cheese not a bogus one?

Chapter 2: Social Media and Organisations

It goes without saying that the rise of social media, social networks and social organisations has been one of the most dramatic consequences of the spread of the Internet. Facebook has nearly a billion users (and nearly half a billion of them access via mobiles) and its impact on business will be huge (as an aside, note that Facebook had half a billion dollars in payment revenues in 2011). The impact on the world of identity will be huge, but the impact won't be limited to that. Social media aren't just changing the way we work, they are changing the way we think.

Technologist can't square circles, but we can help – 26/05/2011

What do the politicians, regulators, police and the rest of them want us (technologists) to do about the interweb tubes? It might be easier to work out what to do if we had a clear set of requirements from them. Then, when confronted with a problem such as, for example, identity theft, we could build systems to make things better. In that particular case, things are currently getting worse.

> *Mr Bowron told the MPs this week that although recovery rates were relatively low, the police detection rate was 80 per cent. However, the number of cases is rising sharply with nearly 2m people affected by identity fraud every year.*
>
> *[From FT.com / UK / Politics & policy - MP calls cybercrime Moriarty v PC Plod]*

So, again, to pick on this particular case, what should be done?

> *Mr Head also clarified his position on the safety of internet banking, insisting that while traditional face-to-face banking was a better guarantee against fraud, he accepted that society had moved on. "If you take precautions, it's safe," he said.*
>
> *[From FT.com / UK / Politics & policy - MP calls cybercrime Moriarty v PC Plod]*

Yet I remember reading in The Daily Telegraph (just googled it: 20th November 2010) there was a story about an eBay fraud perpetrated by fraudsters who set up bank accounts using forged identity documents, so face-to-face FTF does not, as far as I can see, mean any improvement in security at all. In fact, I'm pretty sure that it is worse than nothing, because people are easier to fool than computers. I would argue that Mr. Head has things exactly wrong here, because we an integrated identity infrastructure should not discriminate between FTF and remote transactions.

I think this sort of thing is actually representative of a much bigger problem around the online world. Here's another example. Bob Gourley. The former CTO of the U.S. Defense Intelligence Agency, poses a fundamental and important question about the future identity infrastructure.

> *We must have ways to protect anonymity of good people, but not allow anonymity of bad people. This is going to be much harder to do than it is to say. I believe a structure could be put in place, with massive engineering, where all people are given some means to stay anonymous, but when a certain key is applied, their cloak can be peeled back. Hmmm. Who wants to keep those keys?*
>
> *[From A CTO analysis: Hillary Clinton's speech on Internet freedom | IT Leadership | TechRepublic.com]*

So, just to recap, Hillary says that we need an infrastructure that stops crime but allows free assembly. I have no idea how to square that circle, except to say that prevention and detection of crime ought to be feasible even with anonymity, which is the most obvious and basic way to protect free speech, free assembly and whistleblowers: it means doing more police work, naturally, but it can be done. By comparison, "knee jerk" reactions, attempting to force the physical world's limited and simplistic identity model into cyberspace, will certainly have unintended consequences.

> *Facebook's real-name-only approach is non-negotiable – despite claims that it puts political activists at risk, one of its senior policy execs said this morning.*
>
> *[From Facebook]*

I've had a Facebook account for quite a while, and it's not in my "real" name. My friends know that John Q. Doe is me, so we're linked and can happily communicate, but no-one else does. Which suits me fine. If my real name is actually Dave bin Laden, Hammer of the Infidel, but I register as John Smith, how on Earth are Facebook supposed to know whether "John Smith" is a "real" name or not? Ludicrous, and just another example of how broken the whole identity realm actually is.

For Facebook to actually check the real names, and then to accept the liabilities that will inevitably result, would be expensive and pointless even if it could be achieved. A much better solution is for Facebook to help to the construction and adoption of a proper digital identity infrastructure (such as USTIC, for example) and then use it.

The implementation of NSTIC could force some companies, like Facebook, to change the way it does business.

[From Wave of the Future: Trusted Identities In Cyberspace]

That's true, but it's a good thing, and it's good for Facebook as well as for other businesses and society as a whole. So, for example, I might use a persistent pseudonymous identity given to me by a mobile operator, say Vodafone UK. If I use that identity to obtain a Facebook identity, that's fine by Facebook: they have a certificate from Vodafone UK to say that I'm a UK citizen or whatever. I use the Vodafone example advisedly, because it seems to me that mobile operators would be the natural providers of these kinds of credentials, having both the mechanism to interact FTF (shops) and remotely, as well as access to the SIM for key storage and authentication. Authentication is part of the story too.

But perhaps the US government's four convenient "levels of assurance" (LOAs), which tie strong authentication to strong identity proofing, don't apply to every use case under the sun. On the recent teleconference where I discussed these findings, we ended up looking at the example of World of Warcraft, which offers strong authentication but had to back off strong proofing.

[From Identity Assurance Means Never Having To Say "Who Are You, Again?" | Forrester Blogs]

Eve is, naturally, absolutely right to highlight this. There is no need for Facebook to know who I really am if I can prove that Vodafone know who I am (and, importantly, that I'm over 13, although they may not be for much longer given Mr. Zuckerberg's recent comments on age limits).

Friends and relations – 20/08/2011

While I was sitting through a presentation (a very good presentation, I might add) on social media strategy for one of our client's financial services business, it struck me that they were slightly misjudging the more interactive and transactional nature of social media, doing great stuff but treating social media as another customer communication channel. I'm naturally more interested in social media for transactions: social commerce. I've given a couple of talks about this recently, pointing out the opportunities that social commerce opens up.

One prediction says social commerce will top $30 billion globally by 2015 with Facebook-generated sales one of the primary drivers.

[From [Infographic: The history of F-commerce | SMI]]

There are many different ways that financial services organisations can exploit this. A good example, to my mind, is the way in which Amex works with Foursquare.

> *Just after announcing that it passed 10 million users, location-based check-in service Foursquare has said it is partnering with American Express to give members even better deals when they check in at merchants' stores across the country.*

[From [Foursquare partners with American Express for deal check-ins | VentureBeat]]

This is a terrific proposition and it's well implemented (through statement credits, so no coupons or vouchers or anything are needed). And, to follow this example, Amex also has a Facebook page where its large number of fans can come to learn about products and services, share with the community of card holders and so on. Great stuff. And it isn't only financial services organisations that are integrating themselves into social media to create new kinds of social commerce.

> *That is because the well-known mobile service provider is now allowing its customers to log on to Facebook to purchase phone credit.*

[From [O2]]

Wow, that's pretty interesting.

> *Pre-paid subscribers will now be able to access a secure app on the social networking website, where they will put in credit card details in order to purchase top ups.*

[From [O2]]

Credit card details? Not Facebook credits? But you get the picture. Something like Facebook can be used to create a more intimate transactional environment without having to develop software, making it easy for consumers to "friend" and "like" and so forth. Personally, I don't find this sort of thing particularly appealing because to me it's the wrong kind of social relationship: I want something more granular.

Here's what I mean. I don't want to be friends with my bank—after all, I'm a typical consumer so I hate banks—but I do want to be friends with my bank account. Why can't Barclays let me friend my current account so I can see its status updates like "Premium card fee £10.00", "Direct Debit

British Gas £37.85" and "Counter Credit £5.00" and so forth? I quite like the text messages that Barclays sends me but would prefer something more immediate and more detailed (I often call this "streaming commerce") so that I can make decisions and respond.

Similarly, I don't especially want to be friends with MBNA, but I do want to be friends with my MBNA American Express card. If i see a status about about my payment being use, that would be really useful. If I see a status update from my card that appears to have gone on holiday to Kazakhstan while I'm in Peckham, I can press a button somewhere and get straight through to lost and stolen cards. I wouldn't mind if the status updates where now and then promotional messages instead of transaction reports, that would be handy. It would due like my friend telling me that there's double reward points in Sainsbury's today, so something like that. I'm using "friend" generically, of course, I don't mean to imply that Facebook is the one and only way to implement a social media strategy.

> *Facebook usage in the UK fell nearly 4pc in July to its lowest level since 2009, sparking concerns that the social network has hit its peak and may be declining in popularity.*
>
> *[From Facebook]*

I don't use Facebook that much—it's really for sharing with my brother and sister, other family members and a few old friends—and I've not got a crystal ball to see whether we'll still be using it in a couple of years.

> *Many of the smartest people I know are leaving Facebook as well. I predict we'll see many people leaving over the coming months and adopting Twitter.*
>
> *[From The Facebook]*

My idea would work even better with Twitter. Suppose Barclays knew my twitter name—maybe they could ask me when I log in for home banking and get permission to send tweets to me—and connected it to my bank account. Now, whenever Barclays gets a new follower on twitter it can scan its customer database to find out if that twitter name belongs to a customer. If it does, they can start sending out all status changes as Direct Messages (DMs). That would be simple and great.

I'd love to follow my John Lewis MasterCard on Twitter in this way instead of having to log in to find out what it's been up to. Since I use Twitter all day and every day anyway, it would be a much better channel for payment products to develop a more intimate relationship with me. And think of the practical benefits: if I get a tweet from my debit card telling me it's just been used to withdraw money from an ATM in Belarus,

I can call Barclays right away to block it from further misbehaviour. This doesn't seem terribly complex: all Barclays need to know is my twitter name and then it can use the Twitter API to post tweets and only allow me to follow them.

If I could follow my transactional instruments, I could also (in time) feed their tweets, status updates, notifications and so on into other software for mash-ups. I don't know what kind of mash-ups - I'm not smart enough for that - but I'm sure there are people out there who could do great stuff with the data. So a plea to my account, card and service providers: I don't want to be friends with you, because you are corporations and not mates, but I don't want to be friends with my stuff: my money, my cards, my phone. How hard can it be?

Comments

I like the point about the MBNA card. If the bank could delegate fraud monitoring to the account holder then that would get rid of the irritation of false positives that is making me seriously reconsider my relationship with my Tesco credit card and it would also make shifting liability a lot easier too.

Posted by: Jane Adams on 22/08/2011 at 13:49.

I agree with being friends with stuff and not with corporations. But the examples you give almost only focus on security aspects, so probably you won't even receive that many status updates. And maybe that is even better to receive by sms or phone call. Are there also other status updates you would like to receive? Or could think of. Because for things like my current balance or latest transactions I already use a banking app. I am not sure whether I want my bank-account or creditcard-account to be incorporated with the social media I use...

Posted by: Wieske on 22/08/2011 at 16:15.

Facing up to the competition– 28/09/2011

The news is full of Facebook again. The digital money community, just like every other community, must spend time working out what the rise of Facebook means to them.

If Facebook were a country, it would be the third largest in the world, so it figures that the social networking giant is trying to develop its own currency - Facebook Credits.

[From Facebook]

It isn't a country, of course, and we shouldn't get too carried away with that kind of thinking.

> *The privately held Facebook does not disclose its financials, but according to one estimate from 2009, it was generating $550 million of annual revenue, of which $75 million came from virtual payments.*

[From Facebook]

That's going to go up substantially if the estimates for Facebook Credits usage now are anything like accurate, but I still think some of the comments about them (and other alternative payment schemes) can be a little misplaced. For example, here's something from Information Week.

> *For example, if Facebook adds the ability to transfer Credits among users, which was speculated as something under development in 2010, it will do three things practically overnight: create the largest money laundering network in the world since PayPal; become the largest bank in the world; and establish itself as the largest credit card processor.*

[From Dangerous Intersection Of Mobility And Credit - - Mobile]

All three of these statements are incorrect.

Money Laundering. About $1.5 billion in Facebook Credits will be in circulation this year. This is so small as to be insignificant in global money laundering statistics. Money is laundered via cash and through the banking network, not through PayPal (the account limits are too low), M-PESA or Walmart gift cards. There's more money flowing through virtual world and game networks in Asia (look at China where prisoners are used to mine virtual gold) than through Facebook Credits.

Biggest Bank. Payments are not banking. They might be called "Credits" but they are not credit. I've never thought that Facebook might want to be a bank and there is no possibility of it having more money on deposit than, say, Citi in any foreseeable future.

> *If you look at this short video "The Bank of Facebook" from Thomas Power, you can see how more of this kind of thinking. I don't agree with Thomas about Facebook becoming a bank -- that is, a heavily regulated credit institution -- but I do agree that it*

can become a payment institution and, as Thomas point out, a facilitator of peer-to-peer finance.

[From Digital Money: Complacent or short-sighted?]

Card Processor. Even if Facebook Credits purchase volume doubled to $3 billion, this is tiny compared to the overall card processing market.

The US credit card processing industry includes about 2,000 companies with combined annual revenue of about $40 billion.

[From Research and Markets: Updated 2011 Report on the $40 Billion US Financial Transaction Processing Industry - pymnts.com]

Research & Markets estimate the US credit card processing industry is 2,000 companies with a combined annual turnover of $40 billion. But the amount of value they process is absolutely gigantic. Last year, for example, American Express alone handled half a trillion dollars in purchase volume. I just checked in the Nilson Report (March 2011) and it says that the biggest acquirer in the US, First Data, handled 15 billion transactions worth $700 billion.

Facebook Credits are small beer compared to the incumbents, but they are interesting because of what they represent:

The real point here however, is that Facebook is on course to generate $1 billion in revenue this year from social gaming. If that is the case, the social gaming market on Facebook alone is worth at least $3 billion, as they're taking a 30% cut. This is an ecosystem that is only a couple of years old. And it's just for gaming and not commerce.

[From BAI | Banking Strategies | Payments | Remote Payments | Facebook]

They work in places where the alternatives are expensive, inconvenient or absent. And since they work, and customers like them, they are already spreading.

BBC Worldwide will allow Facebook users to rent 29 Doctor Who episodes... Viewers will pay for the digital videos using Facebook Credits

[From BBC Worldwide to show Doctor Who on Facebook]

With a 30% (or whatever) fee, they are currently more suited to digital goods rather than physical goods, but as volume builds and the merchant services charges fall, it will change.

> *Payment launched a Facebook Mall two weeks ago, where consumers can shop among 50,000 retailers and add items to a single shopping cart. Payvment is signing up around 300 new storefronts daily and has roughly 1.2 million items in the mall today.*

[From Will Facebook]

But as I say, it's what it represents that is important. And what it represents is a population scale, non-bank payment solution.

> *Facebook then also has the potential to draw in the unbanked or the underbanked around the world, where the entire infrastructure of having physical money and a place to store it can be leapfrogged in place of a virtual system and marketplace.*

[From Telcos become banks. Facebook]

Facebook isn't going to become a telco, I'm sure, but they could become an M-PESA. They did make an interesting comment about their strategy yesterday.

> *Erick Tseng, head of mobile products at Facebook, reinforced the theme of mobility at the Mobilize conference he was speaking at when he said, "We're going to become a mobile company." He said that Facebook has more than 350 million mobile users (out of 800 million total), and that the proportion will swing to more than 50 percent within the next year*

[From Facebook]

Just as Eric Schmidt at Google said, if you don't have a mobile strategy then you don't have a strategy. There's a lot to be discussed about mobile commerce and which organisations might take up which positions in the emerging value networks, but if we just focus back down on payments for a bit...

> *Not surprisingly, consumers trust incumbent payment brands when they think about the future of mobile payments. Facebook is the least trusted, despite big numbers of consumer who spend a lot time sharing personal information on the site.*

[From Facebook]

What the figures actually show is that about a third of consumers say they would trust Visa, MasterCard and Amex with mobile payments, about a quarter would trust Apple, Microsoft and Google and half of that number would trust eBay or Facebook. Personally I don't care what the public say about anything, but it is a little puzzling to me that the payment brand trust figures are so low. Any theories? Are they tainted by association with banks? If they stay that low, and the trust in Facebook stays high, then maybe Facebook Credits will be more of a competitor than the incumbents currently imagine.

Friends with things - 01/11/2011

I enjoyed the presentation that Christophe Langlois (Visible Banking) gave to the Financial Services Club in London and particularly the enjoyed the question and answer session afterwards. Christophe was talking about banks' use of social media and was comparing and contrasting some different approaches that explored further in his new book "Customer Experiences without Borders" (which I won a signed copy of at the event, hurrah!). During the question and answer session, I made the point about the mismatch in the use of social media.

> *I don't want to be friends with my bank—after all, I'm a typical consumer so I hate banks—but I do want to be friends with my bank account. Why can't Barclays let me friend my current account so I can see its status updates like "Premium card fee £10.00", "Direct Debit British Gas £37.85" and "Counter Credit £5.00" and so forth?*

> *[From Friends and relations]*

This is a point that I amplified in Retail Banker Interactive, finishing up with plea.

> *So a plea to my account, card and service providers: I don't want to be friends with you, because you are corporations and not mates, but I do want to be friends with my stuff: my money, my cards, my phone. How hard can it be?*

> *[From Social media is not just another communication channel - Blogs - Retail Banker Interactive]*

A discussion about this continued over drinks, and I am indebted to David Harris from salesforce.com for bringing a fascinating example to my attention. Apparently, Toyota are going to have a system whereby you can be friends with your car, which is a great idea.

For example, if an EV or PHV is running low on battery power, Toyota Friend would notify the driver to re-charge in the form of a "tweet"-like alert. In addition, while Toyota Friend will be a private social network, customers can choose to extend their communication to family, friends, and others through public social networks such as Twitter and Facebook.

[From Toyota USA Newsroom | Salesforce.com and Toyota Form Strategic Alliance to Build 'Toyota Friend' Social Network for Toyota Customers and Their Cars]

So your friends could be friends with your car too. You might wonder why anyone would want to do this, but consider this: my sister has borrowed my wife's car for a couple of days while she goes looking for another car, so it would be great if my sister could be friends with my wife's car (and it would make sense for me to be friends with my wife's car and vice versa) for a time.

What I'm not sure about is if I would want these connections to be in my hilariously-entitled "real name" or via a network like Facebook. I'm not paranoid, but I don't want to be bombarded with crap all the time because Facebook has noticed that one of my brake pads is wearing a little thin and has sold this information to a hundred different brake pad companies around the world. And I'm sure it will only be a matter of time before some guy tracks down and murders his ex-girlfriend because she forget he was friends with her car so knows where she is.

There's a layer of infrastructure missing here and I hope that the Cabinet Office's Identity Assurance Programme that we were discussing yesterday is going to take this into account. They've finally got a budget so I hope that some of the input from the Working Groups can now be acted on.

Cabinet Office minister Francis Maude has earmarked £10m for implementation of the government's Identity Assurance (IDA) programme,

[From Government earmarks £10m for Identity Assurance and targets over £500m savings - 10/31/2011 - Computer Weekly]

So what has being friends with my bank account got to do with the Cabinet Office? We need an identity infrastructure for things as well as for people. I need to delegate permission to access my wife's car to my sister just as I need to give permission for my sister to be friends with my wife's car for a while. Right now, there's precious little security around people, but even less around things, largely because the "internet of things" wasn't designed with security in mind.

Typically, the person who designs the embedded software system for a car or a power grid system or a generating system are engineers who learn programming maybe as part of their engineering course, but they are not trained computer scientists or computer engineers. The point is that someone whose primary job is understanding control theory is not someone who knows anything about software vulnerabilities.

[From The internet of things | Interviews | Opinion, News, Analysis | BCS - The Chartered Institute for IT]

If this sounds esoteric, it isn't. It's a real issue that should be taken seriously as input to the deployment of devices right now. Here's a straightforward example from Rob Bratby.

The deployment of smart meters is one of the most significant deployments of what is often described as 'the internet of things', but its linkage to subscriber accounts and individual homes, and the increasing prevalence of data 'mash-ups' (cross-referencing of multiple databases) will require these issues to be thought about in a more sophisticated and nuanced way.

[From Watching the connectives | A lawyer's insight into telecoms and technology]

So I should be able to make friends with my electricity meter and under some circumstances I might need to be friends with my father's electricity meter but I don't want burglars and ne'erdowells to be friends with it. It seems to me that we already sort of know how to do this sort of thing: we understand public / private key pairs, tamper-resistant stores for private keys, certificates, selective disclosure and everything else. But we're going to end up using Facebook Connect, because it's all too complicated for the marketing people to understand and we haven't yet found a way of explaining it to them.

I love the way they think – 23/11/2011

The subject of identity infrastructure came up again yesterday and this led on to a discussion about banks, identity providers, attribute providers and business models. When we are thinking about identity infrastructure in the mass market, a very simple identity vs. attribute example often comes to mind. It's the apparently simple case of age verification: how do you prove to a web site that you are over 18 or to a bar in the US that you are over 21 or to a bus company that you are over 65, or whatever. I think this is a pretty reasonable measure of how a system intended for the general public is going to work. Talking about this in the meeting, the example of

Facebook came to mind, where there is an utterly prosaic, immediate and important use case. You have to be 13 to exist on Facebook.

Now, one interesting question is… why? Why do Facebook ban under-13s? I mean why not under-18s? or under-12s? I mean 13 sounds rather arbitrary and there's no obvious reason for it that springs to mind. So I began to look for a rational reason for this, thinking that it was a Facebook policy. But it isn't. The reason for this abitrary and capricious age boundary is, as I should have suspected, a consequence of government regulation of the interweb tubes.

> *Internet companies have set up the rules against under-age users because they must comply with the federal Children's Online Privacy Protection Act (COPPA), passed in 1998, which says web sites that collect information from children younger than 13 must obtain parental consent.*
>
> *Obtaining that consent is complex and expensive, so companies like Facebook and Google, which owns YouTube, reject anyone who tries to sign up using an age below 13.*
>
> *[From Facebook]*

Unusually, across the spectrum of wise political steering in cyberspace, this legislation has not turned out precisely how the politicians and lobbyists intended.

> *The Children's Online Privacy Protection Act is a well-intentioned piece of legislation with unintended consequences for parents, educators, and the public writ large. It has stifled innovation for sites focused on children and its implementations have made parenting more challenging.*
>
> *[From danah boyd | apophenia » Why Parents Help Children Violate Facebook]*

I realise that Facebook-13 seems like a very particular and specific issue, but I think it is entirely representative of a class of problems in the new, online world. The way that people talk about this issue illustrates—I would at least postulate—how they think about stuff like online identity at a deep level and is a rather useful guide to technologists and legislators.

> *In Victoria's fifth-period honors English class, all 32 students said they had faked their birth year to gain access to one site or another… Jerry Ng, Victoria's 14-year-old cousin, agreed. "It's one thing to lie to a person," he said. "But this is lying to a computer."*

[From <u>Facebook</u>]

I love this comment, which is utterly revealing about how the so-called "screenagers" think about the world. A new ethics, discontinuous to our pre-post-industrial moral paradigm. Talking of which, perhaps an alternative to a sophisticated modern identity management system and the new mental models to with it is simply to clear the plebs off the playing field.

> *The Pope has warned of the dangers of social networking sites such as Facebook and MySpace, saying that communication between people online must not stop face-to-face conversations.*

[From <u>Pope warns Facebook</u>]

There's a heritage to this kind of pedagogical panic.

> *Similar concerns arose in the 18th century, when newspapers became more common. The French statesman Malesherbes railed against the fashion for getting news from the printed page, arguing that it socially isolated readers and detracted from the spiritually uplifting group practice of getting news from the pulpit.*

[From <u>A history of media technology scares, from the printing press to Facebook</u>]

God knows what he would make to the newspapers I saw at Woking train station this morning. The front pages included a splash about whether bread is bad for you, voyeuristic photographs up a female pop star's dress (I think she was a pop star - I didn't recognise the name or, for that matter, anything else) and something about the X-Factor. All this at a time when the eurozone is in crisis and people are being machine-gunned on the streets of Syria. But back to Facebook.

> *Whether Facebook is responding to changing social norms or, in fact, leading the charge is an unresolved question*

[From <u>FT.com / FT Magazine - Facebook</u>]

This is very important question. I think that people are disoriented about post-industrial society and confused about the fractal online/offline (or virtual/mundane) boundary. Facebook provides a way to think about some of these things. I don't think its right to say that it it "leading" the change but I think it is fair to say that until a new model emerges, Facebook will continue to provide a kind of substitute. I think that we should have an identity infrastructure that does not have a mundane analogue, where you can prove that you are an adult or a child without disclosing who you are and that this should be the basic test of fitness of any proposed solution. At the moment, Facebook doesn't provide this, because it's still trapped in industrial age identity thinking.

> *Facebook insists on what it calls authentic identity, or real names. And it is becoming a de facto passport vendor of sorts, allowing its users to sign into seven million other sites and applications with their Facebook user names and passwords.*

[From <u>Rushdie Wins Facebook</u>]

I'm sure it does. But doesn't this have dangers associated with it?

> *The information leak can be exploited by social-engineering scammers, phishers, or anyone who has ever been curious about the person behind an anonymous email message. If the address belongs to any one of the 500 million active users on Facebook, the social-networking site will return the full name and picture associated with the account.*

[From <u>Facebook</u>]

Yet another good reason for not having your Facebook account use your real name, as indeed I don't (for either of my accounts). My point is that what Facebook has now isn't the identity infrastructure we need for the information age, but unless someone else gets to work on building it, we'll end up with what Facebook has and we'll be stuck with it.

Comments

> I know when Sony needed kids to re-register for as part of the problem they had with Play Station Network, there was mayhem as you needed to enter your date of birth as part of the process. No kid in the world had actually used their correct date of birth, because that would not have alllowed them access to all the over 18 games content.

Posted by: David Steed on 06/12/2011 at 19:19.

Chapter 3: Political, Legal and Regulatory

It's crazy to talk about the online world as a lawless "Wild West" when it simply isn't. The regulatory framework for electronic transactions, ultimately, determines the path of new entrants. It may be frustrating at times, but the onus is on technologists to try and inform regulators, to demonstrate the advantages of competition and free invention and to help to create a platform for innovation.

Positive Changes in e-money regulation – 08/02/2011

William Long and Kai Zhang, from our friends at Sidley & Austin, present a typically good summary of the main issues raised in the consultations preceding the implementation of the new E-Money Directive (EMD) in the UK in the recent issue of *E-Finance & Payments Law & Policy* (December 2010).

Generally speaking, things look very positive. The capital requirements are being relaxed so that anyone who wants to provide e-money services probably can do with too much trouble, so I predict that you'll see some major companies moving in now. The prime candidates to offer services are probably telecommunications operators and retailers, but transit operators, event managers, corporate "campus" suppliers and others will surely seize the opportunity. Some have already declared their intentions.

> *O2 will apply for an e-money licence this year, signalling its commitment to support contactless payments in the UK in the near future.*
>
> *[From O2]*

The French operators announced a similar move this week. I can't resist noting that this is precisely the strategy that we recommended to mobile operators a couple of years ago (that is, use the upcoming PSD/ELMI changes to start their own payment businesses). Competition is good for innovation, and bringing these new players into the payments business will be very positive for all of us.

The interest of mobile operators is natural, and they have to move quickly to avoid being cut out of the loop by handset-based secure element providers (eg, Apple) who may move quicker than the UICC-based secure element providers (eg, mobile operators). The interest of the transit operators is also natural, since they have the cards out there in peoples' pockets. I still think that we've yet to see the really big plays yet: these will come from the retailers, just as they are in the US.

Kmart has begun testing check cashing, money transfers and prepaid cards in stores in Illinois, California and Puerto Rico, with plans to roll out the services nationally later this year. Best Buy has installed kiosks in its stores for shoppers to pay utility, cable and phone bills. Wal-Mart has opened roughly 1,500 MoneyCenters that process as many as 5 million transactions each week.

[From Retailers offer financial services to 'unbanked']

The use of retailer-issued e-money pre-paid products as a low-cost alternative to bank accounts for the excluded is a win-win. It takes unprofitable customers away from the banks and gives those customers more convenient services. And the retailers could steer customers to use these products at POS, thus saving on their payment processing costs. Personally, I think the prepaid market is not competitive enough (the charges are still too high) but new entrants enabled by the ELMI, new entrants with economies of scale (such as high street retailers), could open up the market and drive down costs very quickly.

Finally, I was also very excited to note in the article that the Treasury is considering my idea of making the balance limit for simplified due diligence (under the Third Anti-Money Laundering Directive) for low-value electronic money "accounts" the same as the value of the largest banknote: in this case, €500. Although they are only looking at this for non-reloadable devices, I think this should be the guiding principle for reloadable devices as well. The link between the two, the "magic number", is entirely symbolic: it doesn't mean anything at all, but it's a good way to focus debate and discussion about the regulatory balance between cash and cash alternatives.

A theory of privacy to help technologists – 10/02/2011

The Institute for Advanced Legal Studies hosted an excellent seminar by Professor Michael Birnhack from the Faculty of Law at Tel Aviv University who was talking about "A Quest for a Theory of Privacy".

He pointed out that while we're all very worried about privacy, we're not really sure what should be done. It might be better to pause and review the legal "mess" around privacy and then try to find an intellectually-consistent way forward. This seems like a reasonable course of action to me, so I listened with interest as Michael explained that for most people, privacy issues are becoming more noticeable with Facebook, Google Buzz, Airport "nudatrons", Street View, CCTV everywhere (particularly in the UK) and so on. (I'm particularly curious about the intersection between new technologies—such as RFID tags and biometrics—and public perceptions of those technologies, so I found some of the discussion very interesting indeed.)

Michael is part of the EU PRACTIS research group that has been forecasting technologies that will have an impact on privacy (good and bad: PETs and threats, so to speak). They use a roadmapping technique that is similar to the one we use at Consult Hyperion to help our clients to plan their strategies for exploiting new transaction technologies and is reasonably accurate within a 20 year horizon. Note that for our work for commercial clients, we use a 1-2 year, 2-5 year, and 5+ year roadmap. No-one in a bank or a telco cares about the 20 year view, even if we could predict it with any accuracy—and given that I've just read the BBC correspondents informed predictions for 2011 and they don't mention, for example, what's been going on in Tunisia and Egypt, I'd say that's pretty difficult.

One key focus that Michael rather scarily picked out is omnipresent surveillance, particularly of the body (data about ourselves, that is, rather than data about our activities), with data acted upon immediately, but perhaps its best not go into that sort of thing right now!

He struck a definite chord when he said that it might be the new business models enabled by new technologies that are the real threat to privacy, not the technologies themselves. These mean that we need to approach a number of balances in new ways: privacy versus law enforcement, privacy versus efficiency, privacy versus freedom of expression. Moving to try and set these balances, via the courts, without first trying to understand what privacy is may take us in the wrong direction.

His idea for working towards a solution was plausible and understandable. Noting that privacy is a vague, elusive and contingent concept, but nevertheless a fundamental human right, he said that we need a useful model to start with. We can make a simple model by bounding a triangle with technology, law and values: this gives three sets of tensions to explore.

Law-Technology. It isn't a simple as saying that law lags technology. In some cases, law attempts to regulate technology directly, sometimes indirectly. Sometimes technology responds against the law (eg, anonymity tools) and sometimes it co-operates (eg, PETs—a point that I thought I might disagree with Michael about until I realised that he doesn't quite mean the same thing as I do by PETs).

Technology-Values. Technological determinism is wrong, because technology embodies certain values. (with reference to Social Construction of Technology, SCOT). Thus (as I think repressive regimes around the world are showing) it's not enough to just have a network.

Law-Values, or in other words, jurisprudence, finds courts choosing between different interpretations. This is where Michael got into the interesting stuff from my point of view, because I'm not a lawyer and so I don't know the background of previous efforts to resolve tensions on this line.

Focusing on that third set of tensions, then, in summary: From Warren and Brandeis' 1890 definition of privacy as the right to be let alone, there have been more attempts to pick out a particular bundle of rights and call them privacy. Alan Westin's 1967 definition was privacy as control: the claims of individuals or groups or institutions to determine for themselves when, how and to what extent information about them is communicated to others.

This is a much better approach than the property right approach, where disclosing or not disclosing, "private" and "public" are the states of data. Think about the example of smart meters, where data outside the home provides information about how many people are in the home, what time they are there and so on. This shows that the public/private, in/out, home/work barriers are not useful for formulating a theory. The alternative that he put forward considers the person, their relationships, their community and their state. I'm not a lawyer so I probably didn't understand the nuances, but this didn't seem quite right to me, because there are other dimensions around context, persona, transaction and so on.

The idea of managing the decontextualisation of self seemed solid to my untrained ear and eye and I could see how this fitted with the Westin definition of control, taking on board the point that privacy isn't property and it isn't static (because it is technology-dependent). I do think that choices about identity ought, in principle, to be made on a transaction-by-transaction basis even if we set defaults and delegate some of the decisions to our technology and the idea that different persona, or avatars, might bundle some of these choices seems practical.

Michael's essential point is, then, that a theory of privacy that is formulated by examining definitions, classsifications, threats, descriptions, justifications and concepts around privacy from scratch will be based on the central notion of privacy as control rather than secrecy or obscurity. As a technologist, I'm used to the idea that privacy isn't about hiding data or not hiding it, but about controlling who can use it. Therefore Michael's conclusions from jurisprudence connect nicely connect with my observations from technology.

An argument that I introduced in support of his position during the questions draws on previous discussions around the real and virtual boundary, noting that the lack of control in physical space means the end of privacy there, whereas in virtual space it may thrive. If I'm walking down the street, I have no control over whether I am captured by CCTV or not. But in virtual space, I can choose which persona to launch into which environment, which set of relationships and which business deals. I found Michael's thoughts on the theory behind this fascinating, and I'm sure I'l be returning to them in the future.

Does mass market eID need a liability model or not? – 14/03/2011

I posted about the silo-style identity and authentication schemes we have in place at the moment and complained that we are making no progress on federation. Steve Wilson posted a thoughtful reply and picked me up on a few points, such as my "idea" (that's a bit strong - more of a notion, really) of developing an equivalent of creative commons licences, a sort of open source framework. He says:-

> *CC licenses wouldn't ever be enough. Absent new laws to make this kind of grand identity federation happen, we will still need new contracts—brand new contracts of an unusual form—struck between all the parties.*

> *[From comment on Digital Identity: The sorry state of id and authentication]*

But isn't that what CC licences solve?

> *It's complicated by the fact that banks & telcos don't naturally see themselves as "identity providers", not in the open anyway*

> *[From comment on Digital Identity: The sorry state of id and authentication]*

Well, I'm doing what I can to change that (see, for example, the Visa), but on the main point I happened to be reading the notes from the EURIM Identity Governance Subgroup meeting on 23 February 2011, talking about business cases for population scale identity management systems. The notes say that:-

> *It is alleged that the only body with the remit, power and capability needed for assuring and recording a root identity through a secure and reliable registration process is Government.*

The notes then go on to talk about case studies such as the Nordic bank-issued eIDs though. These arguments are to some extent circular, of course, because the e-government applications in the Nordics are using bank-issued eIDs, but the only reason that the banks can issue these eIDs is because they are using government ID as the basis for KYC. In the discussion about this at a recent roundtable in that Visa/CSFI "Identity and Financial Services" series, someone made a comment in passing (and I'm embarrassed to say that I can't remember who said this, because I noted the comment but forgot the commenter) that all of this takes places in a model **absent liability**. That is, as far as I understand what was said, the government accepts no liability from the banks, and vice versa. So if the bank opens an account for me Sven Birch, using a government "Sven Birch" identity, but it subsequently transpires that I am actually Theogenes de Montford, then the bank cannot claim against the government. Similarly, if I used my bank eID "Sven Birch" to access government services, but it subsequently transpires that I am actually Theogenes, then the government has no claim against the bank. (If this isn't true, by the way, I would appreciate clarification from a knowledgeable correspondent.)

So what is the situation? Must we have a liability model, or can we all agree to get along without one. Or do you have to a have a more consensual society, or perhaps one with fewer lawyers per head of population?

Joint approaches – 14/09/2011

More activity in the world of mobile financial services, and I've been in a few conversations with people recently about changing regulatory structures. I've been fairly consistent in arguing that there are sound reasons why mobile operators will want to provide some services themselves and not work in partnership with existing banks. Now this:

> Rogers Communications, the largest mobile operator in Canada, has applied for a licence to offer banking services, according to a filing it has made with the country's government. If successful, the operator would be "primarily focused on credit, payment and charge card services", according to its application.

> [From Canada's Rogers wants to be a bank, Articles | Mobile]

Why would anyone want to be a bank, unless it's to get some kind of government handout? I can see why an operator might want to run payment services, but they should leave the provision of credit to banks. Of course, I imagine this is what's really behind their decision. You need to consider the regulatory context. Rogers have to apply for banking licence, even though they have no intention of taking deposits, because there's no other construct for running payment systems. Perhaps a lawyer can inform us, but I imagine that in order run certain kinds of payment services in Canada, you have to be a bank because there's no separate regulatory category that's the equivalent of the European Payment Institution (PI).

The European telcos are not applying for banking licences, instead they are applying for Payment Institution (PI) licences. These allow them to offer the retail payment services that they want to and in a regulatory structure that is much "lighter" (and therefore less expensive) than for banking—which is why, as an aside, I expect banks to form subsidiaries with PI licences as well. In France and Germany, the operators are moving ahead with their own schemes.

> *Operator-backed Buyster will launch its payment service, which aims to make online transactions more secure using mobile phones, on Sept. 13... Buyster was born in February, when operators Bouygues Telecom, Orange, SFR and IT services company Atos formed it.*

[From <u>French Operators Launch Mobile</u>]

The French multi-operator service is launching with a relatively simple security layer on top of card payments.

> *To use the service, mobile subscribers first need to register with Buyster, which enables a bank card to be linked to the user's cell phone number in a secure way. To make an online payment, users first enter their mobile phone number and password. They then receive a message with a one-time password that is entered on the website to finalize the transaction*

[From <u>French Operators Launch Mobile</u>]

I wonder if security is a good enough play for the mass market? I know the French market is different from the UK, and consumer attitudes to PINs, cards and risk are different, but I would have thought that the average consumer sees security as the banks' problem, not theirs. A convenience-based play strikes me as being the way forward. Which isn't to say, naturally, that Buyster isn't convenient. Compared to messing about typing in card numbers, it's much easier.

The German mobile operators have joined together to launch a more ambitious scheme because they are going after the physical point of service (POS). Remember that the French operators are already involved in a scheme with French banks to target the physical POS and I understand that several transactions have already been made in the Nice area, where 3000 people were given NFC phones, although it seems to me unlikely that the AFSCM (the French mobile proximity association) projection of a million handsets by the end of this year will be met.

The three operators - Vodafone, Telefónica and Deutsche Telekom - are planning to launch under Mpass brand in early 2012. Mpass is an existing SMS-based service which German consumers can use for Internet shopping and charge their purchases to a pre-registered bank account. Recognising the shortage of NFC phones, the new Mpass service will start with NFC stickers.

[From Celent Banking Blog » What Do The German Telcos Know That We Don't?]

Stickers are the future!! So Mpass is similar to AFSCM except that Mpass uses stickers and AFSCM uses handsets and it's similar to Buyster except that it uses bank accounts whereas Buyster uses cards. It makes sense: everyone in Germany has a bank account but card usage is lower than in France. In Deutsche Bank's September research note on this, they say that:

German customers are likely to be even more cautious when shopping by mobile than at a desk-bound PC when big-ticket items are involved and with certain processes that they already have reservations about (such as credit cards in Germany)

The German approach, then, is based more around bank accounts and the short-term expedient of stickers. But this makes for a major barrier

In contrast, the German operators clearly aim to introduce a new payment brand, mpass, and expect to sign-up enough merchants to create the necessary acceptance infrastructure. Instead of working with banks or existing card schemes, it plans to work with prepaid payment services providers, such as easycash.

[From Celent Banking Blog » What Do The German Telcos Know That We Don't?]

They're setting themselves a difficult problem - persuading merchants to sign up for the new payment scheme - but if they can crack it then their higher risk and reward curve looks pretty interesting. I'm sure that Mpass will be much cheaper than conventional card-based schemes and it will set them a useful competitive challenge.

All of this makes the situation in the UK really interesting. The operators here are forming a joint venture to make it easier for service providers to exploit the new proximity technology but they are clear that payments are only one part of the proposition: advertising, coupons, loyalty and so forth are all part of the mix. It's an interaction as well as transaction play. I say "the operators", incidentally, but this doesn't include "3", who are taking legal action

Mobile operator 3 is mounting a campaign to scupper a mobile payments joint venture between its bigger rivals, urging regulators in Brussels and London to block the plan on competition grounds.

[From Payments joint venture under attack by 3 - FT.com]

Therefore in the UK, France and Germany we have three entirely different examples of joint ventures involving the operators to try and exploit mobile proximity technology: NFC with a focus on card payments and ticketing in France, NFC stickers and bank payments in Germany, NFC value-added wallets with card payments in the UK. Great stuff: there will be lots to learn from these different approaches over coming months.

Part 2 – Networks

Chapter 4: Finance and Banking

Electronic transactions have been at the heart of the finance and banking sector since the first Western Union wire transfer in1871. Whatever technologists might think about the sector, we need to understand its dynamics and response to new transaction technologies and the new business opportunities they provide.

Time to experiment with new ATMs – 09/02/2011

There has been another spate of cash machine fraud, near where I live, entirely coincidentally. The police have instructed us to... well, let them tell you.

> *Officers have advised members of the public that if possible they should not leave the scene if their card is retained*
>
> *[From BBC News - Cash machine users in Woking warned over thefts]*

So, essentially, if an ATM keeps your card (this has never, ever, happened to me) then you should stay by the machine and call for help. Who you are supposed to call is not made clear, but I will call one of our local police stations. These are open from 8am to 10pm. As an aside, when I last went to one of our local police stations, I was ushered into a small room with a telephone, from where you are connected to the same call centre as if you had just stayed at home and phoned them, so come to think of it I may just as well call the call centre directly. Perhaps it's time to rethink the "hello 1966" card plus 4-digit PIN system and either get rid of ATMs completely or improve their security. Perhaps we should look further afield for ideas for new ATMs.

> *The Intelligent ATM comes equipped with a camera that recognises the customer's face and sends details of the facial dimensions to a database for verification... Its use could also reduce the now common incidents where carjackers force their victims to empty their accounts at gunpoint, often taking the card and the personal identification number (PIN).*
>
> *[From Daily Nation: - News |Your face is all you'll need at an ATM]*

I think this is unlikely: it would simply replace customers being forced to hand over their ATM card at gunpoint with customers being forced to go to an ATM at gunpoint, which strikes me as being more dangerous!

Relatively few people are carjacked and shot dead in Woking at the moment—this generally happens up the A3 in South London—- but it could all change. Mind you, you've got to be pretty brave to use an ATM at all in the UK.

> 'We were surprised by our results because the ATM machines were shown to be heavily contaminated with bacteria; to the same level as nearby public toilets... In addition the bacteria we detected on ATMs were similar to those from the toilet, which are well known as causes of common human illnesses.'

[From Cash machines 'as dirty as public toilets' | Mail Online]

Yuk. It's time to stop the silly 1960s fashion for putting things in slots and touching filthy keypads. This might help prevent fraud as well as the propagation of intestinal disorders.

> The future may lie with RFID chips and mobile phones. If a mobile phone replaced the ATM card and withdrawals could be performed only by placing an RFID phone near an ATM then cell site analysis (plus E911 and E112 compliance) would greatly limit the scope of fraud against banks. But such a secure deployment needs investment - and in these difficult times this looks doubtful.

[From Forensic Computing Expert and Barrister - Automated Teller Machines]

Maybe Barclays, who have issued millions of contactless debit cards in the UK, might want to start experimenting with ATM de nos jours. After all, I want to leave home without a wallet, with only a phone, but there are still backward and underdeveloped parts of the world (eg, Woking) where many retailers do not yet have contactless terminals and so there is the need for occasional recourse to the hole in the wall, but it's difficult to get my iPhone in the slot, especially when it is fitted with anti-fraud devices. Consider this appealing alternative: take splendid new Barclaycard/Orange mobile phone with NFC, open card application and enter numerical passcode and amount of money required. Then hold phone next to ATM and wait for the money to come out.

Why is card fraud in the UK apparently so much worse than elsewhere? – 11/02/2011

Our good friends at ACI Worldwide have just released their annual Global Card Fraud Survey, which contains some rather bad news: the UK has more card fraud than many other countries. We're up there with the US, with three times as many people affected than in Germany and the Netherlands. So a third of us have been victims of card fraud compared to only a tenth in Netherlands. Why? Are the Dutch more honest than Brits? Are their cards more sophisticated? No. I think there are two main reasons for this discrepancy.

First of all, while chip and PIN has cut fraud on the high street, card-not-present fraud is still a big problem. In the UK, cards still account for a big portion of online payments. In the Netherlands, and some other countries, they don't. More than two-thirds of Dutch e-commerce purchases are made with iDeal, a bank-based scheme that has no equivalent in the UK (or the US, or pretty much anywhere else for that matter).

Second, UK credit cards have high limits. In the last couple of weeks, both of my main card issuers have written to me raising credit limits (I didn't ask for this in either case). If you're going to steal some card details, you'd go for cards that are likely to be some way from their limit.

The survey wasn't all bad news, by any means. I found it interesting that the proportion of people who had been victims of card fraud but were satisfied with the response of their issuer had actually increased slightly, to almost four-fifths, which isn't bad. Personally, like the majority of people surveyed, the last time there was a strange charge on my card, the bank took off the charge then cancelled and reissued the card.

> *The agent informed me that new cards for me and my wife would be Fed-Ex'd, to arrive today or tomorrow. What followed were a series of texts from merchants that have my credit card on file for automatic billing, delighting me with the knowledge that I won't be able to use such services as the Bay's FasTrak toll lanes or uninterrupted cable service until I update my records.*
>
> *[From I'm a five-time ID Fraud victim; How crazy is that? - Javelin Strategy & Research Blog]*

Think how expensive this all this though: cancelling and re-issuing cards, call centre seats, letters and whatever else. So we still need to do better. Only around a third of people (fewer than before) said that they would switch financial institutions because of card fraud, which is bad news for people trying to sell anti-card fraud solutions to high street banks.

> *The poll of 970 UK adults, part of the bi-annual global Unisys Security Index, reveals that cyber-security is the public's chief concern, with 85% of respondents worried, and over 50% "seriously concerned", about bank card fraud and identity theft.*
>
> *[From Finextra: Brits switching banks over security and privacy]*

This is odd, I think. I couldn't care less about bank card fraud, since it's the banks' problem and not mine. I never use a debit card for anything, offline or online, so I'm totally protected by the legislation around credit cards. I'm more worried about identity theft, because it's more time consuming to put right, but that's a different issue (being discussed at the CSFI yesterday, as it happens).

The press release also noted that 81% of people have confidence in their issuer protecting them from fraud. I think that this may be a little simplistic, for that very reason: had I been asked for the survey, I would have said that I don't really care about Barclays' ability to prevent fraud on my splendid OnePulse credit card because it's their problem.

Mobile payment and mobile banking are different and complementary – 23/02/2011

Mobile payments and mobile banking are not the same thing at all and, as I have long maintained, there is no reason to think that mobile payments should be provided by banks, nor that mobile operators want to get in to banking. This is why I maintain the much of the comment around these topics is misleading. For example:

> Geo-strategic and political consultant at Nova-Comm Strategy Group, Brett Goldman, says: "With M-Pesa... Essentially, what you are doing is eliminating the need for a bank,"

> [From *Near field comms: How are mobile payments changing traditional banking? - 2/22/2011 - Computer Weekly*]

Well, up to a point. They are not eliminating the need for a bank, they are eliminating the need for banks to run payment services. And this is not bad for banks, or customers, because M-PESA don't need to eliminate banks in order to improve the banking infrastructure as it demonstrates with the example of the M-KESHO service, launched with Equity Bank, that allows M-PESA customers to transfer money to and from savings accounts.

> With the M-Kesho Account, customers will be able to get pre-qualified personal accident insurance, access to short-term loan facilities ranging from KES 100, and interest on the mobile account from as little as KES 1. The application is built with the ability to score a customer's credit rating using a six-month history of his M-Pesa balances.

> [From *Safaricom, Equity Bank launch M-Pesa bank account - Telecompaper*]

How interesting is that? The transaction history built up inside M-PESA provides a straightforward mechanism for financial inclusion, simply not available in a cash economy, and an apparently entirely viable alternative to credit history. The service has been tremendously successful.

> *He noted that some 21 percent of M-PESA users in Kenya now use the service simply to store money and earn interest. The savings service – branded as M-KESHO and in partnership with Kenya's Equity Bank – has effectively set-up 750,000 new bank accounts in Kenya since launching in May with deposits totalling KES900 million (US$10.7 million).*

[From Vodafone]

Scatchamagowza! They're on their way to creating a million new bank accounts. Far from taking customers away from banks, M-PESA is bringing customers to them! As far as I can see, this is pretty conclusive proof that banks are wrong to lobby regulators to insist that mobile payments can only be provided by banks and that regulators are wrong to listen to them. (In Europe, fortunately, this is not true because of the Payment Services Directive: O2 have applied for a payments licence in the UK, for example). So, an efficient and effective mobile payments platform adds value to mobile financial services by making those financial services more accessible at lower cost. And while stimulating this, operators can make money too.

> *Aite says mobile payments will account for $214 billion in gross dollar volume by 2015, up from only $16 billion in 2010*

[From The Smartphone Payments Train's Leaving the Station - Bank Technology News]

That means lots of transaction fees. It's interesting to note how M-PESA's transaction fee income has held up.

> *As the use of M-Pesa spread, Kenyans started using it for smaller and smaller transactions. The average amount sent through M-Pesa declined from the equivalent of about $50 in March 2007 to less than $30 by March 2009.*

[From Fascinating Stat and Lesson for the US About Mobile]

So Kenyans are sending smaller amounts and are paying transaction fees that amount to larger fraction of the transaction (around 7%) because they still find it more convenient to do this than to use any of the alternatives. Once again, we see the mobility premium in action and a new value network that enables mobile operators to provide profitable payment services (because of that mobility premium) while simultaneously enabling bank, insurance companies and others to provide profitable financial services using mobile payments as a conduit.

More important than the mobile payments business itself will be the businesses that it enables. Just like M-KESHO, there will be new financial services businesses that only make sense on the mobile payments platform. In the UK, initiatives such as O2 Mobile Money and Orange Cash should provide some useful early indications as to how the market might evolve: if third-party financial services offer new products using these payments (eg, SME payments, media subscriptions, that kind of thing), then I think that will show that the pie will get bigger instead of getting sliced

P.S. By way of an experiment in the service of readers, I have instructed no.1 son to go mystery shopping for an Orange Cash card and will report here in a couple of weeks.

We already have the cheque replacement technology – 24/02/2011

There's a fun piece by Mark Kitto in this month's *Prospect* magazine. It concerns a chap who was visiting a friend in Shanghai. The visitor borrowed some cash from the host and wanted to repay it, so he posted a cheque drawn on a major international bank (which took 34 days to arrive). In order to cash the cheque, the host had to go through a time-consuming and expensive process, which culminated in having to open a bank account that now lays dormant (my good lady wife had to go through a similar process in the US a couple of years ago).

The piece is bylined "Shanghai is the financial capital of the far east. But just try cashing a cheque."

Surely, I thought, reading this piece that only someone with virtually no understanding of retail payment systems and completely cut-off from modern technology would write a cheque in these circumstances? I then realised that I'd missed a clue at the start of the article: the visitor was described as "a banker friend from Britain".

A cheque? Crackers.

I'm actually writing this article while visiting China, and tonight I'm going to dinner with an English friend who is visiting here from Thailand. (To be fair to British bankers, he did tell me that his HSBC Beijing account and HSBC Bangkok account do play together nicely.) Anyway, if I end up owing him money I will either PayPal it to him, post U.S. dollars in an envelope or leave him a Travelex prepaid Visa card which I'll load for him via the internet, or if he (like all wise travellers) has a spare pre-paid card in his back pocket, I'll top his up for him. Or I'll top up his Thai mobile using my credit card, or I'll load an Oyster card for him to use next time he comes to London, or…

Anything but a cheque, actually. It's time we started to get serious about getting rid of them: British bankers who write cheques should be made to feel silly. When the UK Payments Council announced a roadmap for getting rid of cheques, the reaction was predictably, well, reactionary. Here's some typical stuff, in the case from The Guardian, for example.

> *I'm a sole trader who runs a window cleaning business, and many of my customers pay me by cheque. What am I going to do?*
>
> *This group is expected to see the biggest impact when cheques disappear in 2018, not least because many won't be able to invest in the technology the industry is relying on taking over from cheques.*
>
> *[From Cheques out, but what does it mean for everyday payments? | Money | The Guardian]*

What? Sole traders don't have mobile phones? What a load of old rubbish. In a list of "8 Things Your Phone Will (Probably) Replace", the payment terminal shows up as no. 4 and I can't say I disagree.

> *Handsets already connect to the same networks as mobile payment terminals so to think they will be able to mimic the same functionality isn't too hard to imagine.*
>
> *[From 8 Things Your Phone Will (Probably) Replace - Consumerologist's posterous]*

We already have the cheque replacement technology in our hands. What many people don't yet have are cheque replacement systems, but we're getting there as more non-banks move to open up this sector, as has long been obvious to most non-bankers. Of course, cheques are only one part of the payments business that could be replaced by non-bank alternatives.

> *Indeed, banks have been extremely slow to meet the evolving customer demands of the digital age. With the rise of these new Web 2.0 business models we are experiencing a complete change in the way money is transacted. In the future, it won't be the banks that are sending out thousands of cheques or triggering tens of thousands of micro bank transfers to these users.*
>
> *[From Financial World Online]*

This isn't bad for banks - as we were discussing with reference to M-PESA - provided they have a strategy for using these new payment systems to everyone's advantage.

Criminals have to adapt their strategies too! 14/04/2011

I'm giving a keynote at the Smart Card Alliance conference in Chicago in a couple of weeks. It's going to be about EMV in the USA. I've just been mulling it over, and once again looked at Deborah Baxley's neat summary of the immediate future for the US cards business:

> Banks scrambling to replace lost fee revenue will likely shift focus to credit and prepaid, impose DDA and other fees, along with new account services and comprehensive pricing packages.

> [From Changing the Game in Cards - pymnts.com]

It's not just banks who have to rethink their strategies because of developments in the payment sector. I note that in the UK, according to the Centre for Economics & Business Research reported in Fraud Watch 6(18), nearly 100,000 people were victims of direct debt fraud last year, a direct consequence of the use of chip and PIN at retail POS. As card fraud has become more difficult, the criminals have shifted their focus. Direct debit fraud was one basis point of identity fraud cases a decade ago, now it is a tenth of all cases. Criminals have to adapt to chip and PIN just as banks and merchants do.

> A group of seven postmen intercepted letters containing credit cards, switched the microchips of the cards with fake ones and then delivered them to the applicants... the syndicate also had the help of a National Registration Department (NRD) officer who supplied them with the names of the mothers of the real credit card applicants

> [From 7 M'sian postmen nabbed for credit]

It's interesting to think like a criminal. Well, sometimes. In Chicago, two men were shot by guards while trying to rob a cash transit.

> The dead suspect was identified as Jimmy Townsend, 52... a convicted felon and was sentenced to 10 years in prison for two separate armed robbery convictions.

> [From 2 suspects shot, one fatally, in armored truck heist - Chicago Breaking News]

Armed robbery is a bizarre crime. I think I'm right in saying that in the UK the average sentence is longer than that for murder. In the US, Mr. Townsend spent years in jail for it, and then got killed doing it again. How dumb did he have to be to go back to trying to rob armoured cars. If only he read the Digital Money Blog, he would have known that there are much easier targets.

> *The heavily-armed gang made off with the tournament jackpot of 242,000 euros ($327,000; £217,000) in early March. Police said a 28-year-old Lebanese man, the fourth arrested in connection with the raid, had been detained on Sunday.*
>
> *[From BBC News - German police arrest poker tournament heist suspect]*

OK, so not all of them got away, but casinos are not a bad idea for enterprising criminals. They do have lots of cash, and often the people in them will not report cash as stolen.

> *Masked men have stormed a packed casino near the Swiss border city of Basel, making off with hundreds of thousands of francs, prosecutors say.*
>
> *About 10 raiders pulled up at the Grand Casino in two cars just after 0400 (0200 GMT) and smashed their way in, brandishing machine-guns and pistols. The French-speaking gang ordered the 600 guests and employees to the floor while they emptied registers.*
>
> *[From BBC News - Switzerland casino is robbed by armed gang]*

Criminals follow the path of least resistance. I hope Bankerstuff don't mind me quoting from a marketing e-mail they sent me concerning a forthcoming webinar.

> *A Former Bank Robber Shares Security Insights During Live Webinar on April 28 from 2:00 - 3:00pm Eastern. Troy Evans pursued a career as a self-employed addict, drug dealer, gambler and thief for more than 15 years. Ultimately, his disregard of values and discipline resulted in a 13 year federal prison sentence. Facing the obstacles, pressures and violence of prison life, he was determined that his time behind bars would not be wasted... Having met and interviewed over 300 bank and credit union robbers he is able to give us a "look into the mind of the enemy". Troy answers questions such as... What can financial institutions do to deter a desperate criminal?*

I would have thought than an obvious idea would be to not have any cash since, as another bank robber famously remarked, he went "where the money is"? When it comes to card payments, the money is in getting hold of card details and (because of the switch to chip and PIN) PINs. Here, the criminals soon adapted their strategies to deal with the new instruments.

> Victorian Police believe international crime syndicates are bribing shop workers in return for access to EFTPOS terminals as part of an elaborate scam. They believe criminals have stolen as much as $80 million from Australian bank accounts over the past year...
>
> The syndicates install cameras in ceilings to film people entering their identification numbers.
>
> [From EFTPOS scam costs Australians $80m - ABC News (Australian Broadcasting Corporation)]

They're using these PINs (since they can't make counterfeit chip and PIN cards) with the card details to withdraw cash from ATMs. Once all of the cards and ATMs are chip-only, this avenue will be closed to them. Thus while chip and PIN isn't perfect, it's good enough to push criminals into other channels. So: a thought experiment...

Suppose we improve the security of payment systems to the point where they cannot, effectively, be broken. Theft, fraud and hacking are not possible. Where would criminals go next? I think they're spoilt for choice, so relatively small improvements in payment security would send them off to pasture news.

> The poll of 533 firms shows that 55% experienced fraud in the last 12 months, with 61% of these hit more than once, a similar picture to the previous year. In total, 75% of the businesses participating in the study experienced online account takeover and/or online fraud.
>
> [From Finextra: Account takeover fraud]

SME account takeover seems much easier than armed robbery and much more profitable. The so-called man-in-the-middle attacks on OTP systems for remote access to baking accounts are an established attack vector.

> According to BillingScore, 19.4% of the value of all transactions in the U.K. premium rate sector are fraudulent, or roughly £1 on every £5 spent. "With the premium rate sector in the U.K. mobile industry currently worth in the region of £700 million, this

equates to £135.8 million per year being lost to fraud in the U.K. alone," the company said.

[From UK mobile operators 'hide' £136m annual fraud]

A fifth? As opposed to a few bp in cards? I predict that any forward-looking criminal in this scenario will be eyeing up the telecommunications opportunities. So let's look at what some forward-looking criminals are doing. I think criminals in Eastern Europe are a useful barometer, because they tend to be well-educated and computer-savvy. And they get arrested for time to time so we can see what they get up to. Here's the stash of Romanian hackers arrested last year. You will, of course, note that it does not include low maximum balance prepaid cards or accounts.

77,350 euros, 49,000 U.S. dollars, 64,860 pounds, 60,645 lei, a luxury watch, a rifle, three pistols and 150 grams of gold. 70 laptops, 165 mobile phones, 35 desktop computers, 15 modems, new servers, 10 blank cards, 2425 SIM cards...

[From CyberCrime & Doing Time: Nicolae Popescu, Romanian hacker, at large!]

So not only the usual euros and dollars, but also gold (clearly the hackers were diversifying) and also two-and-a-half thousand SIM cards. Two-and-a-half thousand! Here are people taking the messages of convergence, future-proofing and cloud payments quite seriously. As Eric Schmidt said when still with Google, if you don't have a mobile strategy then you don't have a strategy. Now, if you're like me, you will wonder what on Earth they are going to do with these SIMs. Then I remembered something that I'd read a while ago.

Only days after almost two million Bulgarians registered their SIM cards, the Interior Ministry warns that new forms of abuse are appearing... the Interior Ministry as saying that it expected a flood of SIM cards, registered to Romas and homeless people, to appear on the market in the coming weeks.

[From Interior Ministry warns of trade in registered pre-paid SIM]

Mystery solved. The answer to why there should be a significant value attached to SIM cards that you can buy for virtually nothing in any shop is, naturally, government policy. After pocketing their windfalls from selling their SIM cards, the homeless and Roma presumably went off to celebrate their good fortune, whereas the criminals went off to figure out how to create a mass supply instead of having to negotiate with individuals.

...only four months into 2010, and organised crime groups already have found ways of beating the system... Radio host Borislav Borissov found out that he was the "proud owner" of about 200 different SIM cards, all registered to his name and personal social security number.

[From Bulgarian criminals 'beating the system' of pre-paid SIM]

I know where I'd invest my criminal dollars! Mobile is the future! No, of course, I'm just joking to make a point. If I really was going to invest dollars in a criminal enterprise, it would be in Somali pirates, except for one sticking point. I'm afraid my strict ethical position will not allow me to deal with these people.

The al Shabaab group, which professes loyalty to al Qaeda, said mobile money transfers (MMT) helped feed Western capitalism and were turning Somalia's Muslims against Islamic banking practices.

[From Somalia's al Shabaab bans mobile money transfers | Top News | Reuters]

I cannot do sufficient violence to my conscience to support a group who are against mobile payments.

Banks aren't generally the place to look for innovation – 26/04/2011

Around the world, when faced with new products in the payments space, banks naturally crank up their innovation departments and produce super new products and services to wow customers back. I'm joking, of course. What they actually do in many countries is to going whining to the regulator and force competitors to use the banks' legacy infrastructure. This is what just happened in India, which really ought to be a huge and dynamic market for e-, m- and new payments of many kinds.

merchants in India cannot receive payments from abroad of over $500 per transaction. In addition, merchants will no longer be able to use any balance in their PayPal accounts to buy goods or services. Instead all payments must be transferred into Indian bank accounts first.

[From Finextra: RBI forces PayPal]

Now, I'm not saying that banks are the only people who react to innovation in this way: that is, by trying to stop it. This goes on all the time.

For the last fifty years, hard disks have been increasingly super-charged gramophone records: at their heart, there is still a real disk rotating very fast on a real spindle. That's not the only way to store data, as the memory stick revolution shows, but until now, solid state drives (which have no moving parts) have been too small and expensive to replace traditional hard disks as the main storage device for a computer. Now that's changing, with real advantages for users as a result... Seagate's response is to threaten to sue all the new entrants for patent infringement, while insisting that their existing market is not threatened.

[*From* Public Strategy: Innovator's irony]

At the dawn of the industrial revolution, the steam engine delivered the fundamental business school case study in this topic, something that I wrote about when I was invited to speak at the European Patent Forum back in 2009.

In his keynote address, the Czech Prime Minister Mirek Topolanek said that we had to find a balance in the intellectual property system, that it was right to let Stevenson patent his steam engine but not the screwdriver he used to build it (he didn't explain why..).

[*From* Patent error | 15Mb: yet another blog from Dave Birch]

In fact, as I discussed in this post, history teaches the opposite lesson because the patent system held back the evolution of the steam engine for a generation! But back to our business. What kind of innovation is relevant to the payments industry? This is not clear to me. On the one hand, it seems reasonable to say that...

What would be refreshing is if the focus of innovation could be pegged to the value that it delivers to the entire ecosystem, not just the engineers who get a kick out of building cool new toys.

[*From* Payment Gadgets at The Catalyst Code]

But is this true? When Apple put together the iPod, it didn't benefit the "entire ecosystem". The disruptive innovations in fact devastate parts of the ecosystem, like forest fires that allow new shoots to grow. I hate to harp on about the M-PESA example, but I think it illustrates this point well. The banks complained about M-PESA and tried to stop it but fortunately failed. Now that M-PESA has 13m customers and 20,000 agents, the banks are able to deliver new services to new customers using the platform. Were they devastated by the forest fire? No: it gave them space for new shoots as well.

Tomorrow's Transactions—The 2012 Reader

Where do we look for the next new shoots then? Not in banks, generally speaking, but elsewhere in the ecosystem. The payment innovations to come will be technology-enabled, which is why it's important for businesses throughout that ecosystem to understand the new technologies relevant to payments and, just as importantly, understand the business model ramifications of seemingly dreary technology architecture decisions being made by nerds right now. While they will be technology-enabled, though, it's the sustainable new business model that is the key. A good example of this is

> ..*if Square can provide just enough added-value with their app to get traction in the small business sector (they are already processing a million dollars a day), then when new payment technologies come along (eg, NFC phones that can accept payments from contactless cards) the merchants will just expect Square to handle them for them. We have long been advising clients that the key disruptive role of mobile phones in the payments world is the ability to* **take** *payments, not to* **make** *them.*

[From Digital Money: Hip to be Square]

And we still do, in fact. I think Square is an interesting innovation case study. It does not compete with existing acquirers, but opens up the market so that more people can accept card payments.

> *So where is Square seeing the most traction? Without a doubt, small businesses, independent workers and merchants comprise most of Square's rapidly growing user base. The technology only requires its tiny credit card scanner that fits into your audio jack and Square's app. The device and the software are free, but Square takes a small percentage of each transaction (2.75% plus 15 cents for swiped transactions).*

[From Square]

In a way, this is a real-world PSP and a fascinating niche play in a large volume-driven acquiring market, one that can be seen to adumbrate mobile disruption and our projection that the mobile-phone-as-POS meme will be more revolutionary than the mobile-phone-as-card meme. But there's something else to it as well. Conventional acquirers use conventional methods to assess applications.

> *Square's qualification rules are more relaxed than those of standard credit card processors, There are no initiation fees, monthly minimums, and when merchants apply for a reader, Square doesn't just focus on a credit check, but also takes into*

account the influence a company holds on Yelp, Twitter or Facebook.

[From Square]

That, it seems to me, is more of a window into the coming economy based on the reputation interweb (or web 3.1, as I propose to call it, to avoid clashing with web 3.0). Can you imagine Barclays Business or Streamline giving you a merchant acquiring account according to the number of twitter followers you have rather than your trading history or bank references?

By the way, I can't remember if I've blogged this before but one of my favourite stories about accepting merchants for acquiring accounts goes back more than a decade to the hazy days before the LastMinute flotation. I was doing some work over at what was then NatWest Capital Markets, who had invested millions in Lastminute, when they went beserk because NatWest Streamline wouldn't give LastMinute a credit card acquiring account because it didn't have two years' trading history!

Games are quite a serious business – 04/05/2011

It was obvious a few years ago that not only were virtual worlds going to be big business, but that they would have an impact on the payments market. I used put things like World of Warcraft into product and service roadmap discussions for our clients in the financial services space, and I'm sure that they thought I was doing it just for fun, just to get some discussion going. But having played around in the space, I could see it would lead to some new thinking. When you're sending World of Warcraft gold pieces to a friend in Asia via an elven intermediary (quicker and cheaper than banks, by the way) you can't help but wonder at the "real world" instruments to hand. This from three years ago...

> *Well it wouldn't surprise anyone then, that most of our partners report they have a completion rate of 0.5-1% when they present a credit card payment page to their users for virtual goods...Mobile on the other hand... takes 15 seconds, and off goes the user to his virtual good or points that will enhance his game or app experience immediately without ever leaving the environment of the app.*

[From Virtual Goods / Currency and Mobile]

Note that figure: one in a hundred transactions complete. People playing at being virtual farmers want to buy some virtual cows, so they click to buy, but when they see a credit card payment screen, they can't be bothered. So there was a demand for a new kind of payment instrument that was not being met by the banks. Look how much things have changed since then, with the incredible boom in app store and in-game payments. There's no doubt that the retail payments roadmap is indeed being affected by the world of games.

Now I'm not implying that it's only payments will be impacted, because in the longer run it will be many kinds of financial service, including banking.

> *The publisher of the online science-fiction game "Entropia Universe," set on the planet Calypso, received a banking license from the Swedish Financial Supervisory Authority last week and plans to open a real bank within a year, albeit one without physical, walk-in branches.*
>
> *Players of "Entropia" already exchange real money for a virtual currency that is used for their expenses on Calypso. And virtual money they make in the game, through hunting, mining, trading or other activities, can be cashed out into real money.*
>
> *[From The Associated Press: Online game gets real-world banking license]*

A healthy development! My younger son spends a lot of time online with his friends at the moment, hanging out not at the mall but at the WoW auction house (this is where he learns about economics, I'm happy to say). That's where our clients' next generation of customers are learning about money, payments and financial services. This from two years ago…

> *Today, Facebook application developers monetize their games and other applications by accepting payment directly using PayPal, Google, Amazon FPS, or SocialGold. Or developers may opt to receive direct payment via mobile phone via Zong, Boku, or another mobile payment provider… game developers in particular, often accept payment via a prepaid card sold in retail establishments, such as the Ultimate Game Card. The social and gaming web is exploding with virtual currency offerings, yet thus far no one model or payment brand dominates.*
>
> *[From Purchasing Facebook]*

Now, forward-looking organisations could see what was going on and began to target R&D appropriately.

> *Google is developing a micropayment platform that will be "available to both Google and non-Google properties within the*

next year,"... The system, an extension of Google Checkout, would be a new and unexpected option for the news industry as it considers how to charge for content online.

[From <u>Google</u>]

The idea was then that micropayments would be a payment vehicle available to both Google and non-Google properties within the year. The idea was to allow viable payments of a penny to several dollars by aggregating purchases across merchants and over time. Google planned to mitigate the risk of non-payment by assigning credit limits based on past purchasing behaviour and having credit card instruments on file for those with higher credit limits and using proprietary risk engines to track abuse or fraud. Merchant integration through Checkout would be extremely simple. Google, in fact, subsequently decided to purchase an in-game payments company rather than build it themselves.

Facebook and Google are poised to challenge the banking industry in online payments.

[From <u>Facebook</u>]

Is this really true? I think the answer is yes and no, in the sense that I can't see any reason why Facebook or Google would want to be a bank, unless it's to get some sort of government handout, but I can see why they might want to get involved in payments in order to make money (not from the payments, where margins are thin, but from new products and services that have payments integral to them). This is why the news that Facebook had also begun experimenting with a payment system was hardly unexpected, but was notable nonetheless. There was an expectation that the existence of a secure and convenient micropayment scheme for Facebook users (of which there now more than 600 million) would stimulate the development of a new marketplace within Facebook's "barbed wire". This seemed plausible to me—if it had been up to me, I would have added a spurious green element to the proposition somehow (getting merchants and other organisations to give out Facebook credits to reward environmentally desirable behaviour)—and I was sure it would do well. I wondered in a number of forums as to who else might enter this more competitive currency market?

In the coming months, facebook users will be able to obtain facebook Credits using MOL points purchased through MOL's network of more than 500,000 outlets, which are mainly in Malaysia, Singapore, Indonesia, Philippines, Thailand, India, Australia and New Zealand. In addition to outlets such as 7-Eleven stores and cybercafes, customers will be able to purchase

Credits through MOL's network of online banks in these countries.

[From Finextra: Facebook]

I gave a talk last year when I mentioned that I thought that Facebook credits would become the biggest virtual currency in the world fairly quickly. Unusually for my glib and sweeping predictions from the conference platform, this one appears to have come true, and even more quickly than I had imagined.

By the end of the year, Facebook expects that Credits will be used to buy the vast majority of virtual goods sold on Facebook. The fast-growing market is expected to reach $835 million on Facebook this year, according to the Inside Network... Through Credits, Facebook will take a 30 percent cut... To bolster that market, Facebook began selling Credits gift cards at Target stores across the country this month.

[From Facebook]

Now this will one day become a standard business school case study. Talking of which, a few years ago, as part of a course I was teaching at Visa's Bank Card Business School, a colleague and I mocked up a future Visa card that drew on a World of Warcraft account rather than a fiat currency account. This was photoshopped up to make a point, and at the time it was supposed to be a totally out-of-the-box crazy picture of the future. About two weeks after we made it up, I read that a US bank was issuing a Visa card with cashback in World of Warcraft gold. Oh well. It did help to make one of the points that I was trying to get across, which is that the future of payments will extend beyond the "traditional" bank, consumer, merchant and acquirer for 4-party model.

Vegetable company Green Giant is offering an unlikely reward for purchasing their products: virtual currency in Zynga's hit social game FarmVille.

[From Wacky: Zynga Gives Away Free FarmVille Cash With Purchases Of Real Life Vegetables]

That was bad timing, coming just as Zynga (the people behind Farmville) caved in to Facebook and agreed to replace Farmville cash with Facebook credits, but it was an interesting development nonetheless, showing that virtual money is just as valuable as "real" money. Facebook's tactics show they undoubtedly have a strategy in this field.

First Facebook turned off notifications for applications, taking away the primary mechanism for social games to go viral. Now if a company wants a massive audience for a new game, they almost certainly have to buy it through Facebook advertising.

Now Facebook is rolling out Credits as the preferred method of payment for games on their Platform, and taking a 30 per cent cut of the transactions. That's a much larger percentage than the social games companies were handing over to the small payment companies that had sprung up to fill this niche, and higher than the fees charged by PayPal and credit card companies.

[From Zynga says it's not leaving Facebook]

Now there's something to be said for the creation of a single currency area as a way to encourage trade and therefore prosperity.

Besides leading the creation of a more people-centric web, it could also end up having the dominant virtual currency, according to an early adopter of Facebook Credits. PopCap Games has been using the service, which is still in the beta testing phase, as the sole payment method for Bejeweled Blitz on Facebook. The game is free to play and attracts 11m monthly players, 3m of them playing it daily. PopCap sells extra power-ups, which boost players' capabilities, and is moving onto sales of virtual items. It has decided to ignore offering other virtual currency options and only accepts Facebook Credits. Users can buy them with credit cards, Paypal or through their mobile phones in $5, $10 and $20 increments for 50, 100 or 200 Credits.

[From Facebook]

These are all useful case studies, showing how a new currency can develop and evolve.

Facebook has certainly tried to guide the development of its online economy, almost in the way that governments seek to influence economic activity in the real world, through fiscal and monetary policy. Earlier this year the firm said it wanted applications running on its platform to accept its virtual currency, known as Facebook Credits. It argued that this was in the interests of Facebook users, who would no longer have to use different online currencies for different applications.

[From Social networks and statehood | The future is another country | Economist.com]

I think I've seen the playbook before.

> *That means all Facebook game developers will be able to start using Credits as their payment system for virtual goods — in fact, Facebook is requiring them to make the switch by July*

[From All]

This comes from the Great Khan's playbook for monetary and fiscal policy. Not Genghis Khan. His fiscal policy was confused: when he took control of China in 1215, his pacification plan was to kill everyone in China, no small undertaking since China was then, as now, the world's most populous country. Fortunately, one of his advisors, a man who ought to be the patron saint of Finance Ministers everywhere, Yeliu Ch'uts'ai, pointed out (presumably via a primitive Treasury model of some sort) that dead peasants paid considerably less tax than live ones, and the plan was halted. In 1260, Genghis' grandson Kublai Khan became Emporer of China. He decided, much as Mark Zuckerberg has, that it was a burden to commerce and taxation to have all sorts of currencies in use, ranging from copper "cash" to iron bars, to pearls to salt to specie, so he decided to implement a paper currency.

> *Here's what Marco Polo had to say about it…*

[From Digital Money: Lucky, for me anyway]

His monetary policy was refreshingly straightforward and more robust, even, than Mr. Zukerberg's: if you didn't accept his money, he would kill you. Naturally, in a short time, the new single currency was established and paper money began to circulate instead of gold, jewels, copper coins and metal bars. If you think talking about a new currency is crazy, take a look at Facebook Deals. According to Facebook, at launch, you will not be able to buy physical goods with Facebook Credits. Rather you will be able to get things like vouchers that you can redeem at events: now this is, frankly, a paper-thin distinction. I can't use Facebook Credits to pay for, say, a Coke at a pop concert but I can use them to pay for a voucher for a Coke at a pop concert. I am not an economist, but…

> *When beloved national retailers start offering goods and lower prices to customers who pay with a new, virtual currency - that's when said virtual currency becomes a force to reckon with. Somebody call Congress and the Federal Reserve - it's time to start having some serious conversations.*

[From Facebook]

There's a warning from history here! Unfortunately, the Khan's paper money ended in disaster because the money supply was not managed: it collapsed in hyperinflation, because in the days after Yeliu Ch'uts'ai, the temptation to print money was just too great for the monetary authorities too resist. Let's hope that the Emperor of Facebook finds an advisor of the calibre of Yeliu Ch'uts'ai.

One possible future might be that, just as China turned in on itself and stagnated, leaving technological and commercial progress to other people, Facebook will become an inward-looking economy while others take up the torch! Perhaps competition in currency, not only in payment methods, is needed to keep an economic space vital.

> *The new program, announced today at SXSW, is called RewardVille, which will give players zPoints and zCoins in CityVille, FrontierVille, FarmVille, Mafia Wars, Zynga Poker, Café World, Treasure Isle, YoVille, PetVille and Vampire Wars.*

> *[From Zynga Rolls Out New Virtual Currency in Addition to Facebook]*

Competition. This is the American way, not going complaining to Senator Durbin.

Improving authentication in the mass market using two, three (and four?) factors – 10/05/2011

I had an annoying problem with my PayPal account that ended up with me being posted a password, all quite tedious and strangely manual. As I observed at the time, it seemed odd that in 2011 we hadn't got anything figured out when it comes to authentication. Why couldn't I use my Barclays 2FA PINSentry to prove who I was to PayPal? In fact, why couldn't I use it for 2FA in general, since moving from passwords to 2FA involving tamper-resistant hardware would be a simple way to improve security across a range of services. We don't use 2FA, and we should.

> *But that might be changing [recently] Google launched two-factor authentication for Google Accounts—the credentials you use to log in to all Google services, including Gmail.*

> *[From Two-factor authentication: Gmail's new system offers more security than just a password. - By Farhad Manjoo - Slate Magazine]*

This is a good step. I use gmail, and I'd actually prefer to use it with 2FA than without, provided that the 2FA is based on something I already have, such as my phone, because I don't want to carry another dongle. Unfortunately, my mobile operator doesn't provide any sort of identity management or authentication services, so I can't use my phone. I do already have a tamper-resistant chip that I have with me most of the time, and that's in my bank card. Why not use that in some way?

Alternatively, you could slide your credit card through your phone's card reader—or simply wave your credit card so that it can be recognized by the "near-field communication" chip in your phone. Are these things too far out?

[From Two-factor authentication: Gmail's new system offers more security than just a password. - By Farhad Manjoo - Slate Magazine]

I'd say not really, especially since I've seen SecureKey's system for doing just this work perfectly with Google, using a USB key NFC reader and the customer's contactless bank card to provide the second factor. Today I read about someone pitching iris recognition via USB device as a potential third factor as well. But are three factors enough?

I saw a discussion over at the Identity Management Specialists Group on LinkedIn that set me wondering about authentication factors. Traditionally, us experts have referred to three authentication factors: something you know, something you have and something you are (or, as Ben Laurie once told me, something you've forgotten, something you've lost and something you were). The LinkedIn discussion was about whether location might be a fourth authentication factor, because it is independent of the other three and can be determined in isolation.

So does this make sense? Is location an alternative third factor, another kind of "something you are" or is it genuinely something new that adds an additional degree of authentication power. The conclusion in the group discussion was (I think!) that location isn't an authentication factor because where you are doesn't change who you are, but that it is an authorisation factor because you may wish to assign different capabilities to an identity depending on where the physical person is (ie, are they in the office or at home?). I'm not so sure about this: it seems to me that corroborating your location obtained from your mobile phone with, say, a password, does indeed strengthen authentication. There are plenty of options, so a workable strong authentication scheme must be getting closer. right?

Could bank account numbers be portable like mobile numbers? – 23/05/2011

The Independent Commission on Banking recently published an interim report on their Consultation on Reform Options. This interim report raises the subject of bank account number portability. Section 5.17, to be specific, says that:

> *Beyond improvements to the existing system, full account number portability would enable customers to change banking service providers without changing their bank account number. This would remove the need to transfer direct debits and standing orders, which remains the main area where problems may arise. In the past, portability has been rejected as overly costly, but if no other solutions appear effective and practicable, it should be reconsidered to see if this remains the case given improvements in IT and the payments system infrastructure.*

It seems reasonable for the Commission to wonder why customers cannot port their account number from one bank to another the way that they can port their mobile phone number from one network to another. That seems a plausible request for 2011, but phone numbers and account numbers aren't quite the same thing. A phone number is an indirect reference to your phone (well, your SIM card actually) whereas the account number is the "target". Thus, we shouldn't really compare the account number to the phone number, but think of it more as the SIM. Each SIM card has a unique identifier, just as each bank account has an international bank account number (IBAN). When you turn on your phone, essentially, your SIM tells your mobile operator which phone it is in and then "registers" with a network. I am writing this in Singapore, where I just turned on my iPhone, so now my O2 SIM card is registered with Singtel. When you call my number, O2 will route the call to Singtel, who will then route it to my phone. But how does the call get to O2 in the first place?

In most developed nations there is what is called an "All Call Query" or ACQ system: there is a big database of mobile phone numbers that tells the operators which mobile network each number is routed by. In order to make call connections as fast as possible, each operator has their own copy of this database that is regularly updated. Note that for reasons that are too complicated (and boring) to go into there, in the UK there is a different scheme, known as indirect routing, whereby when you dial my phone number 07973 XXXXXX it is routed to Orange (because that's where all 07973 numbers originated from) and then Orange looks XXXXXX number up in its own database to see where to route the call to (in this case to O2). This is why calls to ported numbers in the UK take longer to connect than they do in other countries.

It's entirely possible to envisage a similar system working for banks, whereby we separate the equivalent of the mobile phone number — let's call it the Current Account Number (CAN) — from the underlying bank account and have an industy database that maps CANs to IBANs. This database would be the equivalent of the ACQ database. (I rather like the branding too: if the banks decided to operate this cross-border, they could label it the international current account number, or iCan.) So the bank sends your salary via FPS to the iCan, and the database tells FPS which actual IBAN to route it to. No matter which bank accounts you use or change to throughout your employment, the employer always sends the salary to the iCan and thus reduces their own costs.

There is an analogy to this is in the way that some of the new contactless payment cards work. In the US, American Express credit cards give up what is called an "alias PAN". The PAN, or primary account number, is the 16-digit number on your credit card. When you use your Amex card via contactless, the 16-digit number it gives up is not the actual plan but an alias PAN. Only Amex know which actual PAN this alias PAN refers to. The advantage of doing this is that if criminals get hold of the alias PAN, they can't use it to make a counterfeit magnetic stripe card, because the alias PANs are only valid for the contactless cards (which they can't counterfeit, because the contactless cards have computer chips in them).

In the UK, we route by sort codes. Any account number beginning 20- is known to be Barclays, so a payment switch will send the payment through to Barclays. We might decide, say, that sort codes beginning with 00 are iCans. When you get your first bank account, the bank sets up the IBAN and iCan. For your salary, direct debits, standing orders and so forth, you give the iCan. BACS and FPS will be told about iCans, so when a payment to an IBAN beginning "UK00-" enters one of those systems, they go to a shared database and look up the IBAN to route the payment to.

In the world of payments, a related discussion has already sprung up. This is the discussion about Legal Entity Identifiers (LEIs) that have been going on recently. Many interbank payment messages have account identifiers only and the some law enforcement agencies want to stop this and have banks validate the names as well (it will help to track funds to and from suspects I guess).

A global standardized Legal Entity Identifier (LEI) will help enable organizations to more effectively measure and manage counterparty exposure, while providing substantial operational efficiencies and customer service improvements to the industry ... The LEI Solution is a capability that will help global regulators and supervisors better measure and monitor systemic risk.

[From Legal Entity Identifiers]

I'm sure I'd heard somewhere before, possibly at the International Payment Summit, that the plan was to use the SWIFT business identifier codes (BICs), but apparently that's no longer the case. Fabian Vandenreydt, the new Head of Securities and Treasury Markets at SWFIT, recently said that the International Standardization Organization's Technical Committee 68 (ISO TC68) has concluded that developing a new code would help avoid ambiguities that might be involved if existing codes are used. The BIC is made up of eight to 11 alphanumeric characters with four letters for the bank, two letters for the country, two digits for the location, and three digits for the specific branch but ISO TC68 want we we nerds call an MBUN (a "meaningless but unique number").

I don't think this is way forward for people, though. LEIs are unique corporate identifiers: a corporate identity has one, and only one, LEI. Fortunately, or unfortunately, depending on your view, there is no unique identifier for British persons (and nor is there likely to be under the present administration), nor Europeans, nor citzens of the world. And I don't think we would want the financial services industry to develop its own sort-of-identity card scheme. We just want a simple, portable, pointer to a person that can be used to index into their KYC'd persona.

The easiest way to do this would be to assign a unique financial services identifier (FSI) to a person or other legal entity the first time that they go through a KYC process. I might have the FSI "citizendave!barclays.co.uk", for example. Once someone has one of these FSIs, then there would be no need to drag them through "know your customer" (KYC) again. This would greatly reduce industry costs and make the process of obtaining a new financial service — a new bank account, a new credit card, a new insurance policy, a new accountant — much simpler. Imagine the simplicity of applying for in-store credit for that new sofa by just giving them your FSI and watching the application form magically populate by itself on screen.

It doesn't matter if a person has multiple FSIs, because each FSI will have been obtained as the result of a KYC process. If the FSI Directory ends up with two "Dave Birch" entries, so what? It's not an ID card scheme, it's a "save money for the financial services sector and make life easier for consumers" scheme. And it wouldn't matter either if both of my FSIs point to different iCans: I might, for example, have a personal persona and a small business persona—let's say citizendave!barclays.co.uk and citizendave!rbs.co.uk and that point to my personal and my small business accounts—and I want to use them for different purposes.

Picture this. You are fed up with the appalling service you get from your bank, so you walk into a branch of New Bank. You ask to open an account, and are directed to the ATM in the lobby and asked to request a balance from your existing current account. You put in the card and enter the PIN. While the ATM is carrying out the balance enquiry, the FSI (obtained from your card) is sent to the Directory and within a couple of seconds both your account balance (from your bank) and your picture (from the FSI Directory) are on the screen. The New Bank agent presses a button and a pre-filled application form is printed out for you to sign and, once you have, the existing system for transferring accounts is triggered.

There might be another useful spin-off from the FSI as well. Suppose you could designate a default account against the FSI: generally speaking, your iCan, but it could also be a prepaid account somewhere, or your PayPal account or whatever. Then someone could send you money by giving your FSI: no need to type in names, sort codes, account numbers. Anyone could pay anyone by entering the FSI into the ATM, or their internet banking screen, or (most likely) their mobile. Simple.

Entering the new age of money – 01/06/2011

There's a lot going on in the world of payments in Denmark, sparked in part by SEPA, but with other factors as well. Many people think only of Denmark in terms of its principal exports—such as bacon, Lego and sperm—but it means only one thing to me: Danmont, the first of the European smartcard-based e-purses to try and take on cash half a generation ago.

> *In a statement, PBS says Danmont has not been adopted by the Danes as a preferred way of making small payments... the debit card Dankort has taken over from Danmønt in areas where the e-purse was formerly used as a form of payment. The scheme will continue to operate until 31 December 2005.*

> *[From Finextra: Danish e-purse Danmont to close]*

Now everything is changing again, because the domestic debit scheme can no longer discriminate against "foreign" cards and there needs to be a new national payment strategy. This is why its such an interesting time there and why I was so delighted to be invited by the Copenhagen Finance IT Region, a "cluster organisation" with 13 partners including the Danish Bankers Association, to come and talk at their event looking at the future of money. I was invited along with Alberto Jiminez, the Mobile Payments Global Leader at IBM, and Roslyn Layton from KLEAN, a Danish consultancy. Alberto was talking about mobile, Roslyn was talking about the internet, and I was talking about mercantilism, Kublai Khan and Facebook Credits.

Alberto divided the world into developed (North America, Western Europe, South Korea, Japan, Australia and New Zealand) and developing payment markets, a simpler model than the "quadrants" that we use at Consult Hyperion. Anyway, he pointed out that in the developing countries where there are real opportunities only a handful (Kenya, Philippines, South Africa, Pakistan, Uganda) have reached scale, which he defined as being more than a million users. He explored the benefits of opening up mobile payment markets which, in the IBM model, fall into three categories: the revenue opportunities, cost savings and the "indirect" benefits. This last category—which includes social inclusion, government agendas, brand benefits and so on—I find really interesting, probably because it's the least understood. He also mentioned government agendas, something that has come up in a few recent discussions that I've been involved in.

In her talk, Roslyn touched on one of my very favourite topics, which is the online games business and the growth of what she called "funny money". But she was also taking about the permeable boundary between loyalty schemes and pseudo-currency. In particular, she drew attention to a Lufthansa "Miles & More' scheme that lets you trade in your frequent flier miles for a cash management account (CMA) that can contain both securities and deposits. She also drew attention to the relative size of some markets: online games are a $15 billion business at the moment, sure, but premium SMS (as Tomi never tires of reminding me!) is a $23 billion business and online gambling is a $35 billion business. Great stuff. She finished up, though, by saying that we won't go to an entirely virtual economy, because people ultimately want to keep their money in banks.

Well, up to a point. There's a big difference between keeping money in the bank and keeping bank money, one of the points I tried to bring out it my discussion about the "ages of money" and the shifting implementation of the functions of money. I think the main point that I was trying to get over was that while new technology means real change in payments, it also means real change in money itself. All in all, a really enjoyable event, where I learned a lot and had fun too. Many thanks to everyone involved.

We should be using the end of cheque clearing as a stimulus to innovation – 07/06/2011

The House of Lords (for foreign readers, this is the unelected second chamber of government, stuffed full of government placemen - so many, in fact, that the Lords are begging the government to stop sending more of them) has been getting into a bit of a tizzy about cheques.

Lord Sassoon: the criteria which the Payments Council itself put forward and which the previous Government welcomed back in December 2009—I echo that welcome—was that the new system had to be generally available, generally acceptable to its users and widely adopted. There also has to be, in the view of the Government, a paper-based system

[From Hansard - Lords \ Houses of Parliament]

For foreign readers, Lord Sassoon is James Meyer Sassoon, Baron Sassoon, the Commercial Secretary to the Treasury, a minister in the UK's finance ministry. Note his words: the British government wants to replace the current paper-based system with a new, dynamic, forward-looking, white heat of new technology 21st century paper-based system. Hhhmmm....

Surely we can do something more interesting than that. Cheque replacement was a subject of much conversation in my vicinity last week. Consult Hyperion were one of the sponsors of this Intellect / Payments Council conference on Driving Change in Payments, and an excellent event it was too. Mobile was one of the recurrent themes. Alastair Lukies, the CEO of Monitise, was one of the speakers and one of the subjects he touched on in passing was the potential for mobile to provide the replacement for cheques in the UK. This is a hot topic, since the Payments Council has announced its plan to end cheque clearing in 2018. This, in turn, caused a predictable response from the reactionary press and various interest groups, all of whom want to retain the current system of expensive cheques subsidised by people like me who hate them.

Just to give you a snapshot of the views of the British public—which are of no interest to me, naturally, but may serve to frame the debate here—I cut a few comments from a recent article about this on the Daily Telegraph website,

If cheques are expensive to process then increase the price, I think I already pay 35p per cheque

[From *Plans to phase out cheques*]

Businesses do, but personal customers have grown used to what they perceive to be free banking. I'm all for transparent pricing. If the Payments Council decides to retain cheque clearing but charge full cost recovery to users, that would be a reasonable outcome. However, this would mean that cheques would cost probably even more than 35p each, and once again the pleading for special interests will become the substitute for the real debate.

If cheques go then genuine charities should be given free transfer by card or someone should think of another method of paying small amounts at no cost

[From *Plans to phase out cheques*]

It is plausible, although I don't think it is likely, that the government might impose a social obligation on banks and payment institutions to execute low-value transactions (those, say, of a value less than the largest banknote in circulation, €500) for free as a social obligation in return for their licenses. The root problem is that people think not only that payments should be free but that someone payments are free. This is wrong, but you can imagine the newspaper headlines about the charity for sick children being forced to pay outrageous processing fees by the evil financial sector. (The impact on charities came up a few times in casual discussion around the topic at the recent event.) Some people are worried that this will even put an end to some charities.

> *The Institute of Fundraising has warned that the plans could be disastrous for charities, some of which receive up to 80% of their income through cheques.*

[From *Finextra: Dumping cheques*]

I don't understand what they are thinking. Getting rid of cheques will save them a fortune. Charities in countries without cheques—eg, Finland—seem to be able to raise money without too much trouble. I've already made a perfectly sensible and reasonable suggestion as to how to set up unique financial sector identifiers that can serve as payments addresses for mobile and online payments and for the 0.1% of the population who don't want to use these (eg, my mother) they can just call an 800 number and effect the transfer with voice authentication (or something similar). Why on Earth should we be targeting paper-based replacement? Doesn't this discriminate against people who can't read or write? Let's set the bar higher.

It must be further noted that in the Telegraph, as well as a couple of other papers, the particular issue of paying the gardener was also seen as being an important payments use case in the UK. I thought at first that this might be something to do with the English class system, but it turns out that paying gardeners is an issue around the world!

> *I live in Belgium at the moment and have not used a cheque in years. All the transfers are immediate, not 3 days later which is just a scam by the UK banks to use your money for free for three days. If I pay the gardener its cash or a virement (transfer) easy.*

[From *Plans to phase out cheques*]

Look, I'm sure there will be a small number of people who will find it hard to use mobile payments, or web payments, or whatever, just as there are a small number of people who find it hard to use cheques right now, but that's no reason for the Payments Council to get fainthearted. The end of cheques in 2018 should be a stimulus to innovation in UK payments. Except, as I said before, it isn't the end of cheques.

Cheques aren't being outlawed in 2018, but cheque clearing is going to stop. If Associated Newspapers wants to apply for a Payment Institution (PI) licence and operate its own cheque system, then good luck to them

[From Digital Money: Cached]

Surely the noble Lords can contribute some seed capital to assist the Daily Mail, Saga, Oxfam and the House of Parliament Tennis Club in creating the new paper-based system that they want.

The FATF report on New Payment Methods has very sensible conclusions – 08/06/2011

I thoroughly enjoyed popping along to the recent conference on Mobile and meeting up with friends from around the world there. I was on the Strategy Panel covering financial inclusion, and this coincidentally, the day after I had been quoted in Warren's "Washington Internet Daily":

Mobile payment systems are often treated with a lighter regulatory touch than mobile banking, to reach as many users as possible, Birch said. The need to integrate the "unbanked" into society should "tip the value" toward less regulation of low-value transactions, he said.

An entirely accurate representation of my views. A correspondent wrote in response:

Very sensible words! Not sure if you have actually read FATF's NPM report from October 2010, but it is actually pretty good, and recommends the right thing: a light KYC regime (including no verification) for specific low risk accounts, praising the power of transactions limits and monitoring.

As it happens, I hadn't read the FATF New Payment Methods report, so I downloaded it to take a look and discovered some surprisingly sensible conclusions. By "New Payment Methods", or NPM, the FATF means specifically internet payment systems, mobile payment systems and prepaid card products. My correspondent had noted, to my surprise, that some of their conclusions echo my own ranting on the topic: that is, a light-touch KYC regime (including no verification for specific low risk accounts), with attention paid to setting the right transaction limits and appropriate monitoring and reporting requirements. The report is based on a number of case studies, so the conclusions are based in practical analysis, however it must be said that they are probably not statistically utterly sound.

> *The project team analysed 33 case studies, which mainly involved prepaid cards or internet payment systems. Only three cases were submitted for mobile payment systems, but these involved only small amounts.*

Personally, I found many of the case studies in chapter four of the report uninteresting. Yes, in some cases prepaid cards, or whatever, were used as a part of a crime, but in many of the frauds so were cash and bank accounts. One of the case studies concerned the use of multiple prepaid cards by an individual found to have 12 legally-obtained driving licences in different names (and $145,000 in cash). I'd suggest that cracking down on the driving licence issuing process ought to be more of a priority! The issue of access to transaction record is, I think, much more complicated than many imagine. You could, for example, imagine transaction records that are encrypted with two keys—your key and the system key—so that you can go back and decrypt your records whenever you want, but the forces of law and order would need to obtain a warrant to get the system key. Sounds good. But I might not want a foreign, potentially corrupt, government department to obtain my transactions for perfectly good reasons (like it's none of their business).

The report says very clearly that the overall threat is "difficult" to assess (so some of the rest of it, I think, is necessarily a trifle fuzzy) but also that the anti-money laundering (AML) and counter terrorist financing (CTF), henceforth AML/CTF, risks posed by anonymous products can be effectively mitigated. I agree. And I also strongly agree with chapter three of the report notes that electronic records give law enforcement something to go on where cash does not. This is something that I've mentioned previously, both on this blog and in a variety of other fora, because I think it's a very important point.

> *I said that I was not sure that keeping people out of the "system" was the best strategy (because if the terrorists, drug dealers and bank robbers on the run stay in the cash economy, then they can't be tracked, traced or monitored in any way)*
>
> *[From Digital Money: Anti-anti money laundering]*

The report goes on to expand on the issue of mitigation and, to my mind, deals with it very well. It says that:

> *Obviously, anonymity as a risk factor could be mitigated by implementing robust identification and verification procedures.*

But even in the absence of such procedures, the risk posed by an anonymous product can be effectively mitigated by other measures such as imposing value limits (i.e., limits on transaction amounts or frequency) or implementing strict monitoring systems.

Why is this so important? As well as keeping costs down for industry and stimulating the introduction of competitive products, the need for identification is a barrier to inclusion. This link between identification and inclusion is clear, whatever you think about the identification system itself. India is turning out to be a fascinating case study in that respect.

The process would benefit beneficiaries of welfare schemes like old-age pension and NREGA, enabling them to draw money from anywhere as several blocks in Jharkhand have no branches of any bank and would save them from travelling to distant places for collecting money.

[From Unique numbers will save duplication in financial transactions]

But I can't help cautioning that while customer identification is difficult where no national identity scheme exists, but there is a scheme it may give a false sense of security because obtaining fraudulent identities might be easier than obtaining fraudulent payment services in some jurisdictions or where officials from dodgy regimes (like the UK) are at work…

Prosecutor Simon Wild told the court Griffith abused his position by rubber stamping work permit applications that were obviously fake or forged using false names and references.

[From British embassy official 'nodded through scores of visa applications' | Mail Online]

For low risk products, then, the way forward is absolutely clear: no identification requirements, potentially strong authentication requirements and controlled access to transactions records. One small problem, though, that the report itself highlights: there are no uniform, international, cross-border standards for what constitutes a "low risk" product. But that's for another day.

Finally, I couldn't help but notice that the payment mechanisms that scored worst in the high-level risk table (on page 23) and therefore the one that FATF should be working hardest to crack down on is **cash**.

Will banks and operators be able to work together more effectively in the future?– 14/06/2011

A few days ago I was at Experian's annual Payment Strategies conference, where I had been kindly invited to provide a closing keynote. In it, I made a few predictions about the next phase of evolution of the European payments business, and in passing I mentioned that I felt that some progress had been slow.

> Birch lambasted traditional banks and payments providers for their failure to grasp the nature of the opportunities presented by mobile technologies, which has led them to miss the boat. "I'm almost embarrassed to stand before you and say that I thought that banks and mobile operators could work together," he told the conference. "It was a stupid fantasy for which I apologise."

> [From _Identity is the next big thing for payments_ | _Banking Technology magazine_]

This isn't a new rant, but a considered opinion. In fact, I wrote about this last year, round about the time I made some similar remarks at an event at the GSMA, reflecting the fact that I think that mobile operators should have been quicker in to the NFC space and with more open models, and that I think banks should have been quicker to develop and implement mobile approaches other than "windows on to the web" or "cut down ATM" solutions.

> All of my experience over the last few years has served to reinforce my opinion from those ancient times that it's much harder for banks and operators to work together than either of them might think. So perhaps this part of the [Booz Allen Hamilton] 2001 vision for 2010 may never become reality.

> [From _Digital Money: Let's put the future behind us_]

The reference to Booz Allen Hamilton, a management consultancy, is because the post was discussing a magazine article by them from a decade ago: "Why banks and telecoms must merge to surge" from the Booz Allen Hamilton _strategy+business_ magazine that I'd filed away back in 2001. I took some comfort from it, because it meant that I wasn't the only one who had expected banks and operators to get together, but I was commenting on the cultural factors that meant that it had proved very difficult for them to co-operate effectively.

> The infrastructure to develop than he'd predicted, but more importantly, banks are still missing out: only recently, banks in the US had told him that there is no business case for subsidising

the installation of contactless readers in retail premises, just as Google was announcing that it will.

[From Identity is the next big thing for payments | Banking Technology magazine]

It is absolutely true that I (as well as number of other consultants) were at an event with US banks earlier in the year where this opinion was expressed. But there was nothing special about it: the banks had said exactly the same thing in public to retailers.

Representatives of three of the country's largest banks, Bank of America, Citigroup and U.S. Bank, attended a meeting last month organized by the Merchant Advisory Group... to talk about the new opportunities that mobile technologies, such as NFC, will create for the payments industry. "You know what they (banks) told us? There's just not a business case right now," Dodd Roberts, head of the merchant group, said last week.

[From Digital Money: Inception]

But back to the 2001 article, which agreed with me about one particular strategic element. That is, that while banks have a strong hold over payment systems, mobile network operators would be challengers.

Today, banks are at another competitive crossroads. This time the new contenders in financial services are telephone companies, specifically wireless telecoms.

[From Why Banks and Telecoms Must Merge to Surge]

The Booz Allen Hamilton article finishes up by saying that it would be logical for "mega players" such as Vodafone and Citi to combine. This hasn't happened and I can't help but observe that Vodafone's most successful mobile payment service, in fact, probably the world's most successful mobile payment service, M-PESA, doesn't involve banks at all except as a secure repositories of funds.

So why did my comments about banks and operators working together sound so harsh? It's because we (Consult Hyperion) have been involved in a number of projects, going all the way back to the Orange/NatWest joint venture, and so have seen at first hand what works and what doesn't in these relationships. And, yes, things are improving: but it may well be the case that having let a couple of years evolution slip away, the idea of the bank/operator partnership as the central organising principle for mobile payments is over. European operators have started to apply for their own Payment Institution licences, while I expect banks to focus more on developing value-adding services for the retailers and consumers and less on the "bare" retail payments (where the downward pressure on transactional fee income will continue).

Incidentally, I wonder if both the banks and the mobile operators held back because they'd been listening to their customers? If you had done a survey of consumers asking them if they wanted an iPod, the day before hte iPod had been invented, you would never have launched it.

> In an interview with the Daily Telegraph in February 2005. The founder of Amstrad said: "Next Christmas the iPod will be dead, finished, gone, kaput."
>
> [From Bill Gates and Sir Alan Sugar made some of worse technology predictions of all time - Telegraph]

Predictions are difficult, as the saying goes, especially ones about the future. Of course, you do have to understand what it is that you are predicting, and in many cases people don't really understand the proper context. This is why I read surveys like these with a raised eyebrow.

> Just One-in-Five Brits Currently Interested in Paying by Mobile
>
> [From Just One-in-Five Brits Currently Interested in Paying by Mobile]

Now this might be interesting news if I cared what the public think about anything (I don't), but I wonder if it's the sort of thing that causes mass market players to slow down? It caught my eye because it tallies with the revealed consumer preferences of Japanese consumers, where mobile proximity payments are mainstream. Indeed, only around one in five or six people in Japan use their proximity handsets for payments. But then only one in five or six people here pay for things using credit cards (debit cards dominate in Europe) and that's still a business. The headline intends to be negative, but what it says to me is that the potential for mobile payments is such that ten million people could be using them in the UK in the not-too-distant future, if banks and operators (or someone else?) can come up with the right proposition.

The UK has taken another step backwards by giving cheque clearing a reprieve– 12/07/2011

I was totally shocked to arrive home from work the other day to find my good lady wife celebrating with her tax rebate cheque. Apparently HMRC miscalculated millions of Her Majesty's subject's tax bills and we were one of the lucky overpayers. We are a couple of gallons of petrol better off than before. But a cheque! HMRC must have our ethnic background on file as "Amish". Despite the fact that since time immemorial (for me) we have paid our tax bill online via internet banking, the creaking hand-cranked contraptions at the Revenue are apparently unable to use any form of payment invented after the Act of Union (in 1701).

To be honest, I've always been puzzled by the Amish, the strange religious sect in America made popular by the noted screen actor Harrison Ford in his 1985 film "Witness". The Amish reject "modern" technology, but they seem to me to have a rather arbitrary definition of what constitutes "modern". Why, for example, do they use wheels? Or nails? Or chemical fertilisers? What's the cut-off point? 1750? Why not the invention of the transistor in 1948? Or the synthesis of urea in 1828?

> *The Amish, particular the Old Order Amish—the stereotypical Amish depicted on calendars – really are slow to adopt new things. In contemporary society our default is set to say "yes" to new things, and in Old Order Amish societies the default is set to "no."*
>
> *[From The Technium: Amish Hackers]*

Speaking of reactionary sects that eschew the modern world to remain in the comforting cocoon of a romanticised rural past, I read in the Daily Mail that:

> *Plans to scrap the use of cheques from 2018 were dropped today after the UK Payments Council admitted there was no better paper alternative.*
>
> *[From Cheques will not be scrapped in 2018 but because there are no better alternatives | Mail Online]*

Well, the wrinklies have triumphed again. Another minor skirmish in the intergenerational war for resources has been won by Joan Bakewell's generation and our children are going to be made to subsidise a paper cheque system that should have been a distant memory for them. The Payments Council has been forced to cancel the end of cheque clearing (originally scheduled for 2018) and promise to keep cheques:

> *for as long as customers need them*
>
> *[From Payments Council - Payments Council to keep cheques]*

Note that I am specific in the wording, as were the Payments Council. No-one was banning cheques: they were ending cheque clearing. If someone else—the Post Office, Age Concern or the CBI—wanted to run a cheque system, they were free to do so. And, to be honest, that would be a good solution, because then their members could pay for it and those of us who couldn't care less if they never saw another cheque could have ignored them. I suspect that in the coming age riots of 2025, the cheque book will used as a rallying symbol of revolt by our impoverished offspring because the banks (ie, bank customers) are going to have to pay to support paper cheques into the foreseeable future. This is ridiculous. If some people (eg, my mum) want to carry on using cheques, it should be on the basis of full cost recovery: if you want a cheque book, you should pay for it, and if you want to cash cheques, you should pay £2 (or whatever) to do so.

> *The Government is aware that, although there are declining numbers, 54% of adults still write cheques, and on average every adult write 13 cheques and receives 4 cheques each year.*
>
> *[From Frequently asked questions on the closure of the cheque system - HM Treasury]*

Yes, but that misses the point. When I last wrote a cheque to my son's school, I didn't want to. I would much rather have used PayPal, internet banking, my debit card or M-PESA. I don't want to receive cheques either, from HMRC or anyone else.

> *When someone sends you a cheque, it's like being set homework.*
>
> *[From Digital Money: I could imagine using this]*

So what happened? In recent weeks I've had some conversations with people countries such as the Netherlands, Belgium and Denmark where no-one has seen a cheque for a generation asking me why the UK is different. It's the British disease: faced with the end of cheque clearing in a generation, the British response is not embrace electronic alternatives, for charities to look at inventive and efficient online and telephone giving, for small businesses to exploit the Faster Payment Service (FPS) or for the Post Office to create its own paper-based alternative but to moan and complain and demand that everything be kept the same as it is. What happened was that reactionary press comment, entrenched interests, publicity-seeking MPs and a fragmented industry have combined to conspire against the forces of rationality and modernity. And they won.

But why stop there? Cheques are quite modern invention and I don't understand why the Commons Treasury Committee and the Daily Telegraph want to turn the clock back only to the 17th century. They are not true conservatives, whereas I am. I have therefore decided that my only course of action is to appeal to the European Court of Human Rights to force the Payments Council to reinstate the tally stick system that was prematurely ended in 1834. My great-great-great-great-great grandfather was perfectly happy using tally sticks and was, I'm sure, most distressed by the end of the scheme and the burning of the sticks in the Houses of Parliament furnaces which, as you may recall, resulted in the fire that destroyed the medieval palace and a splendid painting by Turner. It is most unfortunate that Associated Newspapers and Saga did not exist at that time, since I feel they might have been able to spearhead a successful campaign against the introduction of foreign methods (such as double-entry bookkeeping).

Tally sticks had numerous advantages over paper cheques. They were much harder to forge, for example, and were understandable by a largely illiterate population (a situation soon to be restored in this United Kingdom). The sticks were far more durable than cheques are, cheques being made out of flimsy paper instead of fine English wood. Why was this sound and practical system swept away for the convenience of bankers! It is my right to continue to use the tally sticks developed under William I for as long as I need them and quite reasonable of me to demand that the rest of society bears the costs. I hope The Telegraph will support my campaign with vigour. And while we're at it, why haven't farthings been legal tender since 31st December 1960? I tried to use some when out shopping the other day and they were refused: outrageous.

Comments

Why set a date years in advance just so that people can moan at you from now until then? By 2018, cheques will have withered on the vine anyway; as will their users.

Posted by: Neil McEvoy on 12/07/2011 at 22:33.

The Inland Revenue don't want to stop cheques because the alternative is CASH in most cases. Cash is non accountable to some businesses therefore NO TAX would be collected. NO TAX = No society.

Posted by: Lynne on 22/07/2011 at 07:59.

Lynne, I think society functioned perfectly well before cash and money, it's just that the current materialist society we have experienced since our birth cannot perceive a world without money.

a) Money has been in human existence a very short time

b) I bet people according to Cameron's new happiness index were happier before money

c) With 7.6 billion people trying to sustain a $500 trillion debt which can never be paid back, I'll wager that Fiat money has got a "short" future ahead.

d) Cash "alternatives" are going to proliferate in my opinion so "they" better wake up to the fact that income tax (which incidentally isn't part of the US Constitution) will have to go. It will be unsustainable in the hyper-inflationary world we are now entering post 8/8/2011, you cannot tax people who are not earning. But you can tax via purchase taxes.

Posted by: Mark Cross on 07/08/2011 at 20:28.

In the long run, it's all about identity– 21/07/2011

Sam Shrauger, VP Global Product and Experience at PayPal, puts it succinctly:

People couldn't care less which technology a hardware or software manufacturer would like to sell them. They couldn't care less which technology merchants may or may not put in their stores. Ultimately, they just want something that makes their life better when it comes to buying and paying.

[From Why the Mobile]

Now, as it happens, I was chatting with Sam recently so I know he's a smart guy, and I agree with him about many things, but I think that in this particular case he may be underestimating the impact of "tap and go" technology. The point is that tapping is so much simpler, so much quicker, so much more convenient for consumers that it will make a difference to them. People will start looking for the phones that you can tap together to become Facebook friends, or whatever, because that experience blows away bumping, or texting or QR codes or Bluetooth or anything else.

Jukka Saariluoma, development director for Finland-based Hansaprint said QR or other 2-D bar codes are now a common feature alongside RFID tags for any NFC service-discovery projects the company works on… "Using NFC is so intuitive; it is much more pleasant than scanning or taking a picture of 2D bar code, and with NFC you don't need to install anything on your mobile," he said. "As long as you have NFC, you simply touch and it works." But he added "As we all know, the spread of NFC phones is so limited for consumers. It's close to zero."

[From Pioneering NFC Service Provider Adds Bar Codes to New NFC Trial | NFC Times – Near Field Communication and all contactless]

In Europe it isn't close to zero, it's statistically indistinguishable from zero, but that's hopefully about to change as the handsets finally reach the shops. Apart from convenience, however, what else could the technology offer? To be honest, we still don't know, because it's taken a long time to get it into the market and there aren't enough people playing around with it. We need to find ways to open up the technology and get creative people experimenting with it. Here's what i wrote five years ago:

> *I was of the opinion that we should help to operators to develop "internet" business thinking around NFC: open it up and let a thousand flowers bloom, all of which would use SMS, GPRS, 3G or even voice communications, all of which generate more revenue for operators.*

[From Digital Money: NFC "challenges" in payments]

At the same time, based on work we were doing for a number of different clients, I also noted that while most of the focus on NFC was about using phones to make payments, there was another aspect to the technology that deserved attention.

> *A much more interesting, and much more strategically disruptive, integration between the emerging technologies will be the use of mobile handsets as POS terminals (see graphic) because NFC phones can read contactless cards (and other NFC phones of course). As we have been saying for a long time, it is the ability of the mobile handsets to accept payments that is the critical factor in trying to determine the long-term direction of the industry*

[From Digital Money: It's all about density]

This has been borne out by the rapid growth of Square, which has just attracted another $100m of investment following on from the strategic investment by Visa earlier in the year.

> *Keith Rabois, Square's chief operating officer, said the relationship between Square and Visa was a natural one because Square could convert the 27 million businesses that don't accept credit cards into Visa customers.*

[From Visa]

Visa's customers are, of course, banks rather than you or me, but you see his point. As I blogged about Square literally a few hours before this announcement was made:

> *In a way, this is a real-world PSP and a fascinating niche play in a large volume-driven acquiring market, one that can be seen to adumbrate mobile disruption and our projection that the mobile-phone-as-POS meme will be more revolutionary than the mobile-phone-as-card meme*

[From Digital Money: Innovation is technology-enabled]

Square is now processing $4m per day in payments and still growing. So will the long-term impact of NFC be greatest there? I think the opportunities are huge, but they are still not the biggest impact. I think Sam is definitely right to focus on one thing and that's trust. I know it's tedious to keep referring back to snippets of ancient discussions, but I do want to make a point about the kind of advice we were giving to clients back in 2007 when I wrote that

> *Despite the focus on mobile payments and transit, my view of the long-term impact of NFC was unchanged: in the long term, it will be the identity management functionality that changes the world, not the payment functionality.*

[From Digital Money: NFC world]

I also said, at that first NFC World Asia, that no customer would walk into a shop to buy a mobile phone because of proximity payments, although they might because of ticketing. I stand by that: once a consumer buys an NFC phone, then I'm sure they'll appreciate the new payments opportunities. But will they buy it **because** of payments? Not for the foreseeable future. Therefore, it seems to me that we need to have more experimenting and that that experimenting should focus on identity. And here, as in the case of payments, it's the key transformational role of the phone as "acceptor" that will change everything. Its one thing to have an "ID card", but what good is it if only the government, or whoever, can verify it? When the repair guy shows up at my mum's door with his British Gas ID, she needs to be able to verify it - and this is where the phone can make for a new value chain.

NFC phones can be ID cards, but they can also be ID machines. By reading a contactless ID card (or, indeed, another phone) and then verfying the ID (going on line if necessary) they can play a crucial role in making identity infrastructure a simple proposition for mass market consumers. That's how the nightclub bouncer can check that you are over 21, how the retailer can check that you are an EU resident, how the Glastonbury steward can check you have a valid ticket. No more special gates or custom boxes: every phone will be able to do this, just as every phone will be able to accept payments. The only difference will be that everyone will use the ID functions, whereas they may not all use the payment functions.

So will consumers care about NFC? Well, would my mum ever buy an NFC phone so that she can tap and pay in Tesco? No. And she shops in Tesco all the time. Would she buy and NFC phone to collect vouchers to spend in MacDonalds? No. Would she buy an NFC phone so that when people come to the door she can check who they are by tapping their ID cards against her phone? Well, if she wouldn't then I'd buy it for her.

On the grid– 29/07/2011

A day or two ago, I was in an interesting discussion on mobile financial services, and the topic of regulation wandered across the conversation, as it so often does in such circumstances. This led to a question: are payments "financial services" or not? I said that they are not. As I wrote a while ago:

> Just as one might see growing regulatory pressure for some form of narrow banking, I expect to see some pressure for narrower banking that does not include payments. The business of banking will focus more on its core of lending and borrowing and payments will become more of a genuine utility infrastructure.

> [From Digital Money: They're easy, predictions]

I think that, as the economist John Kay has written, payments are a utility and should be regulated as such, in a regulatory framework that is different to, and separate from, the regulatory environment for financial services such as pensions, life insurance and credit agreements.

> The utility element of the financial services system is the payments system. Like the electricity grid or the telecommunications network, failure even for a few hours imposes economic damage. The payments system is inherently a natural monopoly, like the electricity grid or the telecommunications network. There are alternative, and to some degrees competing, payments systems but—as with telecommunications networks—all are ultimately dependent on the core clearing and settlement systems.

> [From John Kay - Should We Have 'Narrow Banking'?]

The electricity grid example came up in our discussion as well. The US National Academy of Engineering calls the electricity grid the "greatest engineering achievement of the 20th century" and it's a pretty impressive machine. Philip Schewe's excellent book "The Grid" tells the story of the US national grid from Edison's first node at 257 Pearl Street in New York to its current state (a fascinating story, by the way), explaining how the grid was originally created by the power companies and that factors that led to the shared utilities (there are actually three grids in the US). The grid may, as an aside, change again in the not-too-distant future, under the technology drivers of high temperature superconductors and distributed, neighbourhood power generation, but that's another topic, except to note that the first superconductor grid elements are already in use.

> *American Superconductor Corp. has teamed with Consolidated Edison Inc. to develop new high-temperature superconductor (HTS) power grid technology for New York City. The U.S. Department of Homeland Security (DHS) will provide up to $25 million of the total project cost of $39.3 million to develop technology for "Secure Super Grids."*

[From NYC's Con Ed to get superconductor power grid]

Perhaps the DHS will have to fund development of a terrorist and banker-resistant payments grid in the future! Anyway, my point was that the electricity grid is a useful way to think about payments: a regulated machine that anyone can connect to with the right, standardised, safety-certified equipment. There's only one electricity cable running into my house, but I can buy electricity from a great many people. I could even put a solar panel on my house and send electricity back along that cable and into the grid. So it's a useful analogy that helps, I think, the discussion about regulation.

> *If there is vertical integration from deposit-taking into transmission, deposit takers will use the economic power that such vertical integration gives them to distort competition in their favour—to advantage a single firm which is owner of the network, or to benefit established firms at the expense of entrants if ownership is collective. That distortion of competition is what currently happens. Narrow banks are institutions that have access to the payments system and take the deposits necessary for that access.*

[From John Kay - Should We Have 'Narrow Banking'?]

In other words, the separation of banking into casino banking and narrow banking, where narrow banking comprises the payment utility plus savings and loans, would be a better economic environment with a less distorted market. I'd go further, and separate the payment utility from the savings and loans, leading to a tripartite structure. This would actually map to John's description of the fundamental requirements for regulation.

Utility: even very brief disruption causes systemic disarray and extended economic loss (e.g. the electricity grid, the telecommunications network).

Essential goods and services: continued supply is necessary but partial or temporary disruption can be accommodated (e.g. food, fuel).

> *Nice to have: free markets can and should generally be allowed to define market price and availability. If the market does not provide, too bad (most goods and services).*
>
> *[From John Kay - Should We Have 'Narrow Banking'?]*

This seems to me to imply that the payments utility should be regulated for what the telco guys would label Grade of Service (GoS) and Quality of Service (QoS) and anyone able to meet those requirements should be able to provide the cables, switches and sockets. The crucial economic functions of savings, loans, risk management and information provision should be provided by banks and, further away from the utility, the investment functions should be provided by investment banks (the casinos).

Golden Moments– 01/08/2011

The price of gold has been climbing steadily: it's gone up a third in the last year, surely a sign that people are disenchanted with other asset classes in general and fiat currency in particular. The fixation on gold has led to a bizarre development: the gold ATM. I remember noting this a while back, but since then yet another swathe of gold-dispensing ATMs have been announced, this time in Turkey.

> *Thus far, all 64 Kuveyt Turk ATMs installed in Istanbul have been upgraded to offer 1 and 1.5 gram ingots of gold bullion as well as banknotes. The bank has contracted with Wincor Nixdorf to retrofit the facility to its national network of 180 machines by year end... The mini gold bars are not dispensed through the banknote output chute, but via a special coin output module that is retrofitted to the ATM. The gold bullion is packed inside a transparent plastic coin roughly the same size as a two-euro coin.*
>
> *[From Finextra: Turkish bank retrofits ATMs to dispense gold ingots]*

There's quite a few of these around. I remember Forum friend Chris Skinner talking about the one he'd come across in the Middle East.

Germany's TG-Gold-Super-Markt installed a gold bar dispensing ATM in the lobby of Abu Dhabi's five star Deluxe Emirates Palace hotel last year, and outlined plans to roll out 500 of the machines in Germany, Switzerland and Austria.

[From Finextra: Turkish bank retrofits ATMs to dispense gold ingots]

How these would fare in the UK I'm not sure - I suspect the ram-raiders and JCB-jackers would be out in force—but there probably are enough people. These are going to become if not commonplace at least not unusual in the US, too.

A German firm that installs and manages gold vending machines aims to introduce them into the United States this year… Thomas Geissler, creator of the Gold to Go brand and chief executive of Ex Oriente Lux, told Reuters on the sidelines of the London Bullion Market Association conference that the company aims to issue a "couple of hundred" machines next year.

[From ATMs That Sell Gold Bars Are Coming Soon to America - CNBC]

The early experiences there seem promising, from the point of view of the provider, and seem to indicate that, however bizarre it may seem, there are people out there who really do want to convert the cash to gold (as well as those who are forced to convert their cash to gold: see here, here and here, for example):

In the US, PMX Gold has set up a banking division with the aim of introducing gold dispensing ATMs nationide follow a pilot run at a shopping mall in Boca Raton, Florida, that saw $270,000.00 in gold sales dispensed through one machine in roughly two and one half months

[From Finextra: Turkish bank retrofits ATMs to dispense gold ingots]

Each time I see one of these stories, it leaves me flabbergasted (my favourite word this week). For example,

An ATM that spits out pure gold nuggets and coins has become such a hit among shoppers that one vendor has had to organise twice-a-week replenishment.

Tomorrow's Transactions—The 2012 Reader

[From gulfnews : Proving its metal: Dubai ATM]

I absolutely do not understand this. Why would anyone want to buy precious metals? I mean actual physical precious metals? It's not like you're going to smelt them or use them to make sophisticated electronic components. By taking home the gold nuggets, the customers are taking home risk.

> *A man who decided to store his precious metals in a vault at his home in Chilliwack, Canada, was robbed of US$750,000 worth of silver bars in broad daylight... The 52-year-old victim is still traumatized after burglars intruded into his house where he had stored his life savings in silver bars. Based on the current silver price at the New York Comex, the silver was valued at about US$750,000.*

[From Robbers get away with US$750,000 worth of silver bars]

Haven't these people ever heard of GoldMoney [disclaimer: my employer Consult Hyperion has provided paid professional services to GoldMoney] or any of the other online services? Plenty of other people seem to: Goldmoney alone has $2 billion in gold under management at the moment. (As an aside: I just worked out that my Goldmoney account has earned me an APR of 23.3% in the four months since I opened the account *)

But back to the Turkish gold ATM. This, it transpires, though, isn't all about currency costs and economic efficiency but tradition.

> *The bank says it wants to become Turkey's leading retailer of gold to consumers, where demand is driven by the local tradition of investing savings in gold and making gifts of gold on the birth of children and at weddings.*

[From Finextra: Turkish bank retrofits ATMs to dispense gold ingots]

I still come back to my point: why would you invest savings, whether for yourself or for your children or grandchildren in physical gold? I just don't see how this can make any sense in a crime-ridden backward-looking primitive economy on the edge of Europe.

> *GOLD coins and bars worth £200,000 were stolen during a daylight robbery of a Brook Green home.*

[From Local News - Fulham Chronicle]

South west London aside, there are some developing economies where gold is not only the mechanism for deferred payment but also a store of value and even the means of exchange.

Gold is a big deal in Vietnam. The average Vietnamese spends more of each Dollar of income on gold than anyone else on Earth. Total gold buying amounted to 3.1% of GDP last year. (By comparison, private gold purchases amounted to 2.5% of India's GDP, while China's were a mere 0.4%.)

[From Gold, Gresham's Law & the Dong - Buy Gold Online with the Bullion Vault - GoldSeek.com]

This is despite the US dollar being legal tender and gold imports being banned since 2008 (the gold is smuggled in) and a series of laws that are supposed to restrict its use inside the country. The measure of the success of these policies?

All told, an estimated 500 tonnes of gold – over $24 billion worth – is hoarded away, reckons Huynh Trung Khanh, deputy chairman of the Vietnam Gold Business Council. It's hidden in mattresses and buried in the garden.

[From Gold, Gresham's Law & the Dong - Buy Gold Online with the Bullion Vault - GoldSeek.com]

The reason why this story caught my eye, though, was because it links to a presentation that I gave at the Copenhagen Finance IT Region, part of the Danish Bankers Association, in May. I was taking about the co-evolution of money and technology and discussing how technology has shifted stores of value (eg, bank deposits) into mediums for exchange. In our pre-industrial economy, this was true of gold, so I was wondering out loud whether technological evolution in the post-industrial economy would take us back to those days or forward to some new kinds of currency.

But gold is not just a store of value in Vietnam. It is also used as a medium of exchange. Which is why, in the day-to-day sense, it also functions as money.In Vietnam you can put gold in a bank and earn interest. People quote house prices in gold, and pay for them with tael gold bars – each bar weighing approximately 1.2 troy ounces. This makes sense when you consider that Vietnam is a largely cash society. A single property can cost up to 4 billion Vietnamese Dong.

[From Gold, Gresham's Law & the Dong - Buy Gold Online with the Bullion Vault - GoldSeek.com]

With the biggest banknote being the 500,000 Dong (about $20), you can see why people would rather use gold than 8,000 of these banknotes to buy a house! But could this happen in developed countries too? If people like Goldmoney manage to make gold sufficiently liquid and convenient at POS then would the consumers who go to gold ATMs go for electronic gold instead or is there something (potentially irrational) about the physical metal?

> *German community bank Fidor is partnering with physical bullion outfit GoldMoney to offer customers precious metals transactions though the FidorPay ewallet.*
>
> *[From Finextra: Germany's Fidor Bank to offer retail access to precious metals via GoldMoney]*

And I note that in the UK, Standard Life now offer gold (again via Goldmoney) as part of their pensions portfolio. It's surprising to think, but there are some people out there who, frankly, don't trust the financial system at all and so want all of their pension holding in gold.

> *The wife of Tunisia's ousted ruler has fled the country with 1.5 tonnes of gold worth more than £35m, it was revealed today.*
>
> *[From Tunisian president's wife Leila Trabelsi fled riots with £35m in gold bars | Mail Online]*

What a wise pension decision! Since she used up her baggage allowance on the shiny stuff, her holding has gone up about £10m. She's probably not very good on the interweb, or has trouble remembering passwords, but for the rest of us electronic gold is, I'm sure, a better proposition.

* Please note. This does not constitute investment advice and should not be seemed a recommending any course of action. Anyone who invests in anything at all on the basis of anything that I say in a blog post is, frankly, an idiot and deserves whatever they get.

Comments

Dave, people like the physical because of the US Executive Order 6102: http://en.wikipedia.org/wiki/Executive_Order_6102

"More recently, in January 2010, the SEC approved a new regulation on money markets which would allow for the suspension of redemptions, practically freezing investor's assets for any duration the SEC sees fit." http://news.silverseek.com/SilverSeek/1265765715.php

Gold however is cool in the UK because Queenie must have stacks, hence its Capital Gains free status me thinks. I personally also like Silver. http://silver-shortage.blogspot.com/2011/08/special-silver-roundtable-with-jim.html "USA geologist society have predicted that Silver will be the first element of the periodic table to run out by 2020."

Posted by: Mark Cross on 08/08/2011 at 18:51.

I don't believe those silver stories. I just checked with the United States Geological Service, which says that there are known reserves of 500,000 tonnes of silver, which is at least 25 years production at current rates. And if the price goes up because of a shortage, the reserves will go up too.

Posted by: Consult Hyperion on 11/08/2011 at 18:00.

A new payment instrument for Britain– 17/08/2011

We can all see the broad outline of retail payments in the UK: cash and cheques down, credit cards up a bit, debit cards up a lot. From these figures, it's fairly easy to extrapolate to say, 2018, and see cheques vanish while cash usage continues a steady decline.

Meanwhile cheque usage fell dramatically as consumers and business sought quicker, more convenient ways to pay. In the last three years, cheque usage has fallen just over 30%... Faster Payments grew 47% in the first quarter year-on-year. A total of £48bn of cleared funds was moved instantly by UK account holders, meaning their payees had immediate access to that money, rather than having to wait for a cheque to clear.

[From Payments Council - Debit cards on top with continued spending surge]

Oddly, the continued fall in cheque usage did not, as you might imagine, serve to reinforce the goal of the national payment strategy set back in 2008 to end cheque clearing in 2018. Instead, under pressure from nutty newspaper columnists, egregious elderly whingers and complaining charities, the Payments Council abandoned that goal and determined to keep cheques for as along as people want them (and can force other people continue to pay for them). I thought that in the light of this decision, the Payments Council and the Treasury Select Committee might be interested in an alternative paper-based cheque replacement scheme: the deposit-cheque.

The deposit-cheque scheme works in this way. Customers are given books of cheques that are preprinted with a maximum amount and protected with a simple anti-rewriting mechanism such as perforations with the same amount on them. To avoid the problem of cheques bouncing and the uncertainties related to clearing (and to obviate the need for any form of replacement cheque guarantee card) the value of the cheques given to any customer is against money that is held in an interest-bearing account for them. So, for example, my Dad would ask Lloyds for £100 in deposit-cheques. Lloyds give him a book of ten £10 cheques. The £100 is moved from my dad's current account to an interest-bearing deposit account solely for the purpose of backing the cheques. The cheques would be valid for, say, two years. When my dad wants to pay the window cleaner, he writes out a cheque for £7.50 and gives it to the window cleaner. Once it has been signed by my dad, the window cleaner can use it in lieu of cash, up until the expiry date - no need to pay it into a bank account, which is the time-consuming and expensive part.

I thought this scheme might go down especially well with the Treasury Select Committee and the Old Person's Czar, Joan Bakewell, because it was invented in the 1873 by a Mr. James Hertz, who set up a "Check Bank" on these principles in London, saying that he intended it to become the medium for the "accomplishment of an immense mass of small payments". They had quite a good "ignition strategy" too, because they were targetting business, for whom the payment of wages in cash was an onerous and expensive task. According to the Handbook of London Bankers for 1876, there were 984 banks who honoured the Check Bank's cheques, so they clearly had something going for them, although I have not as yet discovered what happened to the enterprise. All in all, though, I think it fits the bill for 21st-century Britain.

Having said that, though, perhaps this brilliant and innovative paper-based alternative to our current cheque system needs more support. I wonder if the Treasury Select Committee have looked at neighbouring countries to not merely keep cheques in existence, but to drive up their use? Ireland, for example. Ireland has been very successful in resisting modern contrivances such as payment cards.

> However, the Irish still have a stronger attachment to cash than most European countries, using ATMs more than any other EU member, making an average of 40 withdrawals, totalling almost EUR5000 per capita, in 2010. The value of all non-cash transactions totalled 36% in 2010, in stark contrast to the EU average of 96%, where consumers have for many years been using e-payments. IPSO claims that EUR1 billion could be saved a year by switching to electronic and card payments.
>
> [From Finextra: Ireland moves from cash to cards]

One of the main reasons for this is that Ireland actually taxes payment cards.

> *Ireland is still extremely reliant on paper payments, particularly cash and cheques... Ireland has historically had a policy of such usage, and the government has actively discouraged electronic payment until recently by taxing citizens for using debit and credit cards.*

> *[From The Financial Services Club's Blog: In Ireland, it's cash or cheques]*

Russell Burke, Head of Payments Strategy at the Irish Payment Services Organisation (IPSO wrote an article on this in Electronic Payments Law & Policy (EPLP) in which he said that a consequence of SEPA and PSD will be more competition in the Irish payments market and this should mean eliminating the distorting "stamp duty", the tax on credit and debit card ownership—R. Burke. *From cash to card: the need for a national payments plan* in *E-Finance & Payments Law & Policy* (Jun. 2010)— although it has to be said that that hasn't happened so far.. Perhaps we can learn from our neighbours and modernise further by persuading the UK regulators, commentators, lawmakers and pressure groups to put a tax on the use of electronic instruments to incentivise the use of cheques still further.

At last! Now we can start building the legacy system– 22/08/2011

The Federal Reserve Bank of Atlanta's excellent "Portals and Rails" blog asks today

> *Is recent EMV announcement the catalyst the U.S. needs to catch up?*

> *[From Portals and Rails]*

Richard Oliver, Executive Vice President at the Atlanta Fed opened up the Smart Card Alliance Chicago conference with a great talk about the dilemma facing the US payments industry because of the evolution of payments technology. I was really looking forward to hearing Rich talk, for a couple of reasons. First of all, Rich played a big part in Check21, so he understands what it takes to co-ordinate major change across the US payments industry. Secondly, he just co-authored the white paper on mobile payments in the USA that I've been reading. He didn't disappoint.

As an aside, I should say that I thought that the event keynotes worked quite well, and flowed nicely I thought because Rich was looking at the big picture around the US payments industry and then he was followed by Toni Merschen who was looking at the big picture around EMV and then I followed on to talk more specifically about the EMV roadmap through contactless and on to mobile, where I made the point (not exactly new) that the strategy for EMV in the US will depend on mobile, contactless and internet as much as the retail point-of-sale (POS).

Anyway, Rich was looking at the big picture around payments. As he pointed out, payments used to be a rather sleepy segment of financial services, but life is changing. He pointed out that Check21 took six years, Canadian EMV migration took five years, the Single European Payments Area (SEPA) is four years in (and nothing much has happened) but these timescales look absurd to people in the technology sector. This must, it seems to me, mean that the cultural differences between technology businesses and payments businesses will continue to make co-operation difficult.

While organisations in the payment sector are facing a variety of difficult choices in difficult economic circumstances, the sector as a whole is facing a really serious issue about competitiveness. Rich illustrated the dynamics with the case at hand: contact chip and PIN technology. Will the US be late to market and have to change again soon, be addressing a selected subset of the customer base, be betting on near-obsolete (his words, not mine!) technology? Rich called for a new business paradigms. He was illustrating the classic "disruptive innovation" dilemma, whereby companies listening to their existing customers can innovate their way into oblivion, because meeting the requirements of existing stakeholders (e.g., banks, regulators and networks) does not result in new ways to do business. I was thinking about what Rich said in Chicago after seeing the Atlanta Fed's comment on that announcement about EMV in the USA by Visa (more on this later).

Rich was very funny talking about the great visions from people who have never implemented anything, but was using a few examples to make a general point about the fragmented, pilot-oriented, evolution of new payments before he went on to talk about the Industry Mobile Payments Forum that has been organised by the Boston and Atlanta Feds. The white paper that has come from this Forum (which I intended to blog about, but have still only half-finished the post) introduced the idea of a US mobile framework—that is centred on an open mobile wallet that supports multiple payment credentials in a secure container—and is well worth reading, but perhaps its most useful short term recommendation is that there ought to be a collaborative, neutral forum to address common issues such as standards and business rules. In the UK, this was under the auspices of what was then called APACS (now the UK Payment Administration and related bodies—see my who's who), but the US doesn't currently have a similar body and this would seem to be an obvious and sensible step to take.

I noted that Rich also pointed out that the merchants who were members of the IMPF were not against investing in new POS hardware, software and systems (this mirrors my own experiences with clients: merchants like the idea of mobile wallets and are not against spending money on them) but they are not investing at the moment because they don't see a plausible roadmap from the payments industry and they don't want to waste money on technology dead ends. He finished up noting that some members of the Forum think that the US should skip the contact chip and PIN step and go straight contactless, that some members want to skip contactless and go straight to mobile and some want to miss it out altogether. Although that might be a plausible strategy in niches, I don't think it will happen.

One of the key reasons for this is that Visa have just announced that they will require acquirers to support chip and PIN by 1st April 2013 and that they will implement the "liability shift" on 1st October 2015. This means, essentially, that the merchants who don't take chip and PIN transactions will be liable for fraud on magnetic stripe signature transactions. I'm glad to see that Visa also announced that they would bring the Technology Innovation Programme (TIP) to the USA from 1st October this year, but with an interesting twist.

> *Visa insists on the rollout of terminals able to support both contact and contactless chip acceptance, including NFC-based mobile payments. In fact, unlike in Europe, only such terminals will qualify for the TIP incentive.*

[From Celent Banking Blog » Applauding Visa]

This makes the roadmap I presented in Chicago back in March look even more prescient since, as I said, contactless delivers the rails for mobile to run on. I also made the point about internet authentication and I stand by it: in the medium term, the EMV application in the mobile handset will be used for dynamic authentication on the internet and much as it will be used at the retail POS, making for a convenient common platform for consumers. If issuing banks can co-operate on this, there's an opportunity to create a standard identity management with two-factor authentication (2FA) scheme—within the NSTIC framework—that would greatly improve the lot of all stakeholders (who wouldn't want to log on to Facebook securely using their mobile phone?) and raise the bar on internet security substantially.

In summary, what all of this means, I think, is that now that US is on board, EMV is now officially the legacy infrastructure for retail payments and that we can start work on designing its successor.

In England, the phrase "since time immemorial" actually means "since the death of Henry II", who reformed and unified the English legal system... In our world, "since time immemorial" means "since before the Netscape IPO" (9th August 1995). EMV comes from time immemorial.

[From Digital Money: He's losing touch, surely?]

Rich was right. These things take time. But the coming era of innovation in payments no longer depends on the payments industry, so the timescales of SEPA and EMV, Check 21 and 3D-Secure will never be seen again. When work started on EMV, the new technology solution was the smart card and business problem was that networks were unreliable and expensive. Now, the new technology solution is the mobile phone and the problem is that no-one (still) knows you're a dog (or, at least the dog you claim to be). I hope that some of the lessons learned from EMV (for example: never put a PIN into something that isn't yours)

I don't have a crystal ball, but if I were to be looking around for the germ of a successor, I might be tempted to look in the direction of NSTIC, because I think that a standardised identification and authentication infrastructure is the natural platform for future payments. Or, to put it another way, identity is the new money.

Five major trends (not my words) – 26/08/2011

I had the pleasure of meeting Heather Schlegel (who blogs as heathervescent) at SXSW and determined then to persuade her to come to London for the next year's 15th annual Digital Money Forum sponsored by Visa Europe, Barclaycard and Monitise with support from ACI Worldwide. I'm delighted to say that Heather has kindly agreed to attend and present the results of her research on the future of transactions, which I think will really help the debate and discussion to evolve further this year.

My research found five major trends impacting the Future of Transactions

[From heathervescent: Evolution of Currency]

These five factors may not come as a complete surprise to those of you who have attended previous Digital Money events, but Heather's take on them might be. Her research has emphasised the role of communities in the evolution of digital money, a factor that more and more of our clients are looking to bring into their strategies for the exploitation of new technology in the transaction space. Let's begin with the uncontroversial.

Mobile Transaction Technology is exploding. This not surprising to anyone following this industry. But we're watching the explosion of the hype-curve

[From <u>heathervescent: Evolution of Currency</u>]

Absolutely. I've been boring people at conferences with this for years, saying that even if you believed all the hype about the mobile phone, you would still not be grasping the magnitude of the shift coming. The mobile is becoming the focus for transactions of all kinds (and I continue to maintain that in the long run, it is the mobile management of identity transactions that will reshape reorganise not only commerce, but society, the most).

Alternate Currencies (including gaming currencies like WoW Gold, corporate currencies like frequent flyer miles and social capital "currencies" like reputation and wuffie) are being used in their own niche communities. And some of these niche communities have very high transaction rates

[From <u>heathervescent: Evolution of Currency</u>]

One of the topics that has fascinated me the most since I first began to get interested in electronic transactions is alternative currencies, and in particular the idea that once efficient electronic transaction mechanisms are in place in the mass market then the cost of switching between currencies, the cost of experiment with new currencies, falls. In which case, which of the thousand flowers might bloom? Heather once again made me think and reflect by examining the potential from her perspective.

Non-Financial Transactions create stronger bonds. When you have a community that is formed around non-financial transactions (like time-banks or swap/barter/pay it forward) the transactors create stronger bonds than if the transaction was only a financial transaction.

[From <u>heathervescent: Evolution of Currency</u>]

Without hinting at the potential strategies that might be important for some of our clients, I think I can say that ensuring that what they provide is not "only a financial transaction" is seen as an ingredient. There are a number of approaches that are worth trying here: transparency, for example, which is already seen as being a mainstream opportunity (what with open data, mashups and so on).

We want to communicate more information with each transaction. We're rating our restaurant experiences on Yelp. Writing recommendations on LinkedIn. Giving feedback about people on Honestly. And the technology products for more fine grained communication about each transaction are getting developed. We want to share more information about each transaction we have - regardless of the kind of transaction. This last trend is very important - and one of the most subtle.

[From heathervescent: Evolution of Currency]

These well-founded observations, about the elements of a reputation economy, reinforce my own prejudices about the longer term where a cross between eBay stars and NSTIC provide a low-overhead framework for trade, and therefore prosperity. These are all great points and well worth the discussion and debate they will engender at the Forum. But I think Heather's most important trend is this one:

Communities are being created around transactions. Whether this is in these niche communities with an alternate currency, within forums or craigslist for traditional economy transactions or non-financial transactions; communities are being/have been formed around transactions

[From heathervescent: Evolution of Currency]

This is surely correct. The future isn't a single currency but hundreds of currencies, each of them centred on a community. Some of these communities may be geographic, some virtual, some brand-based, some personal. Who knows? The idea that the only community that counts being the nation state is seen many as a physical law, on par with gravity, but it is a construction: money doesn't have to work that way and is in the process of rescaling for both supranational communities (perhaps only for the unit of account?) and other non-national communities.

Comments

I like the post. There is one issue that I believe is often overlooked when discussing alternate currencies. Governments and central banks worldwide make billions yearly by controlling the issuance of currency, through seigniorage. How can we reconcile the future model with the current legal and political framework? I would love to see contributions on this topic, because I fear government intervention will sabotage free market.

Posted by: René Bastien on 26/08/2011 at 20:55.

Person-to-person banking – 30/08/2011

A year ago, I remember reading and agreeing with Javelin that banks would have to start doing something about, amongst other things, person-to-person payments. At the time, I was thinking about UK banks and the need to accelerate the development of interpersonal solutions to reduce cash usage and respond to the 2018 target for the end of cheque clearing (now removed as we have decided that the future is paper after all).

> *Facing limited budgets, increased regulation, angry consumers, and higher fraud incidence, banks must prioritize scarce investments related to customer fee models, mobile channels, social media, P2P, data breaches and PCI compliance, and even new solutions for ATMs, PINs and real-time systems.*
>
> *[From Javelin Strategy and Research » Bankers, Payments and Security Experts: Changes in Technology, Regulation, and Consumer Trust Require Overhaul of Strategies and Business Models in 2010]*

This point is that bank P2P (or, more properly account-to-account payments) would be an obvious replacement for expensive checks and wire transfers. In the US, the banks have (speaking in very broad terms) gone for two responses: some of them have integrated PayPal as their P2P solution and some of them have decided to build a new P2P system. In fact I've just read that the Javelin guys have been playing with the Bank of America and Wells Fargo offering.

> *According to the terms and conditions of this service, this transfer can take up to three days. Three days? That seems a bit long in this day and age. The Wells Fargo recipient received an email which prompted them to enroll their account in the services. The money was quickly debited from the Bank of America account and within minutes the recipient got an email saying that an amount was being transferred to them. A couple hours after the debit, the credit still has not been posted – it will be interesting to see exactly how long this takes.*
>
> *[From Bank Person to Person Payments – small steps - Javelin Strategy & Research Blog]*

Seriously. Up to three days. It's as if transistors and laser beams had never been invented. I'm moved to say WTF, but I don't want to offend (or annoy any of our bank customers). The reason for this implausible transaction time is, of course, that the money is actually being moved through the existing inter-bank electronic funds transfer networks. PayPal, M-PESA and new-kid-on-the-block Serve from American Express don't work that way. They put the money in a big pot and then reallocate it as necessary. This makes transactions instantaneous and inexpensive (because they are just a few bytes in a big database).

The Javelin guys found that the mobile money service didn't seem to work terribly well either.

> *The receiving phone number must be pre-registered online before any transfers could be made to it.*
>
> *[From Bank Person to Person Payments – small steps - Javelin Strategy & Research Blog]*

M-PESA doesn't do this. You can send money instantly to any phone in Kenya. If they are an M-PESA customer, they get an M-PESA notification. If they are not an M-PESA customer, they get a message telling them to go to any one of 28,000 agents to either get their money or to create an M-PESA account. I've said, at the more than one event, that perhaps the "developed" world should examine and learn from "developing" world use of mobile and I stand by it. In some cases, we could be making a big mistake by succumbing to the temptation to add layer after layer on top of legacy networks instead of putting them to one side and building something new.

ROE on API– 27/09/2011

McKinsey's 2011 report on the state of the global banking industry makes the point (as far as I can see) that if banks don't embrace disruptive technologies themselves then someone else will. This is the "standard" Clayton Christensen "Innovator's Dilemma" view of the world, and I have to say that I subscribe to it too.

> *Banks have overcome previous crises by finding innovative ways to increase the top line. Although opportunities may seem to be limited, we see huge scope to improve pricing, to adapt products to the needs of customers, and to find new pockets of growth (taking advantage of the better risk-management processes many have introduced in the wake of the crisis). Opportunity lies in the potential for disruptive technology in both consumer and wholesale banking—yet many of banking's digital strategies are still in their infancy.*
>
> *[From In search of a sustainable model for global banking - McKinsey Quarterly - Financial Services - Banking]*

But what were those "innovative ways to increase the top line"? Did they involve technology? In 2010, according to McKinsey's figures, the US and European banking industries delivered an ROE of just 7 and 7.9 percent, respectively. They say that "At this level, the banks' ROE is still some 1.5 percentage points below their cost of equity". So have banks always been such bad investments? That's not clear: these ROEs used to be considered normal for the banking sector.

> *In the period up until around 1970 ROE in banking was around 7 per cent with a low variance. In other words, returns to finance broadly mimicked those in the economy as a whole . . . But the 1970s mark a regime shift, with the ROE in banking roughly trebling to over 20 per cent*
>
> [From *What do the banks' target returns on equity tell us? | Martin Wolf's Exchange | Economic commentary from the Financial Times – FT.com*]

We all understand the big changes in bank balance sheets that led to these incredible returns: leveraging, and a big increase in risk. But banks have a special place in the economy, and there are a couple of reasons why they can target much higher ROE this way.

> *One is that they can earn monopoly profits. The other is that they are subsidised, principally because taxpayers provide insurance against catastrophic risk, particularly for bank creditors. The two – monopoly and subsidy – are, of course, related. Without barriers to entry, subsidies would be arbitraged away.*
>
> [From *What do the banks' target returns on equity tell us? | Martin Wolf's Exchange | Economic commentary from the Financial Times – FT.com*]

This is, as all observers anticipate, what will happen in the payments sector in Europe as the new regulatory environment begins to reshape the payments value networks. The Commission is so keen to see new entrants create new competition that they are right now considering further legal action to accelerate the process.

> *The EC has opened an antitrust investigation into whether the European Payments Council (EPC) is blocking new, non-bank, players from entering the online payments market.*
>
> [From *Finextra: EC launches antitrust investigation into EPC and e-payments market*]

You can see why this is a problem for European retail banks. There is going to be more competition than ever before. They are faced with competitors such as Google Wallet who appear to play nicely in the short term (by using bank payment instruments) but who could be utterly disruptive in the medium term by obtaining PSD and ELMI licences just as the mobile operators have started to. These are nimble and flexible competitors. This is not a criticism of our bank clients, who are well aware of these trends, but a reflection on the problems that incumbent players face in general (cf Christensen, as mentioned at the start).

> *Google Wallet launched three months after it was announced. On the other hand Isis, first announced in November 2010, is only planning to launch a pilot run in Salt Lake City and Austin in early-mid 2012.*

> *[From Google]*

There's a really serious point behind this, and I think it's central to what many of our clients have to wrestle with as they turn strategy into a tactics. It's very, very difficult for banks and mobile operators to work together (a topic for another day) and for both of them the process of bringing new products or services to the mass market is slower than they would like. The mobile operators have been wrestling with this for some time, struggling to avoid being "just a pipe".

> *Telecommunications carriers, facing increased competition from companies taking advantage of the global Internet, cost pressures and consumer demands must restructure now, or resign themselves to being utility providers, says Gartner principal analyst Will Hahn.*

> *[From ITWeb :Gartner tells telcos to adapt]*

If we focus on banks, there are smart people who are developing strategies and understand the environment, but their organisational IT spending goes almost entirely on operations and compliance. Therefore banks have to focus their "skunk works" very tightly into areas where they might expect to have some sustainable competitive advantage. It's not clear to me that this is in payments. Suppose that in payments terms the banks are "just a pipe"? Then it makes sense to become an operationally-efficient and profitable pipe and forget about putting value-adding services on top. They should just open up their APIs and let other players come in and build new products and services.

> *Putting everything into an Application Programming Interface (API) is how Facebook, Paypal and others are working today and, if they didn't, they would be dead. This is Craig's contention*

for banking. In other words, banks should throw their functionality out there for anyone with the gumption to plug and play with and integrate into their apps, websites, mobiles ... anything.

[From The Financial Services Club's Blog: Banks should build their business models as APIs]

I can think of a million reasons not to do this from the incumbents' position, but they probably have no choice. Look at the innovation that PayPal unleashed by opening up its API.

One thing that struck me about PayPal's "Innovate 2010" conference in San Francisco, in (I have to say) fairly stark contrast to many of the events I attend in the more traditional banking world is just how much innovation was actually going on.

[From Digital Money: Innovate and innovation]

So suppose my Google Wallet could have direct access to my Barclays account via an API, and Twitter could get my Barclaycard transactions via an API, and... Wow.

Square might be a first step towards cashless– 03/11/2011

Remember way back when, over a year ago (that's a decade in internet years), Square came align with their cute little device to save you from having to type card details into your iPhone...

Square, an application that turns a smartphone into a mobile cash register, is open for business. Created by Twitter co-founder Jack Dorsey, Square uses a free download and plastic card reader to let users accept credit card payments.

[From Mobile]

Square has gone through the roof. Its real innovation wasn't that you could read the cards with a smartphone (other people make excellent devices for that: Verifone and Intuit for example) but that you didn't need a merchant account with a bank. You could just sign up and start taking payments. This opened up a whole new market, especially for SMEs, micro enterprises and individuals.

Businesses with many small transactions should look at Square closely, while businesses with high average ticket size should get a competitive merchant account with interchange plus pricing.

[From Should small businesses use Square]

Surely this is only part of the comparison though. The school fete cake stand can't have a merchant acquiring account, whatever their transaction mix. Just trying call your bank and asking them "hey I've been asked to run the lemonade stand at the village fair on Saturday and I'd like to accept card payments, can you send over a POS device" to see how far you get. Anyway, customers reveal preferences tell the story.

Square's Keith Rabois also revealed a number of growth statistics for the company, including that the payments service is now processing $2 billion in payments volume per year. To date, Square has been activated by 800,000 merchants

[From Square]

I was reading a story about Square on the web the other day and I found the comments quite interesting, because they tell you what the consumer users think about it rather than what people like me think about it.

I use my Square reader all the time to get reimbursed for utilities in the house I share with three other guys; the small hit I take for the fees is nothing to get the cash right away (and not have to mess with checks).

[From Square]

It's these kinds of prosaic applications that have taken Square into all sorts of interesting new areas. In retrospect, it's easy to see that the demand was there and not met.

On Saturday, I was at the Middle School, manning the snack booth for the regional band competition. I did pretty well - over 50 sales! But what fascinated me was that three people asked, somewhat plaintively, if I took debit cards... They were all young moms.

[From Maybe Cash Really Is Going Away? — Payments Views from Glenbrook Partners]

I may not be in the same demographic, but I'm certainly of the same sentiment. In fact, I'd go a bit further. When I was buying something to eat at one of the stands at Waterloo station the other day, I was positively annoyed when I couldn't pay for a £4.95 snack by just tapping my contactless credit card but instead had to insert the card, enter the PIN and wait for authorisation. Who has the time?

> He said that his entire cab fleet converted to Square at the request of the company's owner. After four months of use, he loves the device. "It's a lot quicker and easier," Mabyae said. He also noted that relative to their old way of accepting credit cards, it seems more secure for passengers.

[From Square]

Secure, convenient, affordable and able to pass the most severe of cash replacement tests, the cab driver. That's pretty impressive! I take my hat off to them, but I would also note at the same time that Square isn't really that radical. It runs on the existing rails. It makes them better, but it doesn't make them cheaper or more flexible. There's an argument that says that the incumbents will only allow in competitors who do not disrupt the existing infrastructure.

> Square, a payments company that is a media darling frequently cited as a leading innovator, does not disrupt the financial infrastructure in any way. In fact, Visa just invested in Square directly because it does such a good job of propagating the status quo.

[From In Fifty Days, Payments Innovation Wi... by Aaron Greenspan - Quora]

So Square almost certainly isn't the end game because there's plenty more disruption to come. But it is plausible to postulate that Square is a first step into making cash seem inconvenient, insecure and expensive? What if people really didn't want to take cash unless they absolutely had to? What if using cash became seen as being socially irresponsible, like drunk driving? Well, what if that were true?

Unexpected? Not to me – 08/11/2011

There's a front page story in today's New York Times titled "As People Shun High Bank Fees, Wal-Mart Unexpectedly Gains".

> Americans say they are fed up with banks. They are protesting on Wall Street and raising a ruckus over outsize fees. Now there is a surprising beneficiary: Wal-Mart.

Tomorrow's Transactions—The 2012 Reader

[*From Wal-Mart Benefits From Anger Over Banking Fees - NYTimes.com*]

Two things struck me about this story. The first thing is that use of the word "unexpectedly". This is a little harsh on Wal-Mart, don't you think? It makes it sound as if they had invested considerable time and money developing their Money Center businesses just in the vague hope that they might attract some business in future. Come on - credit (sic) where credit is due. Wal-Mart saw a business they thought they could compete in, and went for it. That's competition for you. "Unexpectedly" makes it sound like the weather changed.

The second thing is that what the people quoted in the story are doing at Wal-Mart is not "banking" at all. It is, by and large, payments. The story says, clearly, thank Wal-Mart has "no intention" of reviving its plans to become a bank in the US, although it has obtained bank charters in Canada and Mexico. All of which brings me back to the question about whether payments are part of banking or not, a recurring theme in my blogging over the years. This is being discussed at more elevated levels than my e-jotting.

> [*Simon Newstead, managing director, head of FI market & business strategy, Global Transaction Services, RBS*] *says, "There is nothing like new competition and emerging technology to stimulate a focus on product development."*
>
> [*From Do Banks Have a Place in the Future of Payments? - Bank Systems & Technology*]

This is spot on, and one of key conclusions that I drew from last year's Centre for the Study of Financial Innovation, which was kindly supported by Visa Europe. There was a clear sentiment from the roundtable participants that creating a regulatory environment that allowed more competition around the utility business of payments was more likely to lead to good outcomes than having regulators attempt to determine what the payments business should look like. The European Commission itself has decided the same, which is why it is getting frustrated at slow progress.

> *The EC has opened an antitrust investigation into whether the European Payments Council (EPC) is blocking new, non-bank, players from entering the online payments market.*
>
> [*From Finextra: EC launches antitrust investigation into EPC and e-payments market*]

Personally, I've not seen any evidence that this is case, but that doesn't mean anything really. If there was a top secret conspiracy to prevent innovation new players from taking on the banks, they'd hardly publicise it! My position is that the EPC comes from the world of banking, and banks take a long time to agree on new co-operative platforms. I think the Commission is probably wrong to assume anti-competitive behaviour. The point is that we should be getting more competition, and we are, but the market is moving slowly. Banks, as much as anyone else, need to focus on this because payments are a significant cost to banks.

> *Olivier Denecker of McKinsey... Payments = 30% of the €150 billion cost base of EU banks... What struck me as Olivier talked is that banks don't view payments as a separate product stream.*
>
> *[From The Financial Services Club's Blog: Banking as components or integrators]*

I don't think they're a separate product stream, I think they're a separate business and as time goes by I become more convinced of the case. Perhaps banks shouldn't be running payments anymore than they should be building their own offices or generating their own electricity. Payments are a utility that should be provided in an open, transparent and non-discriminatory way to banks and non-banks alike. Here's some fighting talk that suggests that Wal-Mart and M-PESA might not be isolated cases.

> *Nobuhiko Sugiura, a professor in e-money law and part of the team which developed Mondex, says the reason Mondex failed highlights why European and US prepaid spending, particularly for low-value transactions, has lagged Japan. The emphasis for Mondex, he says, was purely bank-led. His experience in Japan over the last decade suggests that non-financial companies, particularly retailers, often have more to gain from issuing e-money products. They also are able to provide more convenience for end-users.*
>
> *[From Prepaid in Japan: A 'Clicks and Mortar' Approach | MasterCard]*

Setting aside retailers, which we'll come back to in a few future posts, I'm writing from Management World Americas 2011, which is a telecommunications industry event, and telecommunications operators are one obvious category of the organisations other than banks that have something to contribute to the payments world. There certainly does seem to be some correlation (which does not, of course, imply causality) between new payment schemes that are very successful (in Japan, Korea, Kenya, Philippines and so on) and schemes that are not led by banks, whether cards, phones or anything else. Maybe banks are just not very good at low-value, retail payments and have owned the turf only because of a series of historical accidents.

Non-bank payment specialists are cropping up all over the world, using technological advancements to steal a march on the banking industry. But are these companies a threat to the more traditional providers of payments, or do these largely niche businesses present partnership opportunities to banks?

[From Are non-bank specialists challengers or partners to banks? - Reports - The Banker]

If banks did move their payment businesses out into non-bank subsidiaries, and those businesses then moved with their own dynamics to consolidate or fragment, then we might reasonably expect to see a more competitive but also more innovation landscape as a result. In the Europe, we have the framework in place and, while some observers might complain that the pace is too slow, the fact is that a large number of non-banks have obtained licenses as Payment Institutions (PIs) or Electronic Money Institutions (ELMIs) and change is on the way.

In the United States, however, the current laws are designed prevent a Verizon or AT&T from doing what Rogers did in Canada. The Bank Holding Company Act, enacted in the 1950s, prohibits the mingling of banking and commerce and generally limits non-banking institutions from controlling banks.

[From Regulatory Uncertainty Casts Doubts On Legal Status of Mobile]

Not only will this prevent American carriers from acting Canadian, it will also stop them from acting Japanese (where DoCoMo took over Sumitomo Mitsui to offer a credit product) or even European (where some carriers have already obtained the PI licences mentioned above).

Chapter 5: Retail and Transport

Anyone can invent a new payment mechanism, it's easy (or at least it's easy if you know how!). Getting a new payment mechanism accepted, that's the hard part. For the average person throughout the whole world, retail and transport are the places where they spend their money, not on the web or in the cloud, and these are the points-of-sale where innovation needs traction.

Mobile Payments will be huge, whatever the public say - 16/02/2011

Last year, I read a Deutsche Bank Research note about mobile payments that was given to me in a meeting with one of our clients (E-Banking Snapshot 34, August 2010). It highlighted a Forrester Research finding that 74% of European consumers and 64% of US consumers are not interested purchasing goods or services via their mobile phones and said that this means there are substantial barriers to adoption of mobile payments. Well, there are certainly substantial barriers to the adoption of mobile payments, but in my experiences consumers are not one of them. Quite the reverse: in every project that I have been involved in, consumers have loved buying things using their mobile phones. The discrepancy comes, I think, because when you ask consumers about something in new in a field they don't care about (let's face it, consumers don't really spend that much time thinking about payments) they will react conservatively. Say to the average British consumer "would you like to use your mobile phone to pay for cups of coffee" and they can't envisage what you are talking about, especially if they don't live in London and use Oyster all the time or use 2D barcodes for travel tickets or whatever.

> *In a survey of 2,500 members of Springboard UK, the market research experts, on behalf of Vision Critical, half of respondents (51%) reported being fairly or very uncomfortable at the prospect of mobile payments.*
>
> *[From British 'uncomfortable' about making mobile payments - Marketing news - Marketing magazine]*

When consumers are given a mobile payment system that works and is convenient, adoption is rapid. Incidentally, in that survey only a fifth of consumers said they were interested in a prepaid wallet. I've heard this over and over again: one of the arguments against substituting cash (which most consumers don't see as a pre-paid product) with some form of "purse" product is that people don't want to pay up front for good or services that they might use in the future. Fair point. Oh, wait…

Starbucks Corp. customers loaded a record $700 million on to the Seattle coffee chain's prepaid card accounts during its most recent quarter, up 39% from a year earlier

[*From* Starbucks Prepaid Loads Jump 39% - American Banker Article]

Turns out that if you know stuff about marketing, consumer behaviour, distribution, management, convenience, payment choices, advertising, incentives and, above all, retailing then customers are only to happy to go with mobile prepaid. That's how come Starbucks went from a mobile payments experiment...

The ultimate goal of the program is to get customers to trade in their physical Starbucks Cards for the digital variety — it's a time saving exchange for the customer and a cost saving exchange for the company. Already, one in five of all in-store transactions are paid for via Starbucks Card (mobile or physical), and more than $1 billion will have been loaded on to cards by year's end.

[*From* Starbucks in New York Now Accepting Mobile]

...to a national roll-out in a quarter. Our good friend Brett King gave the Starbuck's national mobile payment scheme a try and said that

this is far superior to a current interaction using cash or a card for a number of reasons. This gives us a glimpse of what the cashless society will be like; it isn't risky, it isn't subject to fraud or theft, it is safe, secure and fast.

[*From* Brett King: Starbucks Mobile]

We all know that mobile will be the focus for the evolution of retail payments, and I think the message is getting out. Eric Schmidt's talk at Barcelona— saying that NFC will be profitable—attracted a great deal of attention, mainly from people who didn't listen to what he said when still CEO of Google.

Google wants the next generation of Android phones to replace credit cards, Eric E. Schmidt, Google's chief executive, said Monday at the Web 2.0 Summit in San Francisco. The newest version of Android, Google's mobile phone operating system, code-named Gingerbread, will come out in a few weeks, he said. It will include NFC...

[*From* Schmidt: Android]

There's still a long way to go in the mass market though, and it's fair enough to comment on it. Consumers, journalists, commentators don't yet understand how this new infrastructure is going to work. But I think that's about to change. Britain's biggest retailer is Tesco, so they are a benchmark for the acceptance of new technology, and they are going to go contactless this year.

> *Tony Saunders is the director of marketing for VeriFone in Europe, the Middle East and Africa... Saunders told us that within six months, Tesco will be rolling out near-field communications capabilities to its 35 - 38,000 checkouts across Britain*
>
> *[From The future of the high street: near-field communication (Wired UK)]*

This might be connected with a story that I touched on before in another context, illustrating the point about the ability of retailers to exploit the new contactless technologies in interesting ways.

> *Tesco will relaunch its Clubcard scheme as an online rewards programme as it gears up to reach customers in the digital age. Developing a 'secure, multichannel' smart card, the UK retailer will move the scheme to digital channels in an effort to simplify its rewards programme and cut down on direct-mail costs.*
>
> *[From Tesco will relaunch Clubcard scheme in 2011 : WCJB]*

Incidentally, I didn't quite understand the rest of the Wired story, so I dropped an e-mail full of NFC articles to the reporter who had said that:

> *The only obstacle could be similar, but proprietary, technologies set up by banks—which are known as "contactless" payment options. Barclays' contactless cards are a good example, as are Visa's PayWave cards, which are being trialled in Europe using an iPhone dongle.*
>
> *[From The future of the high street: near-field communication (Wired UK)]*

I shouldn't make fun. The technology might be old to us, but it's new to the mass market. And I should not that it isn't just UK journalists who get a bit confused.

> *For example, special payment stickers are available already that allow merchants to NFC-enable their point of sale terminals by*

simply affixing a sticker to the terminal, Litan said. Such stickers go for as little as $18

[From Analysts: Apple]

Wait, what? I think the journalist got the wrong end of the stick on this one! Let's be clear. The contactless payment schemes are NFC and the cards, phones, stickers, watches, hat, badges or anything else will all work with the NFC POS terminals. The key point here is that the retailers are rolling out NFC at POS not just because they want to accept NFC contactless cards, which many of them don't really care about, but because of NFC contactless phones, which promise an entirely new mobile shopping experience. The retailers want mobile wallets as soon as they are practical, because the value-adding opportunities around coupons, loyalty, location-based marketing and all sorts of other things besides payments are so great.

Parking is a great test case for cash replacement - 28/02/2011

I've often mentioned that car parking represents, to me, the prosaic benchmark for e-money. Car parks are a straightforward and daily example of an environment where cash is a pain and e-money would be a better alternative. This is why I made a big deal of the fact that contactless payments never made it to my local car park, where cards have now been supplanted entirely by mobile payments. This is not true everywhere. I think I've mentioned before that on-street car parking is an obvious place to start contactless acquiring: no keyboard, no slot, low-maintenance, simple. Westminster started doing this last year.

> *From January and over a three-month period, 20 pay and display machines in the West End will be retrofitted with wave-and-pay card readers, so motorists will be able to pay car parking charges by waving a credit or debit card at a meter. According to the local authority, the project is intended to eliminate the need to carry cash around or enter chip and pin details to pay to park.*

[From Westminster Council introduces contactless]

I'm going to try find out what customers think about this approach. Franky, I'm sure they would rather use their Oyster cards, and here's one reason why…

> *The machines also incorporate a security function that requires cardholders to confirm their identification with a chip and pin transaction on a regular basis.*

[From <u>Westminster Council introduces contactless</u>]

Hhmmm. This means having to having both a slot and a keypad, which raises costs significantly, and annoys customers when the contactless transaction fails and they are asked to insert the card and enter the PIN. I'll put in a call to see how this went when I'm back in the office sometime. Meanwhile, the alternative approach, of using mobiles, continues to gain ground, and it's not only in Woking that the mobile has trumped the card.

North Devon Council has replaced its Smart card facility with a more modern, pay over the phone system called 'RingGo'.

[From <u>North Devon Gazette - Council winds up pre-pay parking Smart cards scheme</u>]

It's not favouritism, although I have mentioned RingGo here before, but I can't help but notice that when I first went to see them (to interview them for a podcast) I thought that they were a company to watch. I'm actually one of their customers, because they operate the mobile parking at Woking station.

Councils, rail operators and other car park providers across the UK are ditching smartcard and scratchcard parking schemes in favour of streamlined, paperless RingGo.

[From <u>RingGo Proves the Power of Paperless Parking</u>]

I think I'll try and get some of these guys along to the Digital Money Forum 2012, as it will be useful to learn some of the experiences from the front line. Meanwhile, I can't help noticing that not everyone wants to remove cash from the car park. Take, for example, Wokingham council. It car park machines (according to The Daily Telegraph of 26th February 2011, p.4) took in £982,057 last year but only issued £945,417 of tickets. The discrepancy, as you might expect, comes from the machines that don't give change, a form of institutionalised extortion. Simply arithmetic reveals that hapless motorists are thus facing a 4% service charge for using cash. It's time to take action: councils should start making car parks cash-free as soon as possible and learn to cut their cloth. But if the car parks are cash free, and not everyone is using mobile payments, and the banks haven't issued contactless cards to everyone yet, then how to close the gap? Well, why not have local prepaid cards that function as "town cards" as well.

PXT Payments (PXT, formerly Parcxmart) an electronic payment solutions provider, today announced the launch of its new chip-based, secure smart debit cards, designed to create a safe, local currency that boosts consumer spending in municipalities nationwide. The town of Brookline, MA, will be the first town to adopt both Parcxmart and the smart debit card program.

[From PXT Launches Chip-Based Smart Debit Card for Cities, Towns, BIDs | Earth Times News]

I'm really interested in this kind of thing. It illustrates two points that I have been making for some time: first of all, it emphasises the role of transport in the evolution of new payment systems and secondly, it touches on the role of local parallel and alternative payment systems as a potential growth area. Fortunately both transport payments and alternative payments have their own expert panel discussions set aside at the 2011 Digital Money Forum so we'll be able to explore both topics in detail. (Coincidence? You be the judge!)

The reality of the Japanese retail payments sector - 04/03/2011

At the 14th annual Digital Money Forum this week, Michael Salmony from Equens gave a talk about the reality of retail payments in Japan. Or, as he called it, his holiday snaps! He showed some excellent photos and a video to help us to understand what is really going on. We all know that electronic money of one form and another is huge in Japan, so that's a good starting point for trying to figure out where they are and what it means for other markets.

Most of the population uses eMoney on a daily basis with mobile FeliCa RFID wallet phones to purchase train/bus fare, a beverage at a vending machine, a meal at a local restaurant or a snack at a convenience store. Many local business and convenience stores have their own chargeable eMoney cards as well as loyalty cards.

[From What the U.S. Can Learn from Japan's eCommerce Ecosystems - pymnts.com]

As Michael noted, contactless e-money (ie, prepaid) cards are widely used. There are vending machines everywhere and contactless payments are used for them, in convenience stores, for buying tickets and in many other ways. No wonder that the basic numbers are bullish.

During the first half of 2010, the number of electronic money transactions swelled by 39%

[From E-money - Big, and Getting Bigger in Japan - Japan Real Time - WSJ]

Note, though, that most electronic money transactions are still made with these cards. I tried to find the most up-to-date statistics that I could to match them to what Michael was saying and they do confirm his impressions.

> *In December 2010, 9.8 million mobile users in Japan made a purchase using their mobile as the payment vehicle. That works out to about 10 percent of all mobile subscribers, according to comScore.*

> *[From <u>10% of Japanese Use Mobile</u>]*

As far as I can tell, this means that the use of mobile proximity for payments (although not for loyalty, coupons and so on) has fallen over the last year. I wondered why it was not growing quicker, let alone growing at all. Michael showed a video that might explain why: in order to pay using mobile proximity, the user had to press several buttons and wait for software to load. It didn't seem terribly convenient and, I have to say, it seemed a much worse user experience than the European and US mobile proximity payment systems that we are working on at the moment. This explained to me why the use of cards continued to dominate, but... there has also been a decrease in the number of people using the e-money cards as well. Why is this?

Well, if you delve around in the relevant sources of statistics (at least, the ones in English that I subscribe to RSS feeds for) you find an interesting and plausible explanation which I think has significant implications for the development of e-money services in Europe and in the US, especially given the pressure on debit interchange.

> *My IC card cash gets used on public transport and convenience stores only. All the other shops that accept it also accept the credit card portion, and most of them also award 3% points instead of just 1%, so it's an easy choice. Furthermore, they more often than not don't even ask for a PIN when using credit, so the extra effort required is minimal.*

> *[From <u>Japanese electronic cash card users continue to decrease</u> | 世論 <u>What Japan Thinks</u>]*

Contactless credit cards that give 3% rewards appearing to be winning out over other e-payment mechanisms, particularly contactless prepaid cards, whether they are in a phone or not. It seems as if the march of e-money continues, but the mix is changing (probably, in my opinion, temporarily), and cash is the main victim. We can deduce this because the fall in the use of mobile proximity and card e-money does not seem to have been matched by an increase in the use of small denomination banknotes or coins. In fact the coins in circulation fell again last year.

Michael noted that the use of NFC in phones for non-payment purposes—coupons, loyalty etc—was actually far more prevalent, and I think this probably is one of the key lessons to learn. Customers aren't going to buy NFC phones because they can make payments with them: they will buy NFC phones to do more interesting things than payments but we (ie, the payments industry) must be in position to take advantage of the platform.

> *NTT Docomo has begun the world's first mass market deployment of mobile phones with NFC tag reading capabilities. Sixteen of the operator's new range of mobile phones and a number of existing handsets will be able to perform both Osaifu-Keitai mobile contactless payments functions and NFC tag reading from next week.*
>
> *[From NTT Docomo adds NFC tag reading to wide range of mobile phones | Alan Cheslow's Consumer Electronics Industry News]*

Who knows what kind of services will be successful in Europe or the US. Coupons, like McDonalds club in Japan? Something else? That is the fun area for exploration for our clients right now: what's going to go in the mobile wallet alongside the payment applications and how will it change for national and regional markets.

Why don't all retailers install an ATM and ban cards? - 27/04/2011

In a comment on an article about mobile payments that I was reading, I noticed that someone wrote:

> *I hate it when a retailer tells me they don't accept cards. I feel like I have to remind them what year they're living in. They usually prompt me to use an ATM within their store and accept a 2 dollar or more fees just to get the cash to pay for a candy bar. This results in me leaving the store and finding a 7-11 or some such thing.*
>
> *[From Paying by phone is insecure and unnecessary. - By Farhad Manjoo - Slate Magazine]*

It seems to me that this is the market at work, and I don't see a problem with that. If some retailers and some customers want to carry on using cash, then fine, let them, but don't make me pay for it. So long as they are paying the full cost and I'm not subsidising them, so what? (Actually, there is a so what which is to do with the impact on society, but that's not my point here.) On the other hand, if all stores did this then they could all earn commission from the ATM operators and save the money on merchant fees to banks, couldn't they. But then I began to wonder why the store would need an ATM at all. Wouldn't costs be reduced for everyone if the customer could use their ATM card to withdraw money from the retailer's cash draw? This is the sort of thing that is going on in India.

> As a part of the ambitious Unique Identity (UID) card project, a micro-ATM will be a payment platform that would make use of mobile technology and the customers' UID will serve the 'know your customer' (KYC) norms required by the bank to open an account.

> [From <u>Banks take to the shrinking cash machine - dnaindia.com</u>]

The micro-ATM is a POS terminal-with-knobs-on so that customers can make "ATM" withdrawals at agents but also open accounts and carry out other basic functions. Presumably these don't cost the merchants much more (if any more) than regular POS terminals and they must cost less than an ATM, so everyone's better offer, except for ATM manufacturers.

Perhaps we should stop looking at these band-aids to slap over cash's inefficiency though. It's time to get tough. According to recent research by McKinsey and Wincor-Nixdorf (who make, amongst other things, ATMs), cash "in circulation" from the US to Europe through to Asia Pacific is increasing year-on-year,which has resulted in the global cost of handling cash increasing to more than US$300 billion, and retailers bear the brunt of those cash handling costs compared to banks, cash-in-transit operators,cash centers and central banks. As much as 61% is attributed to the cost of handling, transporting and securing cash in the checkout zone and back office of a retail store compared with 32% for a retail bank. Incidentally, I thought I remembered seeing that $300 billion figure a few months ago, and it turns out I did.

> Eckard Heidloff, president and CEO of Wincor Nixdorf and Dr. Karsten Ottenburg, chairman of the management board and CEO of Giesecke & Devrient, noted that $300 billion is spent annually on cash processing worldwide. And since the euro's introduction, the number of banknotes in circulation in euro-member countries has increased 8 percent yearly.

> [From <u>Wincor Nixdorf and Giesecke & Devrient form a partnership | ATM</u>]

Banknotes "in circulation" going up 8%, while retail sales went up, what, 1% last year? What on Earth are people are these banknotes for? Earlier in the recession, the Bank of England put forward a theory:

> As a share of nominal GDP, the value of notes in circulation declined from 6% in 1970 to a low point of 2.4% in the mid-1990s but has since stabilised and then increased, noticeably over the past two years... Rising demand for notes might reflect some loss of confidence in banks and very low interest rates, which reduce the opportunity cost of holding banknotes as a non-interest bearing asset. Andrew Bailey says that is "...pretty good prima facie evidence that there has been an increase in demand for banknotes as a store of value".

> [From Bank of England]

Yes, but a store of value for who? Certainly not for a normal, law-abiding taxpayer like me. Does anyone you know keep cash at home now instead of leaving it in the bank? This isn't a purely European phenomenon, since the amount of cash has been going up in the USA as well.

> The quantity of US currency in circulation in the world was $2776 per US resident in April 2009. That's a lot of currency - the stock held at any point in time is about 6% of US annual GDP. In case you think that's all held overseas, a study by the Bank of Canada (in the Bank of Canada Review - look it up) shows that Canadian currency outstanding is about 3% of annual Canadian GDP, and most of that has to be in Canada.

> [From Stephen Williamson: New Monetarist Economics: The Use of Currency]

These figures seem about right: the US has far more currency out there per person, because more than half of all US currency isn't in circulation in the US and will never be repatriated, so in the UK, Canada and the US we see approximately the same figure, that M0 is 3% of M4.

Square's innovation path – 25/05/2011

Some people don't really understand the big picture around innovation, and how it takes inventions and turns them into sustainable new value-adding processes. Here's one example.

> Last Friday, Congressman Jesse Jackson Jr. (D-IL) took to the floor of the House of Representatives to decry the iPad as a job

killer, as people are using the device to read books rather than buy them from bookstores.

[From Lesson to Congress: iPad]

But wait a minute: surely books were destroying jobs in the scribe industry. Jesse's job creation scheme ought to be banning books, not praising them. Anyway, many popular books are written by non-Americans—why should American's hard earned dollars flow to J. K. Rowling's UK bank account? Hold on though—scribes were destroying jobs in the storytelling industry. Jesse needs to attack the problem at source: we need to stop people from reading and writing. Unless we're going to do that, we should instead welcome and encourage innovation because we need an economy that adds more value. I'm not smart enough to know what that means for individual companies, although I am lucky enough to have a job that means I can experience many different organisations approaches and learn from them.

In 1994, the dominant global provider of mobile handsets was Motorola: its shares were trading at an all-time high and it was seen as an outstanding innovator and even described by a senior consultant at A. T. Kearney as "the best-managed company in the world"

[From Why Nokia]

That's the thing about technology-based innovation: it doesn't follow the smooth distribution of best practice that is the realm of management consultants. It didn't matter if you were the best urine trampler in the land, when a German chemist synthesised urea you were on the scrapheap. It doesn't matter how good your printing company is when e-book sales exceed printed book sales.

Motorola missed most of these market trends, was slow to invest in digital (it was a classic victim of the innovator's dilemma),

[From Why Nokia]

This "innovator's dilemma" analysis, which says that it's just too hard for companies to invest in their own disruptors, suggests that it may be difficult for the incumbents in the payments world to innovate in the right direction. The case study that everyone is focused on right now is mobile.

Bill Gajda, Visa's head of mobile innovation, is confident that Visa and the other card networks, in conjunction with banks, will be at the center of mobile payments in the future.

[From Leading Mobile]

I understand where Bill is coming from, but have to admit that I can see other scenarios as well, where Visa interconnects non-bank, sector-specific, mobile-centric payment accounts rather than only bank accounts. It must be said though that Visa have made a number of substantial investments in the mobile payments space and have been actively developing products and services. Not all observers think that this strategy is optimal.

> *Visa for you to execute in this space, spin out Bill Gajda and team to build a new network. You certainly have the capital and intellectual horsepower to do it.. Don't think of mobile as a service on VisaN*

[From FinVentures]

In the medium term, the existing players (by which I mean banks, the international schemes and processors) will find it more and more difficult to compete with IP-based alternatives because their cost base is just too high. Therefore, it might make sense for a company like Visa to start building one of these, but use their experience to build a better one. Alternatively, they could look for someone else who is building one, and then invest in it. This is what they have done recently with Square (Visa invested an unspecified amount in Square in April 2011). Square is much in the news at the moment, but what is actually interesting about it? As I wrote before, it is not the stripe reader, it's the niche...

> *So where is Square seeing the most traction? Without a doubt, small businesses, independent workers and merchants comprise most of Square's rapidly growing user base.*

[From Square]

In a way, this real-world PSP is a small but interesting niche play in a large acquiring market, and as we've advised our clients for many years that the mobile-phone-as-POS meme will be more revolutionary than the mobile-phone-as-card meme, it's an existence proof of new opportunity.

> *While merchants have to qualify for the app, Square's qualification rules are more relaxed than those of standard credit card processors.*

[From Square]

Never in a million years would I consider signing up as a merchant with my bank. Yet I went into an Apple Store in the US last time I was there and bought a Square (actually, we bought eight of them to play with). It took a couple of minutes to sign up on the web and I accepted my first payment (in Stuart Fiske's iPad) a minute later!

Pretty cool, although naturally I was outraged when I got off the plane in the UK and discovered that my lovely Square only works in the US. Anyway, Square were making me think about innovation again yesterday. They just announced their wallet product, Card Case. Once you've paid with your card at a retailer once, Square's server stores the card details, so from then on the merchant has only to identify you. They can even do this without you having a card or phone, because they can look up your picture (although I have good reasons for thinking that this won't scale).

> *The obvious idea is to make payments "frictionless"—easier and faster for the user and merchant. (Assuming that the app is fast enough that it is actually more convenient to pay this way than just to have your card swiped. Wireless data networks aren't always reliable, etc.)*

[From Jack Dorsey's Square]

Indeed, they're not. But imagine what this will look like with NFC in place: you have an iPhone, the merchant has an iPad, you place your iPhone on the iPad, they beep, done. And it's a card present transaction. Now, we all know that Square Card Case isn't the only wallet game in town, because anyone with any sense is already developing a wallet proposition since that's what the merchants want. Right now we are helping clients in the financial sector and the telecommunications sector with ideas in this space. Visa, being smart, are of course already in the game.

> *Fourteen US and Canadian banks have signed up for the launch later this year of a multi-platform digital wallet that can be used for e-commerce, m-commerce and mobile contactless transactions and includes mobile payment, NFC and coupon capabilities.*

[From Visa]

But now continue the Square-related thought experiment. Suppose that Square are successful at signing up lots of people, so that people don't want an AT&T wallet or a Citi wallet or a Visa wallet? If all of the transactions are now between the secure element in a mobile phone, via Card Case, to the secure element in another phone, via the Square app, then aren't Square at some point going to get rid of intermediaries and just move the money from one bank account to another, in a retailer-centric decoupled debit proposition (which won't be called debit, because of

Durbin) that is proactively marketed by the retailers? That really would be disruptive.

> *Just as the iTunes store completely upended the sale and distribution of digital media, Square just might upend the entire real-world payments industry—whether it meant to or not.*

[From *How Jack Dorsey's Square*]

So, in response to the e-mails I've had over the last couple of days, let me say that the Square trajectory confirms the strategic advice that we gave our clients some years ago (which is great!) and that is it not a "rival" to NFC but an exploiter of it. Square might be a niche in the payments business, but it shows a really interesting innovation path that sees payment cards going the way of books, and probably without Jesse Jackson Jr. to plead their case. That doesn't mean that Square will succeed, but if they don't, then someone else following that same path will.

Different dreams about The future of POS – 03/06/2011

At the end of March, we learned that there is no business case for moving to NFC at POS in the USA.

> *Representatives of three of the country's largest banks, Bank of America, Citigroup and U.S. Bank, attended a meeting last month organized by the Merchant Advisory Group... to talk about the new opportunities that mobile technologies, such as NFC, will create for the payments industry.*
>
> *"You know what they (banks) told us? There's just not a business case right now," Dodd Roberts, head of the merchant group, said last week*

[From *Big U.S. Banks Look for A Business Case for NFC | NFC Times – Near Field Communication and all contactless*]

That's a shame, because it's a fun technology that consumers like. Never mind. Of course, not everyone thinks that banks can't make a go of it, and going back a couple of years we can find some positive projections.

> *Celent estimates that a 30% cash displacement ratio, or an incremental US$151 per card account, per year is reasonable, with an average revenue increase of US$1.83 per debit card account per year.*

[From *The View from the Mobile*]

Anyway, a month after the US banks told the Merchant Advisory Group that there was no business case, we learned that…

> *France-based POS device manufacturer Ingenico has confirmed that it is working with Google on the development of NFC-based services for retailers*

> *[From Confirmed: Google]*

Was this an "Inception"-style paradox? A fault line between two sets of dreams that don't quite connect? A glitch in the matrix that could be eliminated if we all take the bank's blue pill? Because now someone is offering red pills…

> *The first NFC service launched by Google for its Nexus S phone is an enhancement to its Google Places service. Customers tap the phone against NFC tags embedded in stickers or decals that merchants affix to their storefronts to access information about the local business, including phone numbers, hours of operation, payment types, reviews and recommendations.*

> *[From Checking in with NFC–Some Social-Networking Start-ups to Use NFC | NFC Times – Near Field Communication and all contactless]*

Aha! So now we can see how to resolve the paradox. There's no business case if you only think about transaction revenues (the bank model) but there is a business case if you "ignore" payments and focus on value-added services that retailers will pay for (the Google model). This has got the mobile operators interested enough to start upping the orders.

> *Such Android handset makers as Samsung, HTC and likely LG and Motorola are preparing for NFC, based on keen interest or orders from mobile operators, including South Korean telcos, SK Telecom and KT; China Mobile; as well as American and European carriers, NFC Times has learned.*

> *[From 'Open' Battles Break Out Among NFC Vendors Over Android]*

A characteristically well-informed comment from Steve Mott delves further into resolving the paradox. Perhaps payments are losing their strategic appeal for banks because they are becoming commoditised, utility businesses that just won't generate the cash that they did in the past.

> *Consultant Steve Mott, CEO of BetterBuyDesign, who also attended the Merchant Advisory Group meeting, told me the U.S.*

banks do see the advantages of mobile to increase transactions. But mobile confronts them with an unfamiliar payments landscape at the same time they are being squeezed by regulators with the Durbin amendment.

[From Big U.S. Banks Look for A Business Case for NFC | NFC Times – Near Field Communication and all contactless]

Banks aren't stupid. They know that NFC is coming, that consumers and merchants like it, and that it means disruption. But it is very difficult to change core businesses, especially at a time of great regulatory uncertainty. In the meantime, the non-payment use of NFC will lead it into the mass market. But will the new technology pull in the customers? Sam Shrauger, VP Global Product and Experience at PayPal, puts it succinctly:

People couldn't care less which technology a hardware or software manufacturer would like to sell them. They couldn't care less which technology merchants may or may not put in their stores. Ultimately, they just want something that makes their life better when it comes to buying and paying.

[From Why the Mobile]

Now, as it happens, I was chatting with Sam last month and I agree with him about many things, but I think that in this particular case he may be underestimating the impact of "tap and go" technology. The point is that tapping is so much simpler, so much quicker, so much more convenient for consumers that it **will** make a difference to them. People will start looking for the phones that you can tap together to become Facebook friends, or whatever, because that experience blows away bumping, or texting or QR codes or whatever.

This, I think, means risky time for bank payments. Once people are using their non-bank wallets on mobile phones to execute retail transactions, initially using bank-provided payment schemes, it will be a small step to get them to move to non-bank payment schemes inside those wallets. Banks need more active responses to the changing environment and I hope I won't be offending anyone to say that I know from personal experience with recent projects that banks are losing opportunities right now because they are not able to deliver products in the timescales demanded by other industries.

Debit should be the "norm" in Europe - 28/06/2011

At the Intellect / Payments Council conference on Driving Change in Payments, sponsored by Consult Hyperion, one of the delegates (I think it was one of the chaps from Accenture), raised the topic of surcharging, asking whether the surcharging of non-cash payments might slow the spread of e-payments in general and low-value contactless cash replacement payments in particular. He also mentioned the example of surcharging by low-cost airlines.

> *Perhaps the most obvious example of tender steering in Europe is in eCommerce - where Ryanair (and other low-cost carriers) surcharges considerably for all but a single method of payment (currently MasterCard Prepaid cards)*
>
> *[From Will Retailers Use "Tender Steering" to Control Interchange Fees? |... | LinkedIn]*

While the point about surcharging in relation to the spread of new payment mechanisms is interesting, what's going on with the airlines isn't really surcharging (Ryan Air said specifically that "these are not surcharges", and they are correct). What these charges are are a transaction tax that everyone has to pay (I'd be curious to find out how many people actually pay with Ryan Air MasterCard prepaid cards). Unsurprisingly, a great many people were unhappy about this practice (ie, advertising an air fare as £10 then charging £18 because the customer pays with a credit/debit card) as it smacks of unfairness.

> *A super-complaint is to be launched about the "murky practice" of surcharges levied on customers who pay by debit or credit card.*
>
> *[From BBC News - Credit and debit card surcharges 'are excessive']*

Bear in mind that if you are booking tickets for a family, these transaction fees can easily become significant: if they were folded into the price of the ticket, it would give a more accurate guide to the public.

> *I recently used Ryanair and cost me £30 in booking fees and another £48 in online checkin fees to use my printer and my paper and my Ink. Can anybody explain how that works ?*
>
> *[From Which Launches Super-Complaint Into Credit And Debit Card Surcharges With Office Of Fair Trading | Business | Sky News]*

> *Well, the solution to that seems pretty straightforward: don't book Ryanair. It's not just them, by the way. I understand that EasyJet charges £8 (EIGHT QUID) for a debit card transaction that costs it, what, 15p? Personally, I won't use any of the "low*

cost" carriers, so I don't know what the exact figures are. Anyway, today the OFT ruled on the super-complaint (and I can't wait to Ryan Air's response because they will undoubtedly go bonkers):

Travel companies have been ordered to end the use of hidden surcharges for passengers paying by card. Airline, ferry and rail passengers typically have to click through four to six pages of an online booking before the charge is added to the price. Now the Office of Fair Trading (OFT) has ordered them to make all debit or credit card charges clear immediately.

[From BBC News - Hidden card charges for travel tickets to be banned]

But that, to me, isn't the interesting part of the ruling. This is:

It also wants the law changed to abolish altogether charges for using debit cards.

[From BBC News - Hidden card charges for travel tickets to be banned]

Much as I dislike government intervention in the pricing of anything, unless the costs of cash are to be distributed properly (which they won't be) this is the only sensible course of action. Making debit cards the "zero" and allowing retailers to surcharge other payment mechanisms (including cash) is fair, with one proviso: that pre-paid cards are counted as debit cards. This is necessary to deliver financial inclusion.

Perhaps the European Commission could be persuaded to adopt this as part of its SEPA initiative and make it common throughout Europe so that pre-paid and debit cards become the "normal" way to pay?

Events are conducive to contactless - 04/07/2011

Off to the Barclaycard Wireless Festival for the day. I don't really understand why it's still called that. In the old days, when it was sponsored by O2, then calling it the wireless festival sort of made sense. But now it's sponsored by Barclaycard, they should probably call it the Contactless Festival instead. Anyhow it featured a great many very popular bands, as evidenced by the enormous crowd trying to get in.

Barclaycard had kitted all of the bars out with contactless terminals and were kind enough to give me one of the promotional lanyards containing a contactless card (a Visa gift card preloaded with £20) to go and try out. Which, naturally, I did. And, I have to say, it worked perfectly. As testimony, allow me to present the first beer I bought with it! Being me, I couldn't leave it at that though, and I started to try out some other contactless paraphernalia about my person. An obvious experiment was to try my Barclaycard phone, and that worked too, but oddly it went online, which rather slowed the transaction down. I don't understand why it did this, so I'll ask the chaps when I'm next in the office.

More interestingly, I asked a couple of the bar staff what they thought about contactless and they had both positive and negative observations that I promised myself to report in a spirit of openness and balance…

Positive. It's quick, and you don't have to hand the terminal to the customer for them to enter a PIN. And they thought my phone was really cool. They also said that some customers had been paying with their own contactless cards and not just the promotional lanyards.

Negative. There were two big issues that came up in both conversations with bar staff. One was the spending limit, which the bar staff said was too low at £12 (the limit was actually £15, but the all of the drinks cost £4, so you could buy three drinks at £12 but not the advertised four beers in a drinks carrier, because that costs £16). Surely it would have made sense to have subbed the bars so that four beers plus carrier was a £15 special.

Enough of these scientific experiments (most of which I drank), and off to see some of the popular beat combos on show.

I was reflecting on the security issue later on, because it really seemed a block. I took the time to explain to one of the women at the bar that there was no risk to her as a customer, because the UK banks' were unequivocal about unauthorised use: if someone uses your card without your permission, they will refund the transaction. Yet she was unconvinced and was clearly uncomfortable about the idea of "no CVM" purchase. This has been true since the earliest days. As I highlighted four years ago:

> Among those that are not yet ready to use contactless, security appear to be the dominant consideration. Which means, of course, that whatever we might think about actual security situation we must get better at communicating it.

[From Digital Money: Contactless update]

As I don't know anything about customer communications and public information, I genuinely don't know how to cross this chasm, but I wonder if it's yet more evidence that we should be moving more quickly to contactless phones. The simple PIN code that I need to open up the mobile wallet on my Barclaycard MasterCard phone (the Samsung Tocco that I wrote about before) might well provide the reassurance that people want, even though it doesn't really make much difference to the overall risk (phones are inherently safer than cards because people notice when they go missing anyway).

Overall, the weekend's experiences did leave me with three firm conclusions:

1. Both the public and the merchants liked contactless. In this kind of environment - crowded, quick service - the technology performs very well. These were similar to the results seen elsewhere: the punters like contactless payments.

> *Festival-goers quizzed on the experience, said they were quicker (96%) and easier to use (98%) than credit or debit cards, while a resounding 100% said they'd want to use the PayPass prepaid wristbands again to pay at other festivals, concerts and sporting events.*

> *[From Finextra: Contactless wristbands join wellies and camping gear as festival essentials]*

2. We should accelerate the development of contactless phones, because they help with the security issue.

3. The Horrors are a good band, but not my cup of tea.

Best pay - 19/07/2011

I popped in to Best Buy in Chicago to get a couple of things and when I went to pay I noticed that there was a contactless reader. I tried to pay with with PayPass sticker on my iPhone and the transaction was (correctly) declined because I didn't have the balance (it's a prepaid MasterCard). So I tried my UK Visa contactless credit card and the terminal didn't recognise it. Nor did it recognise my UK contactless Visa debit card nor my colleagues UK contactless MasterCard credit card. The terminals have been configured to only read the non-EMV US "magnetic stripe with dynamic signature verification" (MSD) contactless cards and not EMV cards. No wonder stickers are the future.

> *Bank of America Corp. is building on its mobile payments strategy with plans to issue contactless stickers to its credit and debit card customers next year.*

> *[From mobile-payment-stickers-bofa - PaymentsSource Article]*

If anyone has one of these, I'd be interested to know what they think about them. Similarly, I'd be genuinely interested in customer feedback on these.

> *Discover card today announced that it has begun issuing Discover® Zip®contactless credit cards and stickers, targeted at early adopters of its mobile technology.*

> *[From Discover Financial Services - Investor Relations - Press Release]*

I know I annoy people by continuing the meme - that started as a joke borne out of frustration - that stickers are the future but... anyway, stickers to one side and back to Best Buy. I used my trusty John Lewis MasterCard to pay. The clerk asked me for ID, so I showed her a UK driving licence that shouldn't possibly verify, and then signed the transaction "Carlos Tevez"*. The transaction was completed successfully, thus illustrating the point that Jamie Henry (Senior Director, Payment Services at Walmart) made very well during his presentation to the Smart Card Alliance this year. He said that signature was a waste of time and a waste of paper. (While noting that their chargeback rate for signature debit cards is two hundred and fifty times greater than for PIN debit, he called for an early shift to EMV in the USA.) With the first EMV cards now issued (listen to Merrill Halpern, who issued the first EMV card in the US in this week's podcast) perhaps things are indeed going to change. This reminded me (again) of Deborah Baxley's neat summary of the immediate future for cards in the USA:

> *Banks scrambling to replace lost fee revenue will likely shift focus to credit and prepaid, impose DDA and other fees, along with new account services and comprehensive pricing packages.*

> *Consumers: Australia's example illustrates the consequences of interchange fees capping, in which consumer benefits failed to materialize.*

> *Merchants benefit from lower acceptance costs for debit cards. In a surprising twist, incentives and steering could have the perverse result of driving consumers toward cash and checks.*

> *[From Changing the Game in Cards - pymnts.com]*

I think this is a realistic projection, especially given that merchants don't care about the costs they impose on the rest of society by driving up the use of cash. Let's put the consumer position to one side. Can banks use EMV, NFC, SMS or some other TLA (three letter acronym) to recover some of this money? Cards dominate the non-cash retail POS (more specifically, debit cards dominate the non-cash retail POS) so we should focus on the particular case of EMV. Some people think that this might be the year for EMV to finally get off the ground in the US.

> *Don Rhodes, senior director of risk management policy for the American Bankers Association, says a number of emerging technologies, such as the EMV chip standard, mobile payments and peer-to-peer or person-to-person payments, will soon change the way U.S. financial institutions and merchants connect and transact. And it could all happen in 2011, much sooner than most industry experts expect.*

I'm sure Don is right about mobile and peer-to-peer, but what about EMV? One the one hand, of course, I really hope that EMV gets going in the US: Consult Hyperion have world-leading expertise in EMV strategies for financial institutions and many, many years experience providing independent advice on EMV deployment. There are guys in my office who know as much, if not more, about EMV than anyone else in the world, so a US rollout would be good news for us. But what, I hear you all say, is the business case? There isn't (yet) enough fraud to tip the scales.

> *"If we can envision a world where magstripe doesn't exist, Chip-and-PIN would virtually eliminate all counterfeit, lost and stolen fraud as well as almost 99 percent of PCI costs," said Mike Cook, Wal-Mart's VP and assistant treasurer. "So you no longer have to have your database encrypted. You no longer need to have the secure lines. You're no longer storing data that could be used by somebody else. The PCI costs become significant cost savings."*
>
> *[From StorefrontBacktalk » Blog Archive » Target, Wal-Mart On EMV]*

That's a very interesting new perspective, one that other retailers have echoed, it given the enormous cost of PCI-DSS, could well be enough to tip the scales where fraud can't.

> *Visa recently recognized the importance of chip-and-pin along with PCI DSS compliance when it announced its Technology Innovation Program (TIP). With TIP, merchants will no longer have to go through costly annual PCI DSS validation if 75 percent of their Visa transactions are completed at chip-and-pin-enabled terminals—but TIP is not available to merchants in the United States*
>
> *[From Portals and Rails]*

Interesting. All these years we've been thinking that the EMV migration business case depends on fraud, and now it turns out that it might instead depend on fraud prevention, the cost of which is becoming punitive. PCI-DSS has undoubtedly had a positive impact reducing card fraud, but the cost to merchants is enormous. But there's another factor serving to reinforce the pressure for change. Retailers have terminal replacement cycles, and they may well be wanting to replace terminals for other reasons, at which time the marginal cost of adding the smart card reader is very low.

> *Target's Marc Black, the chain's guest data security director, was asked what it would take before Target would start purchasing EMV-friendly POS units. "Part of that investment decision will be how terminal manufacturers incorporate smartcard readers in their products. We need a firm roadmap, so we can guide our investment. This is not the only new payment technology out there," he said, referring to near field communication (NFC), among others.*

> *[From StorefrontBacktalk » Blog Archive » Target, Wal-Mart On EMV]*

Together, these two issues (PCI-DSS compliance and NFC capabilities) might be actually replace fraud in the business case calculation. But are the US retailers ready? When I'd finished paying in Best Buy, I realised that the POS terminal had a smart card reader, so just out of curiosity I asked the clerk what it was for. She told me that is was ready for the new credit and debit cards that were going to have chips on them but there was no software for it yet. Props to Best Buy human resources.

* I always sign stripe transactions with a bogus name. My rationale is that a thief would sign the transaction using the name on the card, because they wouldn't know which Premier League footballer's name that I am using for the month. Thus, if I dispute a transaction and the retailer produces a receipt with my name on it, then I know it's false.

Comments

> Thanks, Dave - I have pointed out many times that the cost of PCI greatly exceeds the cost of EMV; some of these costs represent good practice but the expensive bits are the bits that would be unnecessary with EMV. If the card numbers and expiry dates that PCI is protecting are really secrets, then banks are criminally negligent in printing them on cards, statements etc. The retail arms of banks long ago decided that account numbers are public information but authentication data must be fiercely protected – this is the correct answer.

Tomorrow's Transactions—The 2012 Reader

Posted by: Mike Hendry on 19/07/2011 at 15:14.

Sign Language - 26/07/2011

At dinner, a colleague mentioned his payment experiences on a recent trip to Greece. Apparently no merchants would accept cards, not even gas stations. My colleague asked if this was because of high fees charged by banks for card payments. Well, I guess it might be, but to be honest I imagine it's got more to do with tax evasion on a massive scale. Greece is an extreme example, admittedly, but one of the advantages of using cash is precisely to evade taxes. Fortunately, in developed nations with stable economies, you don't get that kind of thing and e-payments work everywhere at point-of-service with no problems.

No, wait… I'm in New York right now, and my payment experiences on this trip have been mixed. The good, the bad, and the ugly.

The **good**. I went into Duane Reade and bought a hat. You've no idea how hot is here (actually, it was like 104) and I was going to get sunstroke without protection. They had contactless readers. I tapped by iPhone (equipped with splendid MasterCard prepaid sticker) and it worked perfectly. So perfectly, in fact, that Dominique (the sales clerk) told me that it was "mad cute" and asked if all new iPhones could do it. I told her that they could not, but that one day, all iPhones would be able to do this.

The **bad**. When I tried to use my UK contactless debit card it didn't work so the terminal here are still not configured to read EMV contactless cards (or, for that matter, phones). Couldn't they get started on killing two birds with one stone here! Earlier this year, Scott Loftness said, perceptively as ever, that there's a block on EV deployment.

> Yet, US issuers and the major card networks can't really make decisions to invest in EMV because the business case still doesn't make sense.

[From The Case for EMV*]*

Correct. But perhaps there is another route. Perhaps the transition to EMV can be disguised inside the transition to contactless? If US retailers aren't going to install chip card readers for contact EMV, they might at least configure their contactless readers to accept EMV via the wireless interface.

The **ugly**. I went to a deli with three other people to get some authentic NY dinner. I had gefilte fish, latkes with applesauce and a pastrami sandwich with pickles, served by an authentic Asian gentleman. When I went to pay, I was told "we don't take cards, cash only" and was directed to an ATM at the back of the restaurant. The check was almost exactly $100, so I drew $100 from the ATM, for which I was charged a $2.75 fee. How does this benefit anyone? Had I paid with a card, I would still have paid the $2.75 without having the hassle of messing about with the ATM.

I had the same annoying experience the next day: I went to grab coffee and a snack at lunch time near Madison Park. I didn't have any cash, and the deli wouldn't take cards. There was nothing on the door to warn me about this. They, once again, directed me to an ATM at the back of the store. It I wasn't so dammed English and polite and afraid of embarrassment I would have just put the coffee and snack down and walked out. I'm beginning to suspect that either the US is going backwards when it comes to payments or the rent the store owners get from the ATMs is pretty substantial.

Here is my plea: retailers, please feel free to not accept cards for whatever reason. I don't care if you are sticking it to the man, avoiding taxes, a triad front, engaging in money laundering or paying off the cops, you should be forced by law to put a sign at least six inches by six inches on the door at eye level so that customers can decide not to patronise. Just like you have Visa decals, and MC decals, and Amex decals etc, so there should be a "cash only" decal, perhaps showing someone hiding a pile of notes under a mattress. Perhaps I will make this the art competition for next year's Digital Money Forum!

Comments

> I'm not sure I agree that retailers should be required to tell you up front what payment types they don't accept. I often use American Express and quite a few merchants don't accept it (because they charge significantly higher rates than others). I often ask first before attempting to purchase something whether they accept it. Merchants can't be expected to accept all forms of payment.
>
> *Posted by: Jason on 27/07/2011 at 03:47.*

You've got to pick a pocket or two, boys - 21/09/2011

I don't understand why the London Assembly Transport Committee were questioning Forum friend Will Judge from Transport for London (TfL) about the security of contactless payment cards (watch the webcast), since the security of those cards is the concern of the banks that issue them, not the merchants who use them, whether Tesco or TfL. But whatever.

Giving evidence to the London assembly transport committee about TfL's plans to introduce contactless payment to London's transport network, he answered yes when asked by a member of the committee whether the system was "100% safe" against "invisible pick pocketing".

[From Transport for London says new contactless]

Will is, naturally, correct. If I am able to sneak a bogus reader onto the Underground and surreptitiously hold it against people's pockets to read the card data inside, it's not much of a crime. I have to put the reader up against your wallet. If I want to read your card from the other side of the carriage, I need an antenna the size of a wagon wheel pumping out so much power that the coins in commuters pockets would be sparking.

But even if I can access the card in your pocket, I can't use the data to make counterfeit cards and I can only put spurious transactions through to a merchant account at a bank: I can't "pickpocket" anything, in the sense that I can steal anything of any value. But it seems to me that electronic pickpocketing "meme" is unstoppable.

An ongoing effort by credit card companies to issue 1 billion radio frequency identification chip-enabled contactless cards by 2016 will dramatically increase the public's susceptibility to identity and financial theft from electronic pickpocketing, Identity Stronghold announced today.

[From 'Electronic Pickpocketing' Threat Worsened by Credit Card Industry Plan to Issue 1 Billion Contactless Payment Cards, According to Identity Stronghold - pymnts.com]

Now, I have to say, in all honesty, that I know of no report from a reputable source of any incident of electronic pickpocketing ever having taken place anywhere in the world. Not one. I have never seen an unauthorised charge on any of my contactless cards and if I did see one I would simply call my issuer and have it wiped.

The real question, of course, is security: If a special little reader can take and use your credit card data from your phone, how is Google going to ensure this only happens when you want it to happen?

[From Google]

This is a misunderstanding of the difference between stripe cards and chip card (whether contactless or otherwise). We wrote an Android app to use a Square to read the magnetic stripe data from a credit card, decode it and then send it on. But the problem here is not Square or Android or Twitter but the magnetic stripe. If you read a magnetic stripe, you have all the data you need to make a magnetic stripe transaction. But if you read a contactless card, you **do not** have all the information you need to make a contactless card transaction.

Contactless card and phones, the ones with NFC interfaces like the Google phone referred to above, don't send the data necessary to construct a bogus magnetic stripe and you can't use the data that they do send to make a bogus NFC application because the secret keys that you need to create the secure messages are never transmitted - they stay inside the secure element (SE), just as they stay inside the chip on a chip and PIN card. So the strength of the electronic pickpocketing meme does not come from the technology, nor can it come from experience.

As I've said before about contactless, there must be something about contactless, about wireless interaction, that causes irrational concerns.

> *Among those that are not yet ready to use contactless, security appear to be the dominant consideration. Which means, of course, that whatever we might think about actual security situation we must get better at communicating it.*

[From <u>Digital Money: Contactless update</u>]

I'm at a loss what to do though. If I were the UK banks, I might try to persuade the BBC to get a contactless card story into Eastenders, as that seems to be the standard public education channel these days. Otherwise the stories will just keep coming.

> *At least once a year, the contactless payments industry, indeed all of us, has to put up with someone spreading fear about contactless cards and the ability of someone to scan the card of a passerby with a portable contactless reader. Yes, it's true. It can be done. But who cares? The risk is beyond minuscule.*

[From PaymentsJournal - Non-Existent Monsters in Your Wallet]

If the London Assembly were being really forward looking, they would have asked Will what terrific new services TfL will be able to deliver once customers begin using the coming generation of NFC phones instead of contactless cards. This is only just around the corner now.

> *"Until we see implementations of NFC that allows us to get repeatable transaction times within 500 milliseconds, this is going to be a concern for us," Will Judge, Transport for London head of future ticketing, told NFC Times.*

Tomorrow's Transactions—The 2012 Reader

*[From <u>Transport for London Calls for Faster NFC SIMs | NFC</u>
<u>Times – Near Field Communication and all contactless</u>]*

He also said, at the Transport Card Forum in London in December, that
some "very clever people down in Guildford" are going to make this
happen. Modesty forbids me from providing a link to these transaction
heroes; suffice to say that I fully expect the targets for TfL's Future
Ticketing Project (FTP) to be met.

Comments

I think Walt Ausgustinowich would take exception to the comment
"Now, I have to say, in all honesty, that I know of no report from a
reputable source of any incident of electronic pickpocketing ever
having taken place anywhere in the world."

However I am completely on the same page as you David. e-
Pickpocketing, wedge, man in the middle attacks are just
sensationalist headlines to bash the banks with. I say we move to
NFC asap with a £25 limit and higher transactions with online
passcode validation. Off my soap box now.

Posted by: Steve Beecroft on 22/09/2011 at 12:34.

I have seen many dramatic 'news' segments about electronic
pickpocketing here in North America, and they all have a similar
starting point. Strangely enough, news media seem drawn to the
demonstration made by a so-called expert, who also happens to sell
sleeves to protect against that evil! This guy sure is getting more than
his 15 minutes of fame! I fully agree with you, Dave. My question is:
how can we, as industry experts, teach the media to ask the tough
questions, or to defer to experts that will have a counter point of view?

Posted by: René Bastien on 23/09/2011 at 21:05.

Slick transit - 25/10/2011

Today is a rather special anniversary. A hundred years ago today, the
London General Omnibus Company (LGOC, a precursor of London
Transport) took the last horse-drawn bus out of service in London. The
motor had won.

The last LGOC horse-drawn bus ran on 25 October 1911.

[From <u>Buses in London - Wikipedia, the free encyclopedia</u>]

When engines were first introduced, there was an explosion of variety. Steam, electric, hybrid (yes, one of the first motorised London buses used a generator to power an electric motor - I'm told this was to avoid using gears, which the drivers didn't understand having come straight from horses) and petrol. The first buses merely replaced the horses with an engine, but they didn't redesign the rest of the bus.

It takes a while for a new technology that improves on one part of a system to embed in a redesigned system. It's a well-known phenomenon that the first electric motors were used to replace steam engines, and it took a while for factories to be redesigned so that there were lots of motors where they were needed rather than a big motor in the middle transmitting power via belts and drives. When the modern "one man" buses were first introduced, there was a similar dynamic. The buses were fitted with turnstiles and machines that you had to drop money into in order to get a paper ticket, just as you would have done with the human conductor.

Things stayed this way -- handing over cash to get a paper ticket -- until the contactless smart card came along (although magnetic stripe tickets were introduced on the tube starting in 1964). When the first smart cards with contactless interfaces arrived in London, the "Oyster" cards, they were used to simulate the complex cardboard tickets: weekly and monthly tickets, annual season tickets, staff passes, children and old person's concessions and so on. The real revolution arrived a little later, when they began the "capping" system so that you could ride around on your pay-as-you-go (PAYG) Oyster card but your charges would be capped at the cost of a one-day "travel card". Now, to all intents and purposes, everyone in London has an Oyster card.

TfL spent a lot of money developing the Oyster scheme because one thing hadn't changed from the days of the horse-drawn LCOG buses to today: the banks didn't provide a payment mechanism that was quick enough and convenient enough for public transport, so the public transport operators had to sort things out from themselves. Well, now they do. Since the banks decided to roll out contactless payments, TfL have decided to institute a major programme to accept these bank products for travel in London. Starting next year with the buses, TfL are rolling out new readers so that customers will be able to use their bank cards to travel. No need to buy an Oyster card any more.

> *Contactless credit and debit card payment will be rolled out across the London transport network by the end of 2012, making the capital the first in the world to embrace the system so comprehensively.*

> *[From TfL]*

Tomorrow's Transactions—The 2012 Reader

At Consult Hyperion's recent workshop on Open Payments in Transport, Matthew Hudson from TfL explained to the delegates why TfL is moving to accept these "open" (i.e., Visa, MasterCard and Amex) contactless payment cards on the buses and tube starting next year. Given the thousands of acceptance points, millions of users and zillions of transactions this will involve, it's quite a big deal in our neck of the secure electronic transactions woods. Nick Deere from Consult Hyperion explained how the system will work and the complexity of the reader development.

> The Tri-Reader® 3 supports multiple card schemes – for example, with Oyster in the UK, ITSO and contactless EMV cards can now be read concurrently on the same contactless reader. The Tri-Reader 3 was developed by Cubic on behalf of Transport for London and the company has a worldwide licence for its use for open payments.

[From Cubic receives contactless]

Oyster is a fantastic product and has been a huge success. But Oyster costs money to run and TfL is under significant pressure to reduce costs. As Forum friend Shashi Verma (TfL's Director, Customer Experience), has frequently observed about this before, they see they their job as running a transit system, not a ticketing system. TfL reckon that their overall ticketing system costs them about 14p per £1 collected in fares. Some of this is ripe for reinvention. Product sales alone account for almost a third of costs, and this could easily be halved: monthly and yearly season tickets won't go away for a long time, and since they are efficient products to sell, there's no reason to stop them, but most of the ad hoc non-commuter trips could be shifted to open products. According to a "leaked document" quoted in last night's Evening Standard.

> The move would mean mass ticket office closures and the loss of more than 1,500 jobs. The Operational Strategy Discussion Paper says £2 billion could be saved by 2018.

[From Driverless trains on the Tube by 2021 | News]

That's serious money and an obvious driver for change in the ticketing system. There's another issue as well. While Oyster is a great customer experience that is much appreciated in London, it's not a perfect customer experience. Just to give one example: because the data is stored on the card, it's difficult to give consumers a good customer experience online. With the shift toward multi-channel sales and servicing underway, this is now important.

As I'm sure many of you know, Consult Hyperion has been advising TfL on this project for some time so we share their excitement about it going live in the not-too-distant future. The experience that we have gained in the prototyping, design and certification of card and phone EMV products in a demanding transit environment is literally unique, so we are hardly impartial observers. But I'm sure you'll agree that TfL's decision to set a high bar in terms of functionality and performance has paid off for them and for the industry as a whole.

While I appreciate the history of transport in London, I'm looking toward the future. Another change that will come with open payments is the arrival of mobile payments and ticketing. Since the gates will accept bank contactless card they will also accept Visa, MasterCard and Amex payments via mobile phone and that opens up the potential for value-adding services on the mobile that are simply not possible using cards.

> *Transport for London (TfL) has stated it will support NFC payments on mobile phones in 2012.*
>
> *[From Transport for London to accept NFC payments from 2012 • NFC World]*

It's a big deal. It's not been possible to experiment with Oyster in mobile phones because the chipsets used for NFC do not (yet) support the more secure Oyster cards and the software emulations are too slow for practical use. By going down this route, TfL can avoid this problem completely and start to explore the next smart ticketing revolution, which will be integration of ticketing and mobiles. This is just the sort of thing I'm looking forward to learning about at Transport Ticketing 2012 in London on the 24th-26th January 2012. I've been going along to this event for the last couple of years and found it an excellent way to get an up-to-date picture of what's happening in this space.

Ordinary People - 17/11/2011

I was in a large, typical, American mall and I observed three "payment events" in quick succession. I won't name any of the stores involved because it's not really about them, but here's what happened.

In sportswear Store One, I was surprised (and delighted) to see prominent signs near the registers saying "No Cash: Credit and Debit Only". But when I made it to the register, I saw that the signs also said "Please have your ID ready". Being English, I didn't have any ID, so I couldn't buy anything. Crazy, but that's what happens when you rely on signatures instead of PINs. Incidentally, had I had an ID such as my British driving licence, then the store would have served me even though they had no conceivable way of verifying the ID. How this is meant to reduce card fraud, I have no idea.

> *US retailers rack up around $100 billion in identity fraud losses every year, absorbing nearly 10 times the cost incurred by financial institutions, according to a study from LexisNexis and Javelin Strategy & Research.*

[From <u>Finextra: US retailers face $100bn in ID fraud</u>]

If the retailers had access to an actual, working, useful, 21st-century identity infrastructure then this nonsense would be in the dustbin of history already. In menswear Store Two, I found myself behind an English couple who were being thoroughly confused at the register. The store clerk asked them "credit or debit" and they said "debit" and presented an English scheme-branded debit card which, of course, didn't work. The clerk had clearly seen this problem before, and told them that you have to press the "credit" button, remarking that "it's just the way the computer works". But, said the couple, we don't want any credit, we want to pay from our bank account. The clerk was very reassuring, telling them that "don't worry, the computer will take it from your bank". They were quite upset, but then most people don't really have any idea how the system works, so who can blame them.

> *The research reveals that only one in three people could correctly identify what an APR was. Whilst a worrying seven per cent were unable to recognise any payment terms, such as PIN, ATM and Bacs, when asked to identify them.*

[From <u>Payments Council - Confused about credit</u>]

Luckily, I was on hand with a pad and pencil to explain the situation, and after my very fascinating lecture on the evolution of signature and PIN debit in the US, the mechanisms for card processing and the implementation of Visa/MasterCard acceptance at US POS, the irate customers had calmed down. In fact, they were so calm that they seemed to have dozed off, so I left quietly.

In menswear Store Three, I paid by swiping the trivially-counterfeitable magnetic stripe on a MasterCard chip and PIN card and signed "Yaya Toure". Since no-one looked at the signature, it didn't matter, but it's a useful fraud detection technique for me, since a thief who steals my card will probably sign "David Birch".

> *In payments, plastic works just fine. That's why digital wallets will have to "revolutionize" shopping through innovations in*

loyalty and couponing in order to get consumers to switch their payment patterns.

[From 7 Emerging Payments Themes - Bank Innovation]

The idea that the current card payment system is the most efficient and most effective way to deal with retail payments is simply wrong. I'm hardly talking out of school hear, since people who work in the industry know perfectly well that it remains too slow, too expensive and too opaque, which is why (for example) Visa are spending so much money on developing a wallet proposition. And there are plenty of competitors out there snapping at the incumbents heels, which is why it's such a fun time to be in this business.

Why would retailers or banks, for whom credit or debit card purchases are working well, want to introduce this?

[From Is your phone the wallet of the future? | Circuit Breaker - CNET News]

Who says that they are working well? Not the retailers, who are constantly complaining about the cost of accepting cards (which, indeed, is much higher in the US than elsewhere), and not the consumer who couldn't buy sportswear (in this instance, me). Right now, Google's Wallet, ISIS and Visa's V.me are all about taking existing plastic cards and using virtual versions of them, but this must surely be only a stepping stone to new retail payment instruments. There's plenty of room for innovation.

Comments

Dave, I suspect that the "sportswear Store One" policy of asking for your ID has nothing to do with verifying your signature. I suspect that it is probably a very effective anti-fraud technique. If I steal credit card data via a skimming device or illegal access to transaction data, it may be relatively easy to produce fraudulent plastics. However, it will be much more difficult to produce a "valid" driver's license, passport, or state ID. Unless I steal your entire wallet and look like you, I cannot use your card at that retailer. There is no need for the clerk to look at the signature.

Posted by: Jamie on 18/11/2011 at 04:50.

But how could the store verify my English driver's licence even if I had left it in my wallet? They could not possibly tell whether it is real or not - and since my card was a Travelex MasterCard pre-paid US Dollar card that does not have my name on it anyway - I can't see how that would have helped, if you see what I mean.

Tomorrow's Transactions—The 2012 Reader

Posted by: Consult Hyperion on 18/11/2011 at 15:43.

Retail and the long game - 28/11/2011

The initial response to the new European payments regulatory environment has been mainly from mobile operators, transit companies and so on. But I think that the competition engendered in that environment might not assume item its final form until retailers enter the fray.

> *Andrew Higginson (Chief Executive of Retailing Services and Group Strategy Director, Tesco PLC) also during the "Consumer 2020: What Lies Ahead for the Retail Industry?" panel brought up Tesco's credit card product, stating one in nine transactions in the UK at Tesco is now done on a Tesco card.*
>
> *[From Why Bankers Might Not Be Fond of the Tesco Credit Card - pymnts.com]*

This is why, in a couple of previous posts, I've suggested that a plausible, logical step for retailers will be to abandon the antiquated infrastructure of payment cards—issuing and acceptance, interchange and rules—for new, retail-centric payment mechanisms. Starbucks provides more evidence that consumers are perfectly willing to adopt new payment technologies (pre-paid cards specific to retailers' mobile payments). It also provides evidence, as an aside, that designing new payment systems is hard and demands a level of security that is not necessary in loyalty schemes and such like. The very popular Starbucks mobile payment system is based on the use of a 2D barcode.

> *Sam Odio, a serial entrepreneur who previously sold his photo startup Divvyshot to Facebook, has manipulated Jonathan Stark's now-famous communal Starbucks Card to transfer $625 of the balance to his own Starbucks Card.*
>
> *[From Starbucks Card Social Experiment Hacked by Entrepreneur]*

So it turns out that the barcode displayed on a mobile phone screen isn't quite the same thing as the tamper-resistant secure element inside a handset, on the UICC, in an SD or wherever. Anyone can copy a barcode. This is one of the reasons why I think that in the long run NFC will take over these functions, even though it makes sense to experiment with barcodes. This is an interesting debate at present, of course, because (broadly speaking) barcodes exist and NFC handsets don't.

Air France did address this somewhat in the release. They said "compared with 2-D barcode mobile boarding passes, NFC-enabled mobile phones can even be switched-off or out of battery when communicating with a reader." That's it. That's the ONLY advantage they claim over mobile barcodes.

[*From Air France reveals the name of its NFC mobile boarding solution - Pass and Fly | GoMo News*]

Well, as I think that as the Starbucks case shows, there are one or two other advantages. However, that wasn't the point I wanted to make, which was that organisations such as Starbucks and Tesco can bring innovative new payments into the market whereas, in some cases, banks might find it difficult to introduce innovative solutions that are not based on existing infrastructure, sunk costs and fixed thinking. Therefore, to pick on a very current example, the fact that banks have found a new technology (e.g., contactless) to be a difficult proposition to sell to consumers and merchants does not mean that other organisations might not be able to find a way to exploit the technology more effectively. Retailers must be in pole position to take advantage of this because, as discussed many times before, the value-added services that they want (such as electronic coupons) are worth more than the margin on payments.

How might they do this? To take the example mentioned above, one can imagine that the "Tesco Credit Card" will, in time, disintegrate into the "Credit" part (a banking business), the "Tesco" part (a retail business) and the "Card" part that will vanish into mobile phones (a payments business). Now, who will run that payments business? Surely Tesco will get their banking business to set up a subsidiary with a Payment Institution (PI) licence to do the processing and an Electronic Money Institution (ELMI) licence to do the prepaid and "turbo Christmas Club" stuff. Incidentally, note that Tesco Mobile already has a couple of million subscribers, thus making the integrated mobile-based payment, rewards and loyalty offers straightforward. It's going to be hard to compete with that. At least if you're a "conventional" payments operator. Remember this?

Google also is working with 16 retailers, including American Eagle Outfitters Inc., Walgreen Co., Macy's and Subway, to develop its own point-of-sale service, called SingleTap. Under this system, consumers will be able to pay with credit accounts stored on the phone, redeem promotions and earn loyalty points.

[*From Mobile*]

Only a few months later and customers are already using Google Wallet in retailers right now. How long would it take a bank to get something like this together? I probably shouldn't enjoy pointing out that a couple of years ago I worked on a feasibility study for a European stakeholder putting forward this service scenario and it was shelved by them as having no business case. Saying that makes me a bad person, but we should all be allowed a few "I told you so" moments as long as they're not too frequent. I'm not an entrepreneur - I have no idea how to start or run as business, and I take my hat off to the people who do - but thanks to the kind of work we get involved in at Consult Hyperion, I do have a reasonable view of the retail transaction roadmap, and that's what it looks like: retailer-centric, because the value-added services around the payment are where the money is.

This opens up a vision of the retail POS that is based on APIs and authentication, not cards and contactless interfaces. When you look at what people are already doing with the PayPal X.Commerce platform, you can see how retailers might build their own solutions on top of payment APIs. See, for example, the Toys 'R Us case study unveiled earlier this year.

> *Betsy Poirier, director of digital at Toys R Us takes the stage. She's talking about in-store toy pick-up. Using X.commerce customers can order online and quickly pick-up products on their way home. For conversions, customers can get orders fast in store.*

> *[From Live From eBay]*

Here's a vision then: my Tesco Wallet on my Tesco Mobile contains my Tesco Xmas Club and Tesco Money pre-paid accounts as well as my bank-issued cards (that auto-load the Tesco Money account with electronic cash from Tesco Electronic Money Institution, or T-PESA as we call it, since it allows person-to-person payments). At the POS, the Tesco Payment Institution processes the payments while the Clubcard scheme and Tesco Coupons execute automatically. Far fetched? I don't think so. I'm not, incidentally, saying that retailers in general or Tesco in particular are visionaries and infallible in their projections.

> *Barry Grange, a Tesco director who heads the British Retail Consortium's committee that has talked to the banks, has still to be convinced of the usefulness of [debit cards]. But he acknowledges it could bring some advantages to stores. It ocduld reduce the volume of cash that retails have to deal with.*

That comes from *Will Britain buy electronic shopping?* in *New Scientist* magazine from April 29th, 1984. A long game indeed.

Festive season - 01/12/2011

My favourite presentation at the CFIR "Remaking Finance" seminar in Copenhagen was given by Thomas Keller from the Roskilde Festival. This is an annual eight day rock festival along the lines of Glastonbury but, to judge from his slide show, with much more attractive people.

Cash is a big problem at the festival. The entire trading income of around 150m Danish Crowns (around $30m) comes in those eight days (this excludes the ticket and off-site merchandise sales). The resources needed to manage this amount of cash -- from security guards and cash boxes to armoured cars and staff to count and tally -- are huge and that's even before the shrinkage. Apparently there are some strange atmospheric conditions in this part of Scandianvia and every year somewhere between 5-6% of the cash taken simply evaporates (something to do with the Northern lights?)

They did some early trials at the festival with mobile payments are few years ago. In the end they were happy with the way that SMS payments worked (a bit like the old PayPal mobile) but the SMS payment operators are just too expensive. They tried some other mobile payments but they didn't work because (as is common to all pop festivals and the like) the GSM network is constantly collapsing under the weight of video clips, picture messages and web browsing. So far they haven't managed to get wifi up across the site but they are going to look at this again.

Having examined all of the pilots and experiences, they've settled on contactless debit cards as the best short-term solution, moving to contactless mobile in the future. There's a slight problem, obviously, in that virtually no-one has a contactless debit card (the Danish banks don't issue them) and absolutely no-one has a contactless mobile, so they plan to experiment next year with a contactless prepaid card.

I asked him about other form factors and I mentioned wristbands but he said that they silicon rubber bands are no good because criminals cut them off of the wrists of drunk and sleeping people. If the wristbands stored cash, then they would be cut off all the time. I have to say, I hadn't thought about that, so I told him that stickers are the future anyway.

Thomas reckons that shifting from cash to cashless would save them in the region of 5-10m Danish Crowns per annum, even taking into account the merchant service charges and that would make a real difference to the economics around the event. I'm sure his figures could be replicated. This is a super niche for cashless and I can see that it will be a big growth area in the UK where there is a big festival business. Not only for pop festivals, but for the huge variety of festivals that we all love, and not only for payments but for the ticketing. The potential is huge and the benefits manifold:

> *Avoiding having millions of pounds of cash on festival sites, which is seen as a security risk and is expensive to transport and guard;*

> *Improving security for festival goers - who would no longer have to carry cash around and who could freeze their account if the payment device was lost;*

> *Cutting theft and fraud by staff working at festivals;*

> *Making service quicker at bars, and allowing management to monitor stock levels in real-time*

> *Controlling entry to different parts of the festival such as backstage or VIP areas*

> *[From BBC News - Cash to be axed from UK festivals]*

I can tell you from personal experience that the technology works well for the last case. We did some work for O2 a couple of years ago, implementing a simple VIP access control system on Nokia handsets for the pop festival in Hyde Park and it worked very well.

Now, this is is hardly new thinking. People have been experimenting with various forms of contactless technology in the festival environment for some time, and just this year there were experiments at the Isle of Wight Festival, at the Wireless Festival in Hyde Park (the BBC say that London's Wireless festival is tipped to be cashless by next summer) and elsewhere.

> *Specialist event IT supplier Etherlive has road tested a pioneering cash-less ticketing system at the Womad world music festival in Wiltshire... The test marks the first time the RFID technology has been used successfully at a festival and is the first step toward providing the infrastructure to a cashless event. Womad festival director Chris Smith says, "Womad is an exciting test case for the deployment of RFID at festivals, and I believe it could soon be rolled out in other ways. This is the first step in the journey towards cashless events where festival-goers use their wristbands to pay for their drinks, goods and food."*

> *[From Music Week - Music Week - Music business magazine - Womad tests cash-less payment system]*

One of the complexities in this space is that the value network is complex. The web of artists, promoters, producers, concessions, franchise and so on is difficult to navigate and co-ordinate. Nevertheless, contactless does seem to be gained ground across the network.

> *The world's largest concert promoter Live Nation says it's piloting new digital wristbands to try to combat ticket fraud... Live Nation says eventually it would like to get rid of paper tickets... According to the latest figures issued by the government, one in 12 music fans have been scammed online when they've bought live events tickets.*
>
> *[From BBC - Newsbeat - Concert promoters pilot 'smart-chip' digital tickets]*

This all sounds great -- or at least, potentially great, since there are both smart and stupid ways to implement this kind of value-added identity infrastructure -- but what caught my eye in this announcement was, naturally, the incorporation of payment technology..

> *The passes would allow fans to purchase food and drink using the device.*
>
> *[From BBC - Newsbeat - Concert promoters pilot 'smart-chip' digital tickets]*

Cashless payments in these environments don't just save money because of reduced cash handling, they increase sales because they speed things up. Instead of the Glastonbury phenomenon of people queueing for an hour to get to an ATM so that they can queue for an hour to buy a beer token so that they can queue for an hour to get a beer (this could only happen in England, of course, since in any other country people would quite rightly riot if told to queue for three hours to get a drink) there will be the simple, quick tap and go.

> *Here are some more concrete figures from the Ricoh Arena, the home of Coventry City FC. The cashless payment scheme there has been running at Coventry City's fixtures since 2008. Before the system, the average half-time transaction time was 63 seconds and it is now an average of 22 seconds, which means supporters receive their food and drinks quicker. The number of transactions as a percentage of the attendance has increased from 47 per cent to 57 per cent... "It has also been a commercial success with the average spend increasing in the concourses and corporate areas."*

Tomorrow's Transactions—The 2012 Reader

[From Coventry Telegraph - News - Business News - UK & Coventry Business - Ricoh's cashless system a winner]

Looking at all of the evidence it seems fairly straightforward -- and commercially sensible -- to give festival patrons a contactless card or whatever that functions as their ticket and purse. But actually it could even do more than that.

> *In addition to allowing users to pay for purchases from a prepaid account, the wristbands also serve as a medical ID bracelet. A customer can input information about their health conditions into an Emergency Response Profile using a software program Vita developed. The health information is not actually stored on the wristband; rather, the wristband displays a phone number that emergency responders can call to get the information.*

[From VITAband - Press]

So what's the hold up? Maybe the guys selling hot dogs and beer? There are some losers in the bright cashless future. The concessionaires who under-report sales, the merchandisers who trouser the takings, the tax-evading elements of the value chain who prefer to be paid in cash. They must be the block, because the business case isn't.

As an aside, in Swindon City-of-the-Future, an even more futuristic experiment has taken place. Swindon were one of the first clubs in the country to trial mobile ticketing for their fixtures, and made the first 150 mobile tickets available through Gates 28 and 29 of the Don Rogers Stand for their clash with Brentford last year. I shall next visit the County Ground, home of the mighty Robins, in a month to attend the visit of League newcomers AFC Wimbledon and will report back from this expedition to the future forthwith.

Regulate the right things, please - 23/12/2011

Payment cards made the news headlines this morning. As I was lying in bed listening to the BBC Radio 4 Today programme I was genuinely surprised to hear a lead item about a government proposal to intervene in the retail payments space.

> *"Excessive" fees for using a debit or credit card to buy items such as travel or cinema tickets will be banned by the end of 2012, under government plans. The move comes amid complaints that airlines, booking agencies and even councils were imposing excessive charges for using a card.*

However, firms will be allowed to levy a "small charge" to cover payment processing costs.

[From BBC News - Excessive card surcharges will be banned, says Treasury]

So once we've worked out what "excessive", "fee", "small", "charge", "processing" and "costs" means, there should be no problem. Now, I'm not saying that there isn't an issue. Clearly, there is. People navigate their way through web sites to buy tickets and then find themselves confronted with massive, absurd and incomprehensible surcharges.

Examples of these charges are a £6 per person, per leg "administration fee" charged on all but one card by Ryanair, an £8 per booking charge by Easyjet - plus 2.5% when using a credit card, a £4.50 per booking credit card fee from British Airways, and a charge of up to 17 euros (£14.16) per person by Air Berlin.

[From BBC News - Excessive card surcharges will be banned, says Treasury]

None of these charges, note, bear any relationship to what the companies are being charged by their acquirer. Let's just be clear about that. A debit transaction probably costs an airline about 10p, so adding £15 and then blaming it on the banks is pathetic. But what to do about it? As recent experience in the US shows, if the government attempts to regulate the price that is charged for payment services, then the costs will simply migrate to what isn't regulated. Look what happened with Durbin.

Bill Hardee, owner of the Warehouse Saloon & Billiards in Austin, Texas, says he recently tallied up his savings. The grand total: $1. He figured he paid $74 less on larger debit-card transactions, but that amount was offset by $73 in higher charges that he paid on small purchases.

[From Merchants Take Swipe At the New Debit Fees - WSJ.com]

The real solution to this problem, if you are going to regulate anything, is to insist that companies make the costs of payment choices clear and then let the market do the work. If you are upset y an airline charging you £12 to use your debit card, then use another airline. At least airlines have competition. Other ticket surcharges are to my mind much worse. I find it as annoying as the next person that the headline prices of things on the web (e.g., concert tickets) do not include the unavoidable additional charge. I can't believe that people like Ticketmaster really want me to pay in cash instead of by card, so why not show the cost of the card payment (plus "handling charges" and all that sort of crap) in the price of the ticket?

If the government wants to take action, it should adopt my plan to minimise the total social cost of payments and make debit cards the "zero". In other words, companies should not be allowed to surcharge for debit cards and banks should be required to provide zero interchange debit cards as a condition of holding a retail banking licence. If companies want to surcharge for payment instruments that are worse for society (cheques, cash, credit cards, charge cards, cowrie shells or euros) then that's fine.

> *Much as I dislike government intervention in the pricing of anything, unless the costs of cash are to be distributed properly (which they won't be) this is the only sensible course of action. Making debit cards the "zero" and allowing retailers to surcharge other payment mechanisms (including cash) is fair, with one proviso: that pre-paid cards are counted as debit cards. This is necessary to deliver financial inclusion.*

[From Digital Money: Economy class]

I can see at least one problem on the horizon here though. Regulators are sure to want to extend the protections afforded to credit card users to debit card users. Interestingly, in the UK at least, Visa has extended consumer protection to debit cards for some time and now MasterCard is going to do the same thing with its new debit products.

> *MasterCard is re-launching its debit card portfolio in the UK, offering banks "premier debit" products with the capacity to run sophisticated rewards and loyalty programmes... Loyalty programmes are notoriously difficult to run on the debit platform due to the low interchange revenue, but MasterCard believes that enabling banks to build a rewards platform around their debit portfolio will enable issuers to differentiate their current account offerings significantly.*

> *The network has mandated that all cards be contactless enabled and offer zero liability to the cardholder.*

[From MasterCard]

These things aren't cost free - someone has to pay for those protections since neither Visa nor MasterCard nor the banks will want to do it for nothing and if we raise the cost of debit transactions too high then we get away from the social goal of providing a basic low-cost payment system for the whole of society to use. I notice that regulators are beginning to target prepaid cards as well, thus raising their cost too and limiting their ability to tackle financial inclusion. Why this should be a regulatory priority is beyond me, but there we go.

Although the strict legislation looks likely to curb money laundering, its provisions also mean that prepaid cards can be reloaded up to a maximum of €100 ($133.82). For amounts above that, a full KYC procedure needs to take place every time the card is reloaded with credit above €100. The issuer then needs to archive that information for five years.

[From Germany passes AML laws – restricts prepaid]

But let's assume we can find a way as an industry to deal with this. In the meantime, we can get by with debit cards, can't we? Hhmmm...

O'Connell lists five scenarios in which he feels paying debit should be avoided at all costs:

[From 5 Scenarios When Paying with Debit Could Spell Disaster - pymnts.com]

Personally, I avoid paying by debit at all times and under all circumstances. But it's perfectly reasonable for people who do pay with debit cards to ask why they are subsidising my enhanced consumer protection, frequent flier miles, cash back and so on. The price quoted for goods and services by UK merchants should include all charges for using a debit card, and that's that. It is perfectly reasonable to surcharge me for using my credit card: then I as a consumer can decide whether the benefits of using my BA American Express card to buy a ticket at the British Airways web site are worth £4.50 to me or not.

Back to transit - 11/01/2012

When I went to get on the SF Muni the last time I was in San Francisco, I realised that my Clipper card had only a few dollars left, so I decided to top it up. I went to the BART top-up machine. It said that it accepted debit cards only, so being half-asleep (it was very early in the morning) I put my Barclays debit card in the slot. Transaction declined. Then I realised that they meant "debit" in the American sense of non-Visa/MC scheme debit that has a PIN. I didn't have any cash, so I gave up. But as I was walking to the Muni gate I saw another Muni machine that clearly said credit or debit top up. So I tapped my Clipper, selected the $20 top-up, and inserted my Barclays debit card again, this time selecting "credit" as the payment option. It worked. But then I realised that I hadn't got a $20 top-up, but 10 $2 Muni rides, no good for my ride on Caltrain later. If anyone asks you why we want to use the mobile phone to replace cards when the current system works fine, tell them they're full of it.

What I should be able to do in a civilised society is to not have to care about any of this stuff. I should be able to get off the plane at SFO and walk on to BART by just tapping my phone. There are two ways to do this: load the transit applications into the phone, or get the transit system to accept "open" payment cards (the London solution). I have got a Samsung NFC phone, but sadly there's no way to load a Clipper card into it, because Clipper uses DESFire and the phone NFC chipset doesn't support this in hardware. At some point, I suppose, Clipper will have to upgrade to DESFire EV1 (not implemented in phone chipset either) because DESFire is compromised, but I don't think that will be any time soon. Why will they have to upgrade? It's because of security: you can clone certain kinds of MiFare cards because they rely on a proprietary security algorithm that was broken some time ago.

> The case came to light when a counter worker at an unnamed railway station reported selling 100 cards to the same person, Nos says. Further investigation showed the cards were being manipulated so that they appear to have been uploaded with €150 in cash. The cards are then sold on to third parties via internet sites such as Marktplaats.

[From DutchNews.nl - Public transport smart card fraud]

Oops. Oh well, this doesn't mean you have to panic, abandon the current system and buy a new one immediately. It's about risk management.

> BART says there aren't enough Clipper smart-card transit cheats to warrant card changes. The San Francisco Chronicle says there's been a surge in the number of riders misusing Clipper cards, but officials decided Thursday that the number of cheaters hasn't risen to a level that makes changes to the card necessary. Up to 200 commuters may be cheating the system each day.

[From BART says not enough smart-card cheats for fix]

Transit is actually a very interesting to study when trying to understand the implications of the new network technologies on various stakeholders. For one thing, people in many cities never leave home without a transit card, so it's an obvious focus for those trying to introduce new payment technologies.

Take the specific example of the "hacking" of transit cards. It's not worth spending very large amounts of money on security for transit cards that have to cost very little in order to pay for transit fares that are even less. But if someone else has put a high-security system in place, then you might as well use it for transit: then the payment/ticketing security burden is at least shared and in some cases eradicated. Does transit then define the path for mobile contactless because it provides a clear win-win? Yes and no.

> *My prediction? ISIS and MNO initiatives will be successful in Transit. Retailers will migrate to a new commerce network that steers clear of Visa and MA.*

[*From NFC – Announcements Galore ! « FinVentures*]

This is a very interesting prediction. In the short term, transit is central to many markets but, as I wrote recently, there is every reason to imagine that the retailers, rather than MNOs or transit operators, will shape the longer-term evolution in the space, but we'll return to that another time.

Bore reporter - 24/01/2012

As my life is so dull, when I travel to interesting places I like to waste my time and the time of everyone around me by trying out any new payment schemes, terminals and form factors to hand. Thus, I went to San Francisco not with flowers in my hair but with an array of cards, phones and my splendid new PayPass watch. Which, I have to say, got us off to an excellent start! I used my watch to pay for the cab ride from the airport and it worked perfectly. Unfortunately, from then on, things went downhill a bit. Now, remember, the only reason that I am writing about this stuff is because I care about it. I spend a lot of time sitting in offices looking at Powerpoint and reports, but to me there's no substitute for actually going to the retailers and finding out what is really happening with the contactless roll-out. For many of our clients, the use of mobiles at POS can't come soon enough, but if the contactless rails aren't there then the mobile train won't run.

So… We went to CVS and Best Buy, none of which would accept any of our UK contactless cards: not Visa, MasterCard or Amex. Nor would they accept any other form factor (not my UK phone or my UK watch) and we did check the terminals were working because we paid with a US contactless card no problem. We asked the checkout clerk in Best Buy about the situation and were told that while some people did occasionally try and use contactless cards, they only worked some of the time. However, **unprompted**, he also ventured that some people have paid using Google Wallet on their phone and that seemed to work properly. (Indeed, a colleague used Google Wallet to pay in CVS and it worked fine when our cards didn't). Hhmmmm…

We really need contactless to get on track, but I think we're going to have a little bit of a problem unless we (i.e., the industry) buck up a bit. Back in dear old Blighty, where my younger son elicited an appropriate gasp of astonishment when paying in McDonalds using a watch, things are dragging somewhat.

> *On average, each of the approximately 60,000 contactless point-of-sale terminals in the United Kingdom is used only four to five times per month, said Matt Rowsell, chief commercial officer for Streamline, part of WorldPay, the United Kingdom's largest merchant acquirer.*
>
> *[From NFC Retailers Blog » UK Contactless to Reach a Tipping Point in 2011?]*

I'm sure there are all sorts of reasons why consumers might be slow to start tapping -- perhaps they have security concerns (unlike me), or don't like to use a debit card at point of sale (like me) -- but it may be that the simplest explanation is most likely correct. To wit, none of them know what it is.

> *With interviews from mote than 2,500 respondents online, the study reveals that just 12% of the British population believe they own a contactless card. However, the UK Cards Association reported that there were 19.6 million active cards in the month of November.*
>
> *[From ContactlessNews | Report: Banks and retailers need to do more to increase use of contactless]*

I noticed this at a recent event in the US. I happened to be talking with a couple of American chaps and the subject wandered toward contactless acceptance, as it so often does at my lunch table. Both of them said they had no contactless cards. A little later on, as the discussion continued, wallets were produced and opened. One of them had contactless card from a well-known US issuer. I pointed this out. The chap said words to the effect of "I wondered what that symbol was".

There are going to be a few changes soon. I am reliably informed that the contactless no-CVM limit of £15 will be raised soon (one of the things that retailers have been asking for) and that Olympic year will see renewed efforts.

> *In its second 'contactless barometer', the card giant quizzed 500 contactless users in the UK, 500 in Poland and 500 in Turkey. In the UK 73% agree or strongly agree that contactless technology will ultimately become more commonplace than cash, compared to 79% in both Poland and Turkey.*
>
> *[From Finextra: UK contactless]*

What this survey in fact shows, as do all the others, is that people who use contactless like it, but they'd rather have it in their phone. My suggestion, bearing in mind that I know virtually nothing about the acquiring business, is that a potential stratagem might be to locate contactless terminals at points of sale where cash is a pain (e.g., the car park by Blockbuster in Woking) instead of a points of sales where it isn't (e.g., my dry cleaner).

> *To address what one might call a "flight risk," MasterCard Inc. plans to test contactless payments at 30,000 feet, enabling airlines to accept more secure plastic — and potentially mobile — payments aboard planes.*
>
> *[From Making Plane Sense of In-Flight Payment Risk - American Banker Article]*

This is a fun idea, but it set me wondering why they bother with POS at all: they know your seat number, you had to prove your identity to get on, so for frequent fliers at least then they may as well just bill you. But that's for a future blog post. Back at contactless POS, there are other niches where more effort might yield better dividends than in high-street retail. Events, stadiums, arenas and the like would be an obvious category.

> *From today, the world's busiest arena, The O2, is rolling out contactless technology across more than 250 card payment terminals.*
>
> *[From Barclays]*

They clearly had the contactless terminals up and running double quick (well done Barclaycard) because my boys went to watch the ATP Finals for a day and got some free tennis balls for paying for soda contactlessly (albeit with a prepaid MasterCard sticker on the back of an iPhone rather than a Barclays' card!!).

Comments

> Yes! You're so right! Maybe contactless is still parked in "Innovation" teams in all the banks and hence the Marketing departments are studiously ignoring it. Can anyone enlighten us as to how to get it moved to BAU?
>
> *Posted by: Will Judge on 24/01/2012 at 21:16.*

Chapter 6: Public Sector and NGOs

Digital identity, digital money and digital networks have the long-recognised potential to transform the delivery of public services as much as they have the ability to revolutionise commerce. The nature of public sector organizations, and often NGOs, is that they can be slow to change their ways: even if they adopt new technology, their governance, ethos and budgets can conspire to make them conservative in their use of it. Nevertheless, the way in which the public sector uses these technologies will have a major influence on the way the rest of the economy will use them.

Reflecting on NSTIC - 06/07/2011

I've been reading through the final version of the US government's National Strategy on Trusted Identities in Cyberspace (NSTIC). This is roughly what journalists think about:

> *What's envisioned by the White House is an end to passwords, a system in which a consumer will have a piece of software on a smartsphone or some kind of card or token, which they can swipe on their computers to log on to a website.*

> *[From White House Proposes A Universal Credential For Web : The Two-Way : NPR]*

And this is roughly what the public think about it

> *Why don't they just put a chip in all of us and get it over with? What part of being a free people do these socialists not understand?*

> *[From White House Proposes A Universal Credential For Web : The Two-Way : NPR]*

And this is roughly what I think about it: I think that NSTIC isn't bad at all. As I've noted before I'm pretty warm to it. The "identity ecosystem" it envisages is infinitely better than the current ecosystem and it embodies many of the principles that I regard a crucial to the online future. It explicitly says that "the identity ecosystem will use privacy-enhancing technology and policies to inhibit the ability of service providers (presumably including government bodies) to link an individual's transactions and says that by default only the minimum necessary information will be shared in transactions. They have a set of what they term the Fair Information Practice Principles (FIPPs) that share, shall we say, a common heritage with Forum friend Kim Cameron's laws (for the record, the FIPPs cover transparency, individual participation, purpose specification, data minimisation, use limitation, data quality and integrity, security and accountability and audit).

It also, somewhat strangely, I think, says that this proposed ecosystem "will preserve online anonymity", including "anonymous browsing". I think this is strange because there is no online anonymity. If the government, or the police, or an organisation really want to track someone, they can. There are numerous examples which show this to be the case. There may be some practical limitations as to what they can do with this information, but that's a slightly different matter: if I hunt through the inter web tubes to determine that that the person posting "Dave Birch fancies goats" on our blog comes from a particular house in Minsk, there's not much I can do about it. But that doesn't make them anonymous, it makes the economically anonymous, and that's not the same thing, especially to people who don't care about economics (eg, the security services). It's not clear to me whether we as a society actually want an internet that allows anonymity or not, but we certainly don't have one now.

The strategy says that the identity ecosystem must develop in parallel with ongoing "national efforts" to improve platform, network and software security, and I guess that no-one would argue against them, but if we were ever to begin to design an EUSTIC (ie, an EU Strategy for Trusted Identities in Cyberspace) I think I would like it to render platform, network and software security less important. That is, I want my identity to work properly in an untrusted cyberspace, one where ne'erdowells have put viruses on my phone and ever PC is part of a sinister botnet (in other words, the real world).

I rather liked the "envision" boxes that are used to illustrate some of the principles with specific examples to help politicians and journalists to understand what this all means. I have to say that it didn't help in all cases...

The "power utility" example serves as a good focus for discussion. It expects secure authentication between the utility and the domestic meter, trusted hardware modules to ensure that the software configuration on the meter is correct and to ensure that commands and software upgrades do indeed come from the utility. All well and good (and I should declare an interest and disclose that Consult Hyperion has provided paid professional services in this area in the last year). There's an incredible amount of work to be done, though, to translate these relatively modest requirements into a national-scale, multi-supplier roll-out.

Naturally I will claim the credit for the chat room "envision it"! I've used this for many years to illustrate a number of the key concepts in one simple example. But again, we have to acknowledge there's a big step from the strategy to any realistic tactics. Right now, I can't pay my kids school online (last Thursday saw yet another chaotic morning trying to find a cheque book to pay for a school outing) so the chance of them providing a zero-knowledge proof digital credential that the kids can use to access (say) BBC chatrooms is absolutely nil to any horizon I can envisage. In the UK, we're going to have to start somewhere else, and I really think that that place should be with the mobile operators.

What is the government's role in this then? The strategy expects policy and technology interoperability, and there's an obvious role for government—given its purchasing power—to drive interoperability. The government must, however, at some point make some firm choices about its own systems, and this will mean choosing a specific set of standards and fixing a standards profile. They are creating a US National Project Office (NPO) within the Department of Commerce to co-ordinate the public and private sectors along the Implementation Roadmap that is being developed, so let's wish them all the best and look forward to some early results from these efforts.

As an aside, I gave one of the keynote talks at the Smart Card Alliance conference in Chicago a few weeks ago, and I suggested, as a bit of an afterthought, after having sat through some interesting talks about the nascent NSTIC, that a properly implemented infrastructure could provide a viable alternative to the existing mass market payment schemes. But it occurs to me that it might also provide an avenue for EMV in the USA, because the DDA EMV cards that would be issued (were the USA to decide to go ahead and migrate to EMV) could easily be first-class implementations of identity credentials (since DDA cards have the onboard cryptography needed for encryption and digital signatures). What's more, when the EMV cards migrate their way into phones, the PKI applications could follow them on the Secure Element (SE) and deliver an implementation of NSTIC that could succeed in the mass market with the mobile phone as a kind of "personal identity commander".

Practical NSTIC – 08/08/2011

The last Smart Card Alliance was a good opportunity to catch up with some of the thinking on the recently released National Strategy for Trusted Identity in Cyberspace (NSTIC). I went to listen to a series of talks about NSTIC and got involved in a fair amount of coffee break discussion with delegates. As a result of this, I continue to think that NSTIC represents a real opportunity for digital identity to make a difference in many practical cases.

Personally, as I've said before, I like NSTIC and have been encouraging our clients to develop strategies toward NSTIC. Since virtually none of them spend their entire time thinking about identity infrastructure, I'm trying to find ways to simplify and condense some of the key issues. If we step back to look at the intended prosaic impact, it's about better security and fewer passwords, which translates in the short term into a combination of two-factor authentication (2FA) and federation.

The president wants consumers to use strong authentication, something more than user name and password, which will most likely add another security factor, say officials familiar with the project.

For example, user name and password is one-factor security, something you know. But additional factors can be added. A token or digital certificate can be a second factor, something you have, resulting in stronger two-factor authentication. If you add a fingerprint or other biometric, something you are, it's increased to three-factor security.

[From NFCNews | Potential technologies that consumers may use for online ID]

In that specific exposition, there follows an interesting, but confused, list of options. I'd like to suggest a more straightforward taxonomy, based on a digital identity infrastructure (which doesn't exist, of course). The article, to my mind, confuses the distinct bindings between the virtual identities that exist in the Net and the real identities that are connected to. This is why it is useful to introduce the notion of digital identity in the middle (which would also solve the "real names" problem that is causing so much grief at the moment, but that's another story). So then we get the two categories of technology that might be used to solve the key problems and work within the NSTIC framework to make a real difference to the world of online identity. These are:

- Linking virtual identities to digital identities. The article suggests that digital certificates and PKI might be a good way to do this and I agree. Think of a digital identity as a private-public key pair: so long as there is some tamper-resistant store (which has generally meant a smart card) for the private key then the digital identity is portable and convenient. The natural place for this tamper-resistant chip is, of course, the mobile phone (or, at least, the device-formerly-known-as the mobile phone) because it provides both local (via NFC) and remote interfaces to the chip.

- Linking digital identities to real-world entities. Right now this is largely achieved through passwords or PINs, but the article suggests that passwords will be supplanted by biometrics. I think this is plausible, although it is not an immediate requirement for mass market use. People will want to use NSTIC to log into The Telegraph and the DVLC, not to reset nuclear missile launch codes.

By implementing the right technology for each of these links, we (i.e., the industry) can make NSTIC simple and practical. If we can do this, then I think that the use of digital identity will permeate through almost all of our day-to-day interactions. I think some people view NSTIC and being a kind of non-governmental ID "card" and therefore tend to think of it for a particular set of applications but these are only a start. To get an idea of what might be achieved, have a look at how a technologically-advanced ID card is used.

> *The new Estonian e-ID card features a PKI application embedded in the contact chip and allowing online authentication and digital signature by qualified electronic certificates. This technology enables citizens to execute a large variety of e-government and e-commerce services, and makes it possible to verify and validate the documents in electronic transfer. Additionally, the e-ID card offers the owner access to the local public transport network.*

> *Furthermore, the BRP card contains a contactless chip with special functionalities when travelling within the Schengen area. The application fulfils the most recent ICAO norms for biometric identity documents, such as a fingerprint check.*

> *[From Trüb AG]*

This card-based implementation suggests to me a way of funding the improved implementation of NSTIC as well. If mobile operators would provide this functionality on the UICC and make it available to banks and other to use, the consumers could use that solution—generating data and messaging traffic for the operators—or for consumers who didn't want to use the smartphone app, there would be a card to buy.

It seemed to me at the Chicago event that some of the thinking about the technology platform was underdeveloped. We have some fantastic tools available to us now that we can use to create a digital identity infrastructure that would have been hard to imagine a few years ago. Starting from where we are, the realistic platform is the cloud plus the mobile phone which would turn the mobile into an identity selector and

One factor that will have to be taken into account, though, if mobile operators are going to provide this platform is that of regulation. I can see that one of the real attractions of this business for mobile operators is that as both an identity provider and as the authentication platform, they can assemble an incredible amount of personal data.

> *But as of now, the NSTIC Strategy document and the Implementation Plan lack crucial detail about regulating IdPs. By definition, Identity Providers will be able to link all of an individual's personal transactions. Without regulation, larger IDPs will be able to market, share or otherwise derive value from vast storehouses of transactional data, much like today's credit reporting agencies.*

[From NSTIC]

This is a very good point. We do have to find some kind of balance (which may be through a different basic structure, such as is provided by something like MyDex) to give the stakeholders incentive to create an excellent infrastructure. We also have to find a fair basis for the mobile operators and others to create a working set of relationships.

> *Absent new laws to make this kind of grand identity federation happen, we will still need new contracts—brand new contracts of an unusual form—struck between all the parties. It's complicated by the fact that banks & telcos don't naturally see themselves as "identity providers", not in the open anyway*

[From Digital Identity: The sorry state of id and authentication]

One way to do this might be to see the mobile operator provide two distinct functions via separate business entities: the identity platform that is made available to all (in the great tradition of EU regulation in an "open, transparent and non-discriminatory" manner) and the identity and attribute provider business that uses that platform just as many others (e.g., banks) will. The practical use cases are appealing: you go to log on to your bank, you get a message on your phone, you punch in a PIN or something and you're logged in no problem. Now you go to log on to the DVLA, you get a message on your phone, you punch in the same PIN and you're logged in no problem. Consumers will therefore have access to a highly functional infrastructure without having to understand keys, certificates or anything else.

National Cybersecurity - 07/12/2011

I very much appreciated being invited along to speak at the Cyber Security Forum 2011 in London. I'm sorry that I couldn't get along to the first sessions (the demands of clients trumped the future security of our great nation) but I sat through most of it. When I wandered in and sat down, avoiding the temptation to go to "Iceland - New Opportunities" instead, and I loved that within the first ten minutes I had heard about Machiavelli, the scientific illiteracy of the British civil service and how to get stuff done in ancient Greece.

It wasn't all fun though. A chap from the Institute for Security and Resilience said that the measure of strategic capacity is the capacity to innovate, and he sounded sceptical of UK plc's abilities in this space, making an interesting point about they way in which the British system puts specialists and entrepreneurs under the control of generalists (referring to, I think, the well-meaning but amateur way in which government manages IT).

But to the point. It turns out that the UK has cybersecurity strategy. It's available online from the Cabinet Office (revised version 25th November 2011 PDF), so I quickly downloaded it and skimmed through it in time to get to the panel on the "vision for a cyber smart economy" that featured Baroness Pauline Neville-Jones, who is the UK Government's Special Representative to Industry on Cyber Security. She was great: amongst other things she asked why UK educational establishments are training more Chinese people in cyber security than British nationals...

I spoke on the panel on SMEs chaired by Alex van Someren with Nick Kingsbury and Mark West, and that was most enjoyable, but the highlight of the day for me was the wide-ranging discussion between Joseph Menn of the Financial Times, Caspar Bowden (no longer with Microsoft) and the writer Cory Doctorow. They are very smart and very interesting guys, so hearing them range across software patents, copyrights and privacy was genuinely fascinating. The UK Cybersecurity Strategy doesn't actually mention copyright at all and it only mentions "intellectual property" once (on page 9), but in terms of a vision for a cyber smart economy, I would have thought that informed discussions about this were rather central to that vision.

The reason that they are not is, as was covered in the discussion, twofold. Cliff Richard and his stooges are against internet privacy for entirely sociopathic reasons to do with what economists call "rent-seeking regulatory capture", but he finds a sympathetic ear in the government because the government don't want privacy either - they want to be able to listen in to your internet conversations and if that means leaving them open to Chinese cyberwarriors as well as record companies then so be it - and find sobbing pop stars a useful smokescreen and because it's more fun talking to pop stars than to dreary middle-aged "experts" (e.g., me).

At the end of the event my perspective on all of this was reinforced as essentially infrastructural. In particular, we lack national identity infrastructure, so we're starting from a low base. In the UK, we need to accelerate the Cabinet Office's Identity Assurance Programme to formulate something along the lines of the US Department of Commerce's National Strategy for Trusted Identities in Cyberspace (NSTIC) and then mandate its use for public sector services: no identity, no service. If we don't mandate it, and instead rely on citizens to protect themselves (and the rest of us) then we have no hope.

> *Citibank's Rich Detura... runs global consumer fraud policies, which is an expansion from his previous similar role for Citibank's US-specific role. "Consumers' use of technology is far outpacing their ability to comprehend the security implications of their actions"*

> *[From Great quote from Citibank's Rich Detura - Javelin Strategy & Research Blog]*

If we don't take this kind of action, we're going to end up with two internets, as I've written before. With no end-to-end identity management, the rich will instead turn to secure networks that lock out undesirables (or, alternatively, lock in undesirables who know what they're doing).

> *"The concept of a more secure network that customers or vendors are willing to pay for is probably the only way to provide the security that people want to have," says Ted Schlein of Kleiner Perkins.*

> *[From Founding father wants secure 'Internet 2' - FT.com]*

I don't want that, because I think an open internet is a tremendous power for creativity and innovation. Let's have a working national and international identity infrastructure instead. As an aside, Hugh Eaton (Director Security and Intelligence) said that, as Bruce Schneier always does, that when it comes to security or dancing pigs, you always get dancing pigs. I think this should be updated for the 21st century: when it comes to security or newspaper headlines about security, you always get newspaper headlines about security.

Chapter 7: Telecoms and Media

Apart from being some of the biggest businesses in the world (the telecommunications sector has two **trillion** dollars in annual revenues), telcommunications and media companies are creating the platform for the future of work and play. Choices that they make, about how these platforms work, define the downstream business models that can exist on them and thus we should be paying close attention to services, systems and schemes that they are building.

Identity could be a big opportunity for mobile operators - 22/03/2011

The end of privacy is in sight, isn't it? After all, we are part of a generation that twitters and updates its path through the world, telling everyone everything. Not because Big Brother demands it, but because we want to. We have, essentially, become one huge distributed Big Brother. We give away everything about ourselves. And I do mean everything.

> *Mr. Brooks, a 38-year-old consultant for online dating Web sites, seems to be a perfect customer. He publishes his travel schedule on Dopplr. His DNA profile is available on 23andMe. And on Blippy, he makes public everything he spends with his Chase Mastercard, along with his spending at Netflix, iTunes and Amazon.com.*

> *[From T.M.I? Not for Sites Focused on Sharing - NYTimes.com]*

We'll come back to the reputation thing later on, but the point I wanted to make is that I think this is dangerous thinking, the rather lazy "nothing to hide" meme. Apart from anything else, how do you know whether you have anything to hide if you don't know what someone else is looking for?

> *To Silicon Valley's deep thinkers, this is all part of one big trend: People are becoming more relaxed about privacy, having come to recognize that publicizing little pieces of information about themselves can result in serendipitous conversations — and little jolts of ego gratification.*

> *[From T.M.I? Not for Sites Focused on Sharing - NYTimes.com]*

We haven't had the Chernobyl yet, so I don't privilege the views of the "deep thinkers" on this yet. In fact, I share the suspicion that these views are unrepresentative, because they come from such a narrow strata of society.

"No matter how many times a privileged straight white male tech executive tells you privacy is dead, don't believe it," she told upwards of 1,000 attendees during the opening address. "It's not true."

[From Privacy still matters at SXSW | Tech Blog | FT.com]

So what can we actually do? Well, I think that the fragmentation of identity and the support of multiple personas is one good way to ensure that the privacy that escapes us in the physical world will be inbuilt in the virtual world. Not everyone agrees. If you are a rich white guy living in California, it's pretty easy to say that multiple identities are wrong, that you have no privacy get over it, that if you have nothing to hide you have nothing to fear, and such like. But I disagree. So let's examine a prosaic example to see where it takes us: not political activists trying to tweet in Iran or Algerian pro-democracy Facebook groups or whatever, but the example we touched on a few weeks ago when discussing comments on newspaper stories: blog comments.

There's an undeniable problem with people using the sort-of-anonymity of the web, the cyber-equivalent of the urban anonymity that began with the industrial revolution, to post crap, spam, abuse and downright disgusting comments on blog posts. And there is no doubt that people can use that sort-of-anonymity to do stupid, misleading and downright fraudulent things.

Sarah Palin has apparently created a second Facebook account with her Gmail address so that this fake "Lou Sarah" person can praise the other Sarah Palin on Facebook. The Gmail address is available for anyone to see in this leaked manuscript about Sarah Palin, and the Facebook page for "Lou Sarah" — Sarah Palin's middle name is "Louise" — is just a bunch of praise and "Likes" for the things Sarah Palin likes and writes on her other Sarah Palin Facebook page

[From Sarah Palin Has Secret 'Lou Sarah' Facebook]

Now, that's pretty funny. But does it really matter? If Lou Sarah started posting death threats or child pornography then, yeah, I suppose it would, but I'm pretty sure there are laws about that already. But astrosurfing with Facebook and posting dumb comments on tedious blogs, well, who cares? If Lou Sarah were to develop a reputation for incisive and informed comment, and I found myself looking forward to her views on key issues of the day, would it matter to me that she is an alter-ego. I wonder.

I agree with websites such as LinkedIn and Quora that enforce real names, because there is a strong "reputation" angle to their businesses.

[From Dean Bubley's Disruptive Wireless: Insistence on a single, real-name identity]

Surely, the point here is that on LinkedIn and Quora (to be honest, I got a bit bored with Quora and don't go there much now), I want the reputation for work-related skills, knowledge, experience and connections, so I post with my real name. When I'm commenting at my favourite newspaper site, I still want reputation - I want people to read my comments - but I don't always want them connected either with each other or with the physical me (I learned this lesson after posting in a discussion about credit card interest rates and then getting some unpleasant e-mails from someone ranting on about how interest is against Allah's law and so on).

My identity should play ZERO part in the arguments being made. Otherwise, it's just an appeal to authority.

[From The Real "Authenticity Killer" (and an aside about how bad the Yahoo brand has gotten) — Scobleizer]

To be honest, I think I pretty much agree with this. A comment thread on a discussion site about politics or football should be about the ideas, the argument, not "who says". I seem to remember, from when I used to teach an MBA course on IT Management a long time ago, that one of the first lessons of moving to what was then called computer-mediated communication (CMC) for decision-making was that it led to better results precisely because of this. (I also remember that women would often create male pseudonyms for these online communications because research showed that their ideas were discounted when they posted as women.)

It isn't just about blog comments. Having a single identity, particularly the Facebook identity, it seems to me, is fraught with risk. It's not the right solution. It's almost as if it was built in a different age, where no-one had considered what would happen when the primitive privacy model around Facebook met commercial interests with the power of the web at their disposal.

That's the approach taken by two provocateurs that launched LovelyFaces.com this week, with profiles — names, locations and photos — scraped from publicly accessible Facebook pages. The site categorizes these unwitting volunteers into personality types, using a facial recognition algorithm, so you can search for someone in your general area who is "easy going," "smug" or "sly."

[From ‘Dating’ Site Imports 250,000 Facebook]

Nothing to hide? None of my Facebook profiles is in my real name. My youngest son has great fun in World of Warcraft and is very attached to his guilds, and so on, but I would never let him do this in his real name. There's no need for it and every reason to believe that it would make identity problems of one form or another far worse (and, in fact, the WoW rebellion over "real names" was led by the players themselves, not privacy nuts). But you have to hand it to Facebook. They've been out there building stuff while people like me have been blogging about identity infrastructure.

Although it's not apparent to many, Facebook is in the process of transforming itself from the world's most popular social-media website into a critical part of the Internet's identity infrastructure

[From Facebook]

Now Facebook may very well be an essential part of the future identity infrastructure, but I hope that people will learn how to use it properly.

George Bronk used snippets of personal information gleaned from the women's Facebook profiles, such as dates of birth, home addresses, names of pets and mother's maiden names to then pass the security questions to reset the passwords on their email accounts.

[From garlik - The online identity]

I don't know if we should expect the public, many of who are pretty dim, to take more care over their personal data or if we as responsible professionals, should design an infrastructure that at least makes it difficult for them to do dumb things with their personal data, but I do know that without some efforts and design and vision, it's only going to get worse for the time being.

"We are now making a user's address and mobile phone number accessible as part of the User Graph object,"

[From The Next Facebook]

Let's say, then, for sake of argument, that I want to mitigate the dangers inherent in allowing any one organisation to gather too much data about me so I want to engage online using multiple personas to at least partition the problem of online privacy. Who might provide these multiple identities? In an excellent post on this, Forum friend Dean Bubley aggresively asserts

I also believe that this gives the telcos a chance to fight back against the all-conquering Facebook - if, and only if, they have the courage to stand up for some beliefs, and possibly even push back against political pressure in some cases. They will also need to consider de-coupling identity from network-access services.

[From Dean Bubley's Disruptive Wireless: Insistence on a single, real-name identity]

The critical architecture here is pseduonymity, and an obvious way to implement it is by using multiple public-private key pairs and then binding them to credentials to form persona that can be selected from the handset, making the mobile phone into an identity remote control, allowing you to select which identity you want to asset on a per transaction basis if so desired. I'm sure Dean is right about the potential. Now, I don't want to sound the like grumpy old man of Digital Identity, but this is precisely the idea that Stuart Fiske and I put forward to BT Cellnet back in the days of Genie - the idea was the "Genie Passport" to online services. But over the last decade, the idea has never gone anywhere with any of the MNOs that we have worked for. Well, now is the right time to start thinking about this seriously in MNO-land.

But mark my words, we WILL have a selector-based identity layer for the Internet in the future. All Internet devices will have a selector or a selector proxy for digital identity purposes.

[From Aftershocks of an untimely death announcement | IdentitySpace]

The most logical place for this selector is in the handset, managing multiple identities in the UICC, accessible OTA or via NFC. This use case is very appealing: I select 'Dave Birch' on my hansdset, tap it to my laptop and there is all of the 'Dave Birch' stuff. Change the handset selector to 'David G.W. Birch' and then tap the handset to the laptop again and all of the 'Dave Birch' stuff is gone and all of the 'David G.W. Birch' stuff is there. It's a very appealing implementation of a general-purpose identity infrastructure and it would a means for MNOs to move to smart pipe services. But is it too late? Perhaps the arrival of non-UICC secure elements (SEs) means that more agile organisations will move to exploit the identity opportunity.

In the long run, operators can still succeed in the m-payments race against Google and others - 02/06/2011

I happened to be leafing through my (signed) copy of "Services for UMTS" by Forum friend Tomi Ahonen and his colleague Joe Barrett. In section 7.10, writing a decade ago, they say that "becoming a trusted partner money community should therefore be a strategic priority for the mobile service networks". This was an obvious strategy then, and many people thought that mobiles would become wallets, and many people thought that transactional opportunities would drive the mobile operators to develop a central role in the future of payments. What's more, many people (well, me) thought that the role of the mobile in the future of payments would be so disruptive as to have an impact not just on those payments but on the future of money. Having just seen the most recent figures from M-PESA in Kenya—which show 4.33m net additions in the last financial year and 28,000 agents—this prediction seems accurate. But in the developed world, progress has been slow, because of the need to negotiate a path with existing stakeholders and incumbent players. Nevertheless, there have been a couple of key developments in the past week or so.

> *Orange last week unveiled its Quick Tap service, while rival O2 says it is lining up for a major launch in the autumn. Meanwhile, Google this week launched Google Wallet for Android phones which might soon make the traditional wallet stuffed with cards, notes and coins a thing of the past.*

[From Mobile]

In the UK, Orange and Barclaycard put the first NFC handset with SWP and SIM-based SE EMV payment application on sale. In the US, the news has centred on Google since Isis' announcement that their wallet would be open to Visa and MasterCard applications as well, and the Google announcement of their wallet running on just one handset has caused intense interest and comment. Setting aside the wallet play, and just looking at the payment application, a very significant aspect of the Google announcement (at least to people like me) was the location of the application.

> *Moreover, no mobile operator is believed to be directly involved in the project to put a Citi-issued PayPass application on the Nexus S.*

[From Citi and MasterCard]

This sharpens the focus of the operators, I think. They've been slow to get NFC out into the market and spent a couple of years developing the operator-centric model. If other people are going to put out NFC with secure elements that are not under operator control, then that operator-centric model may not support a business model. In which case, what can the operators do to stay in the payment loop. Well, one way, that I have written about before several times, is (in Europe at least) to find ways to make payments part of the "smart pipe" proposition and stop depending on third-parties (eg, banks) with expensive infrastructure.

> *French-headquartered IT services group Atos Origin has formed a joint venture with the country's three MNOs, Orange, SFR and Bouygues Telecom, to develop an internet payment platform to take on PayPal, Google and Apple.*
>
> *[From French operators, Atos form Buyster e-payment venture - Telecompaper]*

As I've been pointing out for some time, the natural way to proceed is to use the PSD to obtain a PI licence, and perhaps obtain an ELMI licence as well. This is exactly what the French operators have chosen to do, and I absolutely predict that as soon as they get the licence they will join one of the international schemes so that they can issue "cards".

> *The new company will apply with the central bank to become a registered payment service provider and aims to launch commercially before the summer.*
>
> *[From French operators, Atos form Buyster e-payment venture - Telecompaper]*

Now, this would give the operators something to offer RIM, Google and Apple other than the raw bits and a secure element that they don't want.

> *Our sources say there is a lot of internal debate at Google about its payment strategy, with some folks wanting to appease the carriers and have them become the payment options. Others disagree and are insistent that Google develop its own payment system – and rightfully so.*
>
> *[From Et Tu Bedier? Why PayPal]*

You can see why people think like this. The existing mass market payment schemes were never designed for the online world and the mobile operators (aside from the odd exception that proves the rule, like M-PESA) have been slow to seize the opportunity. Therefore, the argument goes, why wouldn't Google just do something themselves and stuff everyone else. Well, yes and no: running payment systems isn't quite as easy as it seems, and I genuinely think that if the operators develop new mobile-centric solutions then they can provide real competition to both the existing systems, the legacy infrastructure and the startups. In the long view, the operators can still succeed.

Conservative? Nein – 05/12/2011

The German payments market is huge, and growing, but very different to the UK market or the US market. This has been a problem for many people who are hoping to develop innovative services for the European mass market: schemes that might succeed in the US won't succeed in Europe's largest economy. Conversely, innovative services developed for that German market find it hard to expand abroad, as noted by a senior person at the European Central Bank (ECB).

> *I would like to mention a web merchant in Germany that offers either prepayment, cash on delivery or payment by Sofortüberweisung (an overlay service). Such slim choice and lack of competition is clearly an obstacle to the growth of e-commerce in Europe.*
>
> *[From ECB: A new voice on a familiar topic – SEPA]*

Consumers (and, it has to be said, banks) in Germany are notoriously conservative when it comes to messing about with payments. Payments cards account for only about a third of consumer spending at retail POS. It's a debit market, so almost three-quarters of those payments are made on debit cards (and about a third of those are made using ELV, which doesn't exist outside Germany). I saw a survey about this today, which had some interesting messages: it's not that consumers and retailers aren't interested in e-payments, but they are worried about security and find them too complicated.

> *Around 86% of Germans consider that security concerns are the biggest hurdle to the use of e-payment systems, according to a survey by German internet economy federation BVDW. Customers raise concerns about security and find e-payment transactions complicated (38%). Retailers complained of the lack of technology necessary for e-payment (53%) and also find that transactions are too complicated (41%). Very few respondents said they lacked interest.*
>
> *[From Germans consider e-payment important but unsafe – survey - Telecompaper]*

What could help to overcome these fears? In the German market, unlike the UK or US markets, help may be at hand from a particular source: the national ID card. Deutsche Bank said that:

> *The new ID will help to significantly boost the general environment for electronic commerce in Germany. For one thing, the new ID enables new types of online business relations and*

more efficient processes. These include, for example, opening an account via the internet or reporting insurance claims online. Some people who have harboured concerns up to now about internet security could presumably be convinced of the merits of online transactions via the use of an eID function.

[From Talking point]

Plenty of German consumers seem to be prepared to use their new eID card online (via a USB smart card interface).

The survey found that Germany's internet users would use the new ID mainly for government services (44%), online banking (38%) and online shopping (33%).

[From Talking point]

While the German card and online payment markets might be conservative, the German market for m-payments seems to be developing quickly, again in different and interesting directions from the US and UK. In the survey mentioned above, almost three quarters of respondents thought that m-payments would be "important" in the next two years. So it seems that the traditionally conservative German consumers seem ready to experiment with new mobile payments services.

The study found that Germans who are already using m-payment services or want to use such services see purchasing public transport tickets as most interesting m-payment application with 54 percent, followed by parking ticket payments with 50 percent.

[From German mobile payment skeptics decrease to 45% - study - Telecompaper]

The German mobile operators have clearly taken note and have decided to get together to accelerate the transition. Not by creating a partnership with banks (as in, for example, France or the Netherlands) but by ignoring them.

Three major German mobile operators plan to launch a trial of their own payment brand using contactless stickers in three cities before the end of the year,

[From German Telcos Plan to Launch Payment Trial with Stickers | NFC Times New – Near Field Communication and all contactless]

It has to be said that operators elsewhere (e.g., Kenya, Japan, Korea) have already discovered that given certain local circumstances, it may make more sense for them to get on develop new m-payment systems rather than work with the banks to offer the existing payment systems over mobile channels.

It made headlines in Europe, but this week's announcement that three major telecommunication companies in Germany have joined forces to bypass supporting banks in handling Mpass mobile-payment transactions is a concept not likely to quickly take hold in other countries, one industry observer says.

[From Germany Mobile]

This is a pretty ambitious initiative by the German telcos and I can't see it begin replicated by Isis or the UK mobile operators joint venture in the m-commerce apace.

The German telcos indicated they would distribute new point-of-sale equipment to shop owners when it is time to convert Mpass to NFC capabilities.

[From Germany Mobile]

I noted another interested development in the German market. As I've often joked in presentations, it makes no sense for an operator to spend money on expensive lawyers to obtain a licence for banking services when banks are so cheap! In Japan, DoCoMo simply bought a controlling stake in Sumitomo Mitsui when they wanted to offer banking services (specifically the provision of credit). Now they've done the same thing in Germany.

In 2009 NTT Docomo acquired German mobile content distribution firm net mobile, which already provides some finance-related services, including operator-billing systems, such as premium SMS payments. The Japanese firm has now committed EUR28.4 million to the German unit, most of which will be used to acquire a controlling stake in Bankverein Werther, a private German bank with strong electronic commerce and payment services.

[From Finextra: Japanese telco NTT Docomo takes stake in German bank]

Fascinating. So while the German market will undoubtedly remain conservative in the e-payment space, with some possible innovation around the online use of the eID card, it seems that it will be far from conservative in the m-payment space.

M-laundering - 15/12/2011

Forum friend Jon Matonis drew my attention to a report called "Shadowy Figures: Tracking Illicit Financial Transactions in the Murky World of Digital Currencies, Peer-to-Peer Networks and Mobile Device Payments" from the James A. Baker III Institute for Public Policy and the Center for Technology Innovation at Brookings. I couldn't help but notice this paragraph:

> It is statistically inevitable that some fraction of the more than 300 million transactions performed using M-PESA in 2010, and of the much larger number of transactions that will be performed in 2011 and future years, will not be legitimate. And some fraction of those, in turn, may involve payments that bear on American national security or law enforcement concerns.

Is this real or is it just scaremongering about new technology? I've no figures to hand, but I'm fairly certain that 99.99% of the illicit activity in Kenya involves cash (such as being shaken down by the police there, which happened to a colleague of mine earlier this year).

> About 100 Narok County council employees have been sent on a one month compulsory leave after they protested the introduction of an electronic revenue collection system at the Maasai Mara Reserve... the employees were opposing the introduction of the e-ticketing at the reserve "to reduce the rampant corruption". "The electronic ticketing system installed at the gates will deny the clerks the opportunity to handle solid cash, which they have been stealing from the council for many years," [a council spokesman] added.

> [From allAfrica.com: Kenya: Smart Card - Narok Workers Fired]

Therefore, any public policy aimed at improving the life of the average Kenyan ought to have cash reduction at its centre. I'm looking forward to seeing evidence to the contrary, but I think that the bad guys' medium of choice is the greenback. I'm sure, for example, that Democrat Congressman William Jefferson of Louisiana would not have used M-PESA had it been available in the US.

> A former US congressman famously caught with $90,000 (£54,000) in cash in his freezer, has been sentenced to 13 years

for bribery and money laundering. William Jefferson, a Louisiana Democrat who served for nearly 20 years, was convicted in August of taking hundreds of thousands of dollars in bribes

[From BBC NEWS | World | Americas | US 'freezer cash' lawmaker jailed]

So let's keep things in perspective. If you want to cut down on bribery, tax evasion and money laundering, then you need to cut down on cash. I'm not so stupid as to imagine that eliminating cash would eliminate crime, but it would at least raise the cost of it somewhat and perhaps tilt the balance in one or two places. If Congressman Jefferson had known that all of his money transfers were being recorded by AT&T, Wells Fargo or Walmoney, it may have swayed his judgement. The report goes on to say:

Given the rate of change of the digital landscape, any set of solutions constructed based on a single snapshot in time will quickly become obsolete. However, by creating the collaborations, regulatory frameworks, and technologies that reflect today's more fluid and diverse financial transaction environment, government and industry will be better positioned to address illicit transactions today and to adapt to address those of the future.

Indeed, and it's much too early in the evolution of mobile payments to say what any collaborations, technologies or regulatory frameworks will end up like. So let's focus on the big picture for the time being: end the cash menace now, and worry about mobile later. Let mobile technology make life better for people.

And the new technology pits mobile operators against banks for the same customers. Working with Equity Bank in Kenya, Safaricom has launched an account called "M-KESHO," explicitly for mobile savings, but it's met with less success. Less than 5 percent of M-PESA users have adopted it. The account bears interest and starts a credit history; it also comes with high fees for deposits and withdrawals.

[From In Kenya, Securing Cash on a Cell Phone - BusinessWeek]

That's, I think, a really important observation. When banks get involved in things, the costs go up. Banks are heavily regulated organisations that have an important function in the economy, although it's no transparently obvious that payments are one of them. But one of the reasons why banks' costs are high is that they have to "police" the system. The cost of Know-Your-Customer (KYC), Anti-Money Laundering (AML) and Anti-Terrorist Financing (ATF) rules and regulations is very high, and the higher you make it the more unaffordable the services become for the less well-off in society. And, just as an aside, the figures seem to show that the stringent KYC/AML procedures that waste everyone's time and money are not really effective in stemming the flow of criminal cash.

> *Last year, the D.E.A. seized about $1 billion in cash and drug assets, while Mexico seized an estimated $26 million in money laundering investigations, a tiny fraction of the estimated $18 billion to $39 billion in drug money that flows between the countries each year.*

> *[From U.S. Drug Agents Launder Profits of Mexican Cartels - NYTimes.com]*

So, in essence, for a massive expenditure and huge drain on the economy, KYC/AML has made to all intents and purposes no difference: it's just become a minor tax on criminal activity. It isn't only e-payments nutters like me who think like this, incidentally. Michael Levi, the respected Professor of Criminology at the University of Wales is blunt.

> *It is difficult, even with hindsight, to work out when and how the view developed that attacking the money trail was a key element in the fight against terrorism.*

> *[From Combating the Financing of Terrorism]*

Look: there is no evidence that KYC/AML/ATF has achieved anything at all in this area. The sums that terrorists require are so small, and the "black" economy so large, that here is no chance of stopping terrorism this way and the the criminals can get round them easily, but by excluding the poor from financial services the harm that over-strict regulations cause is tremendous. We need a concentrated policy effort to get cash out of their lives, and putting up barriers to mobile money shouldn't be part of them.

Comments

> The point isn't whether or not KYC/AML/ATF has been effective. The point is that a person's money should never be used as a method of tracking identity or personal behavior. The right to financial privacy, including identity and user-defined anonymity, is a fundamental cornerstone of human rights.

> *Posted by: Jon Matonis on 18/12/2011 at 18:22.*

Wonder if this whole mobile thing will catch on or not? – 16/01/2012

Most of you will, I'm sure, have read The Economist this week, which says that:

> *As mobile phones have spread, a new economic benefit is coming into view: using them for banking (see article), and so improving access to financial services, not just telecoms networks*
>
> *[From Mobile]*
>
> *Pretty uncontroversial stuff. Mobile banking, whatever. But only yesterday I nearly dropped my iPad on top of my iPhone when I read this article from the management consultants McKinsey talking about mobile banking...*
>
> *The survey of executives at 150 European banks, conducted earlier this year, confirms that mobile is here to stay. Most senior executives reject the idea that it's a fad*
>
> *[From What's the future of mobile banking in Europe? - McKinsey Quarterly - Financial Services - Banking]*

Wait, "most"? Seriously, are you kidding me? You mean there are some "senior executives" of European Banks who do think that mobile is "a fad". You'd think they'd have got the message by now, having seen their butlers and chauffeurs using these new-fangled "mobile telephones" for some time.

The McKinsey article quotes a survey from the European Financial Management and Marketing Association (EFMA) which forecasts that in five years' time, essentially, only a third of younger (i.e., under 25) customers will be using mobile banking. This is seems like a perspective from ten years ago. In fact, it was the perspective ten years ago. Chris Skinner made me laugh when he was having a go about this three years ago!

> *Robin Banks visually trembled and said, "not strictly true sir. When APACS and the industry made this decision, we didn't think mobile telephones were going to be as ubiquitous or usable as they are today."*
>
> *[From The Financial Services Club's Blog: Why mobile banking has taken so long]*

Well, no-one had perfect foresight*. But surely it must have been transparently obvious for the last few years that mobile will be the central channel for future financial services. Not an additional channel, but the central channel. The long-term convergence of the industry toward a single customer experience will take everyone toward the mobile experience. Whether you are in a branch, on the train or in bed you will have your mobile in your hand for all banking transactions.

> *Gartner's senior analyst for the financial sector has cast doubts on whether Australian banks should invest heavily in mobile banking applications and near field communication (NFC) payment systems.*
>
> *[From Gartner casts shadows on mobile banking - Strategy - Business - News - iTnews.com.au]*

Let's set aside for a moment the fact that mobile banking and mobile payments are different businesses. No, wait. Let's not.

> *Money transfers and payments over mobile phones are likely to be among the top 10 most important mobile applications by 2012, according to Gartner.*
>
> *[From Money transfer to become hottest mobile app: Gartner - SiliconIndia]*

If I've interpreted the Gartner runes correctly then, they are saying that mobile payments are worth investing in but mobile banking is not. I don't think that's right.

> *There is a strong case for Mobile Banking ROI. On the costs side, a call center transaction costs the bank $3.75, an IVR transaction costs $1.25. A transaction through the mobile channel costs the bank $0.08. So more frequent use of the mobile channel will reduce calls to the call center and IVR thereby reducing costs.*
>
> *[From Mobile]*

There's a discussion to be had about what kind of mobile banking investments banks might make, naturally. But there is no debate about whether they should have a mobile channel. As in the case of payments, the real and valuable discussion is about which parts of the value network the banks should support themselves and which they should leave to others. In the case of payments, for some banks, that will mean giving up altogether. But in the general case, it's about finding the right mixture.

> *But should banks develop their own platforms or could they share one from a provider such as Swift? After all it is all just about sending a message securely across a mobile network.*

[From Will banks avoid the mistake of DIY internet banking platforms and opt for shared mobile banking? - Inside Outsourcing]

Good question, and not one that I am especially qualified to answer. I can add to the debate by pointing out that, once again, it's been clear for some time

Imagine you are a bank with no branches or ATMs, almost three million customers and only 195 employees in total. This is eBank in Japan.

[From E-bank Japan sets mobile banking example | 13 Oct 2008 | ComputerWeekly.com]

Again, these aren't new observations, but just to reinforce their message, it's that banks won't see much return on investments in mobile if they are just pfaffing around using it as a small browser window.

It's more than just a channel, mobile solutions provide a new way to think about old processes.

[From Mobile]

Couldn't agree more. And if you do that, I strongly suspect, you will end up with a role for the mobile phone that is integral to all transactions, not only mobile ones. The role of the mobile has been discussed many times during my Centre for the Study of Financial Innovation (CSFI) Fellowship on "Identity and Financial Services", to the point where i am convinced that identity management, not payments, is the single main reason for banks to invest in exploiting the technology.

Not everyone has access to the internet. But we are well on the way to pretty much everyone having a mobile phone. And in parallel with that, what those phones can be used for is growing almost as fast.

[From Public Strategy: Channels not so much converging as crashing together]

Or, to put it another way, identity is the new money. The role of the mobile phone in financial services will be disruptive because it brings functions that do not currently exist. Using the mobile phone to look at a bank website isn't disruptive, but using the mobile phone to prove that you are a Barclays' customer, over 18 and resident in the United Kingdom is. I can make, I think, a confident prediction that the synergy between the mobile phone as a personal device and personal identity as a business function is so great that it will mean a revolution.

> *Arguably the largest disruptions in mobile phone use over existing practices have come from the very personal nature of mobile phone ownership: incoming and outgoing communication; social networking; web browsing and media consumption; search queries are now by default a private matter with sharing a matter of choice.*

[From Mobile]

In time, I expect my phone to be an indispensable part of every single banking transaction I do: that's because the mobile phone is going to become my identity **selector** and **authenticator**. Let me stress that this hardly a wild, science fiction prediction. It is based on an analysis of the technology roadmap, the business drivers and the social trends. And, of course, looking at what's happening around the world. Let's go back down under for a moment.

> *The National Australia Bank has confirmed a spike in customers using its retail banking services from internet-enabled mobile phones is likely to lead to it replacing security pass codes - now sent by SMS - with biometric voice prints within a year because of growing security concerns.*

[From CIO > What is next in mobile banking]

Again, another key synergy with the mobile channel: voice recognition and voice authentication mean major, major changes in the way we interact and transact. Mobile isn't a "fad", or an important channel or a nice to have layer on top of online banking. It's the basis for a new way to do banking.

> *It's more than just a channel, mobile solutions provide a new way to think about old processes.*

[From Mobile]

All of which, to finish, means that the evolution of security technology in the mobile world is going to have a fundamental role in shaping the way that all financial services organisations are going to do business in the future. That's why it's so important for the people putting together business strategy to understand the relationship between technology choices (some of which must seem pretty obscure) being made now around mobile architecture and infrastructure.

* Not strictly true. When the Centre for the Study of Financial Innovation (CSFI) published its first report on electronic finance, more than ten years ago, I clearly remember it highlighting the mobile phone as a key channel.

Part 3 – Money

Chapter 8: History and Future

I am convinced that the best way to understand the future of transactions is to understand their past. The complex inter-relationship between social, business and technology developments means that it is very difficult to imagine the impact of new technologies in the transaction space. But we can look back, to examine disruptive (and unexpected) consequences of previous technology revolutions and use them to imagine plausible futures for individuals, businesses and governments.

Cryptography can bring novel solutions – 03/01/2011

In some of the workshops that I've been running, I've mentioned that I think that transparency will be one of the key elements of new propositions in the world of electronic transactions and that clients looking to develop new businesses in that space might want to consider the opportunities for sustained advantage. Why not let me look inside my bank and see where my money is, so to speak? If I log in to my credit card issuer I can see that I spent £43 on books at Amazon: if I log in to Amazon I can that I spent £43 but I can also see what books I bought, recommendations, reviews and so on. They have the data, so they let me look at it. If I want to buy a carpet from a carpet company, how do I know whether they will go bankrupt or not before they deliver? Can I have a look at their order book?

Transparency increases confidence and trust. I often use a story from the August 1931 edition of *Popular Mechanics* to illustrate this point. The article concerns the relationship between transparency and behaviour in the specific case of depression-era extra-judicial unlicensed wealth redistribution...

> *BANK hold-ups may soon become things of the past if the common-sense but revolutionary ideas of Francis Keally, New York architect, are put into effect. He suggests that banks be constructed with glass walls and that office partitions within the building likewise be transparent, so that a clear view of everything that is happening inside the bank will be afforded from all angles at all times.*
>
> *[From Glass Banks Will Foil Hold-Ups]*

I urge you to clink on the link, by the way, to see the lovely drawing that goes with the article. The point is well made though: you can't rob a glass bank. No walls, no Bernie Madoff. But you can see the problem: some of the information in the bank is confidential: my personal details, for example. Thus, it would be great if I could look through the list of bank deposits to check that the bank really has the money it says it has, but I shouldn't be able to see who those depositors are (although I will want third-party verification that they exist!).

Why am I talking about this? Well, I read recently that Bank of America has called in management consultants to help them manage the fallout from an as-yet-nonexistent leak of corporate secrets, although why these secrets be prove embarrassing is not clear. In fact, no-one knows whether the leak will happen, or whether it will impact BofA, although Wikileaks' Julian Assange had previously mentioned having a BofA hard disk in his possession, so the market drew its own conclusions.

> *Bank of America shares fell 3 percent in trading the day after Mr. Assange made his threat against a nameless bank*

[From Facing WikiLeaks Threat, Bank of America]

Serious money. Anyway, I'm interested in what this means for the future rather than what it means now: irrespective of what Bank of America's secrets actually are because:

> *when WikiLeaks, a whistle-blowing website, promised to publish five gigabytes of files from an unnamed financial institution early next year, bankers everywhere started quaking in their hand-made shoes. And businesses were struck by an alarming thought: even if this threat proves empty, commercial secrets are no longer safe.*

[From Business and WikiLeaks: Be afraid | The Economist]

Does technology provide any comfort here at all? I think it does. Many years ago, I had the pleasant experience of having dinner with Nicholas Negroponte, John Barlow and Eric Hughes, author of the cypherpunk manifesto, at a seminar in Palm Springs. This was in, I think, 1995. I can remember Eric talking about "encrypted open books", a topic that now seems fantastically prescient. His idea was to develop cryptographic techniques so that you could perform certain kinds of operations on encrypted data: in other words, you could build glass organisations where anyone could run some software to check your books without actually being able to read your books. Nick Szabo later referred back to the same concepts when talking about the specific issue of auditing.

> *Knowing that mutually confidential auditing can be accomplished in principle may lead us to practical solutions. Eric Hughes' "encrypted open books" was one attempt.*

[From Szabo]

Things like this seem impossible when you think of books in terms of paper and index cards: how can you show me your books without giving away commercial data? But when we think in terms of bits, and cryptography, and "blinding" it is all perfectly sensible. This technology seems to me to open up a new model, where corporate data is encrypted but open to all so that no-one cares whether it is copied or distributed in any way. Instead of individuals being given the keys to the database, they will be given keys to decrypt only the data that they are allowed to see and since these keys can easily be stored in tamper-resistant hardware (whereas databases can't) the implementation becomes cost-effective. While I was thinking about this, Bob Hettinga reminded me about Peter Wayner's "translucent databases", that build on the Eric's concepts.

> *Wayner really does end up where a lot of us think databases will be someday, particularly in finance: repositories of data accessible only by digital bearer tokens using various blind signature protocols... and, oddly enough, not because someone or other wants to strike a blow against the empire, but simply because it's safer -- and cheaper -- to do that way.*

[From Book Review: Peter Wayner's "Translucent Databases"]

There are other kinds of corporate data that it may at first seem need to be secret, but on reflection could be translucent (I'll switch to Peter's word here because it's a much better description of practical implementations). An example might be salaries. Have the payroll encrypted but open, so anyone can access a company's salary data and see what salaries are earned. Publish the key to decrypt the salaries, but not any other data. Now anyone who needs access to salary data (eg, the taxman, pressure groups, potential employees, customers etc) can see it and the relevant company data is transparent to them. One particular category of people who might need access to this data is staff! So, let's say I'm working on a particular project and need access to our salary data because I need to work out the costs of a proposed new business unit. All I need to know is the distribution of salaries: I don't need to know who they belong to. If our payroll data is open, I can get on and use it without having to have CDs of personal data sent through the post, of whatever.

I can see that for many organisations this kind of controlled transparency (ie, translucency) will be a competitive advantage: as an investor, as customer, as a citizen, I would trust these organisations far more than "closed" ones. Why wait for quarterly filings to see how a public company is doing when you could go on the web at any time to see their sales ledger? Why rely on management assurances of cost control when you can see how their purchase ledger is looking (without necessarily seeing what they're buying or who they are buying it from) when you can see it on their web page? Why not check staffing levels and qualifications by accessing the personnel database? Is this any crazier than Blippy?

Categorising the ages of money – 08/04/2011

A few years ago, I was thinking about how to relate the changing technology of money to changes in money, and I thought it would be useful to have some rough categorisation to organise thoughts. At the time, I wrote this:

> *The era of Money 3.0 is just beginning. Its central dynamic is no longer connectivity (since everything is connected to everything else) but community.*
>
> *[From Digital Money: Money 3.0]*

After a while, I realised that my initial categorisation was insufficiently granular to organise all of the thoughts I had on the topic and all of the information I had gathered on the topic. (I'm thinking of writing a book about it, which is why I have been gathering a lot of material on the specific topic of the technology of money.) A little while ago I posted a more sophisticated idea for a categorisation of the ages of money, or money eras. This extended the framework from three to five "eras".

> *Our current era, Money 4.0, can be dated in retrospect to 1971 when Richard Nixon finally ended the gold standard and Visa introduced the Base 1 network for authenticating card payments based on the magnetic stripe. Money 4.0 is bits about bits, but we still apply the wrong mental model, and imagine it to be bits about atoms.*
>
> *[From Digital Money: Another go at categorising money technologies]*

This led me to describe the future as a new age of money, Money 5.0 I suppose, where the abstraction becomes complete and there are wholly new kinds of money that are not based on debt (or, indeed, anything else ultimately tangible) or secured in some conventional way but on relationships. Having had a bit of feedback on this, I think it serves its purpose. Obviously, some aspects are a little arbitrary—starting the information revolution in 1871—but I think I can support the dating of the communications revolution to 1971, since this is roughly when company size peaked in the UK (actually it was in 1973), and anyway it fits nicely with the narrative of the 100 year interlude that I contend still constrains our mental models of what money is and how it works.

This categorisation leads me to think that we should be looking for Money 5.0 where we see private bits, not bits about anything, becoming a means of exchange. Why private bits? Well, at this year's Digital Money Forum, we had a wonderful session on private currency, chaired by the economist Diane Coyle.

> This morning I had the privilege of chairing a fascinating session at the Digital Money Forum run each year by Dave Birch of Consult Hyperion. The speakers were Professor George Selgin of the University of Georgia, and James Turk of the Gold Money Foundation. Both were arguing, from different perspectives, for private money as a competitor to government money.
>
> [From The Enlightened Economist :: Good money, digital or analogue]

George gave a superb talk on the way in which the industrial revolution in England was hampered by a lack of circulating means of exchange, so private companies stepped in to develop new forms of industrial means of exchange (copper tokens) that help commerce and trade to grow to the great benefit of the nation. It strikes me that we are now in a similar position: we have had the post-industrial revolution but we are still using industrial money and it is holding us back. This is why the virtual empires, such as Facebook, have gone on to produce wholly private currencies—everything from the Everquest Platinum Pieces of old to the Facebook Credits of today—just as the giants of the industrial revolution (e.g. Boulton's Factory) did 200 years ago. If you think that sounds fanciful, remember that the wholly virtual economy—that has no industrial analogue—is already of significant size and growing strongly.

> More than 100,000 people in countries such as China and India earn a living by performing 'micro-tasks' in the virtual economy. Jobs include categorising products in online shops, moderating content posted to social media sites, or even playing online games on behalf of wealthier players who are too busy to tend to their characters themselves.
>
> [From Finextra: Three billion dollar virtual economy to fuel developed world - World Bank]

As the World Bank report notes, this economy is already worth several billion dollars. With better money, it could be worth several billion more.

Tomorrow's Transactions—The 2012 Reader

Anywhere, yes, but anyone, no – 08/07/2011

I've been reading Emily Nagel's book "Anywhere". She's the CEO of Yankee Group and the book is about global connectivity revolutionising business. I hope she won't be offended if I say that it's an "airport book", but it's an accurate description, at least for me, because I read it on the plane. There's something that bothers me about it, though. It has lots of stories and examples and narrative about ways in which business is transformed as it goes online, but it doesn't have "identity" or "authentication" in the index and says nothing about the identity problems that will need to be solved in order to realise the full potential of connectivity. As I've often observed before, using my favourite Kevin Kelly classification, connection isn't the problem: it's the disconnection technologies that will shape the medium-term roadmap for transforming new technology into business models: once everything is connected to everything else, the business model shifts to the creation and management of subgroups within that single, giant internet of everything.

Here, things aren't going so well. By coincidence, the Saturday newspaper that I picked up after putting down Emily's book had a technology advice column, and there was a letter from a typical consumer in it. I paraphrase:

> *I have a long list of passwords for home banking, shopping, social networks, magazines and so on. I've put them all in a Word document. How can I encrypt it?*

This is, in a nutshell, the state of the mass market today. We all have masses of passwords, we've been complaining about it since 1994, and nothing much seems to happen, largely (I think) because the costs of our time don't factor into business models. And yet... we don't seem to be evolving any better business models and we don't seem any closer to better identity infrastructure. Should we give up? No! I say we should remember William Samuel Henson.

It is sad that the name of William Samuel Henson is largely unknown today. A man of great vision, he petitioned Parliament for permission to set up an airline—with a business model largely based on post—flying to Egypt, India and China. Parliament turned his proposal down on the grounds that it was 1843 and no-one had invented airplanes yet. Henson knew this, obviously, but could see which way technology was evolving and correctly reasoned that just because he didn't know how to get an airplane off the ground (he had been involved in numerous experiments around powered flight), that didn't mean that no-one else would. And when they did, there would be a new business to build on aviation technology. So he started thinking about the businesses that would make sense and, since the post had just been invented in the UK, he looked at how that might work in the future.

This is a parable of our identity space now. We can't get the technology to work, but we know that someone will, so we're trying to think of business models (I should be clear in our case: we're trying to think of business models for our clients) that will make sense when the technology works. But we're thinking about web browsing and e-mail because these have just been invented and they're our equivalent of the post service. Maybe we should challenge ourselves harder to look at wider possibilities, start from the perspective of social networking, virtual worlds and Twitter rather than Alice sending her credit card details to Bob.

> *Facebook is better understood, not as a country, but as a refugee camp for people who feel today's lack of identity-forging social experience.*

[From Facebook]

I think many organisations should be focusing on the next phase of evolution of online business, and phase that will be fundamentally shaped by the emerging identity infrastructure. But we must be careful not to take what has just been invented (in this case, say, Facebook) and project it into the future as the key to new business models. We have to think more broadly to develop strategic roadmaps for business that can react to the general trends to exploit the technology downstream. An example? Well, it doesn't matter which social network we'll be using in five years time, we'll still need to authenticate ourselves in a more effective way that a Word file full of passwords. It isn't only me that thinks this.

> *The president wants consumers to use strong authentication, something more than user name and password, which will most likely add another security factor, say officials familiar with the project.*

[From NFCNews | Potential technologies that consumers may use for online ID]

There follows an interesting, but confused, list of options. I'd like to suggest a more straightforward taxonomy, based on a digital identity infrastructure (which doesn't exist, of course). The article, to my mind, confuses the distinct bindings between the virtual identities that exist in the Net and the real identities that are connected to. This is why it is useful to introduce the notion of digital identity in the middle. So then we get the two categories of things that might be used to solve the:

- Linking virtual identities to digital identities. The article suggests that digital certificates and PKI might be a good way to do this and I agree. Think of a digital identity as a private-public key pair ... tamper-resistance… smart cards, tokens, smart phones.

- Linking digital identities to real-world entities. The article suggests that passwords will be supplanted by biometrics.

Each of these will be a separate business that operates according to difference scale factors (scale in the first case, scope in the second). I don't know how to make them work, but someone will.

Up a gum tree – 25/11/2011

A surprising story in the national press here in the UK alerted me to an interesting phenomenon.

> *Gangs of Eastern Europeans are stealing chewing gum from supermarkets to use back home as currency. The likes of Wrigleys Extra and Airwaves are being stolen in bulk before taking it home where it has a tangible value as currency - particularly in Romania where it often given as change in shops.*
>
> *[From Eastern European gangs 'steal chewing gum to use as currency in Romania' | Mail Online]*

A reliable correspondent tells me that this also true in Zimbabwe. There are no coins in circulation, so small-scale retail trade is conducted in $1 bills. These bills circulate to the extent that they are barely recognisable. Now, for the wealthy, this doesn't matter. If you buy a bottle of scotch and get a pack of chewing gum in change, you don't really care. But if you are living on $1 per day, then the absence of change is a real problem. It's the big problem of small change that may be the source of monetary innovation. This is precisely what happened in England at the beginning of the 19th century.

> *In his excellent book "The Birmingham Button Makers", Professor George Selgin explains how the British economy faced that same problem during the industrial revolution.*
>
> *[From Digital Money: What is cash actually for?]*

What happened in that case was that there was money for the wealthy (bank notes and gold and silver coins) but there was no money for the masses. You couldn't by a loaf of bread or pint of beer with the banknote or a silver coin, so private industry stepped in to mint copper token money, and this money circulated particularly in industrial centres in order to (very successfully) facilitate wage payments and retail spending. It looks as if private industry is going to have a go in Zimbabwe to. There are several mobile money schemes there, with many banks connecting to the "ZimSwitch" mobile banking platform.

> *It is Econet, however, that might have the greatest advantage in the mobile money market. As the country's leading mobile operator, Econet's customer base makes up more than 60 percent of the mobile phone market, in addition to possessing extensive infrastructure.*
>
> *[From Mobile]*

There is now a new smart card scheme there as well, which is great. I'm a firm believer in letting competition help to consumer.

> *Smartpayment Solutions (Smartpay), in conjunction with South Africa's NET1, will on the 22nd of this month kick off a pilot project of Net1's Universal Electronic Payment System (UEPS) in Chitungwiza*
>
> *[From Bulawayo24 NEWS | Zim moves to cashless society as US$3 million deal yields fruit]*

They are planning to use a multi-purse smart card scheme for a wide variety of primarily payment-related banking services.

> *Services offered via the smart card will range from wage payments, pension payments, social grant payments, cash deposits, cash withdrawals, wage payments, balance inquiries (directly from the card), transaction lists (directly from the card), deposit without card, wallet to wallet transfers (from primary to savings and vice versa), money transfers between smart cards, bank accounts and un-banked people, third party bill payments to registered, linked and once-off merchants, amongst others.*
>
> *[From Bulawayo24 NEWS | Zim moves to cashless society as US$3 million deal yields fruit]*

This is actually the same system that is used by the Ghanaian banks, and it uses fingerprint biometrics for authentication so that it can be used to provide tolerably secure access to money in a mass market with limited literacy (although to be honest I think a lot of perfectly literate people would go for fingerprint biometrics simply as a convenience, irrespective of security.

> *The use of e-zwich money transfer recorded a significant growth in 2010 ending the year with total transfers valued at GH¢ 24.5 million. This represents a growth of 713 per cent over the 2009 figure of three million Ghana cedis.*

Tomorrow's Transactions—The 2012 Reader

[From E-zwich money transfer grows by over 700 per cent in 2010 | Business News 2011-10-01]

It is interesting note that, in comparison, mobile money seems to have a slow start in Ghana.

> *With 6 live branchless banking deployments involving 12 banks, 3 Mobile Network Operators, 2 start-ups and a government entity, the race is on in Ghana to reach the unbanked with branchless banking services. Ghana has 15 million adults and a majority of the population living on less than $2 a day, making it significantly smaller and poorer than the other countries featured in this series. It is a unique market with a regulatory focus on interoperability and interesting dynamics in the bank-MNO partnerships.*

[From Ghana: Aiming for interoperability in branchless banking]

As this CGAP note points out, this makes Ghana a fascinating case study in the co-evolution of card and mobile cash replacement.

> *Airtel is already in partnership with leading international and regional banks including Zenith Bank, United Bank of Africa, Ecobank, Standard Chartered Bank and other corporate institutions notably Databank, DSTV and Gesroto to provide customers with more convenient ways of paying bills, contributing to investments, making deposits and withdrawals... There are also more than one thousand three hundred (1300) Airtel Money dealers, and over hundred (100) branches of partners banks ensuring the widest availability of Airtel Money throughout Ghana.*

[From JOURNALISTS EXPERIENCE AIRTEL MONEY IN GHANA | Mobile]

I wonder if Zimbabwe's experience might be different? For one thing, there isn't an even slightly satisfactory cash alternative to the new technology and for another thing the market share of the leading mobile player might be able to drive adoption in a feedback loop much like M-PESA. It's definitely going to be one to watch to help us to understand the dynamics around mobile money adoption in competitive markets.

Dining out – 09/12/2011

I came across this fascinating newspaper report from "The Hartford Courant" dated 23rd October 1962. It concerns the world premiere of this movie called "The Man From The Diner's Club", which I'd googled because it was the subject of a couple of e-mails from correspondents. Here's the story:

> *The Board of Selectmen unanimously adopted an ordinance Monday night to prohibit the use of money and place the entire town on credit for a day next March 13. Columbia Pictures "The Man From the Diners' Club" will have its world premier at the Strand Theater here that day. On the day of the premiere, all transactions by local merchants will be by Diners' Club cards only."*

How fascinating! So there has already been a "No Cash Day" in the USA!

> *Mayor John E. Lynch said: "I am especially pleased to participate in this progressive experiment in the use of credit which may prove to the business world that the future method of transacting business will be through such a device as a single credit card."*

What a forward looking guy! Anyway, I was so fascinated by the story of what is, as far as I know, the first movie to feature a payment card as a plot device that I actually went online and ordered a copy. I watched it on my iPad in a hotel. It's not a very good movie, although it was quite fun seeing a young Telly Savalas hamming it up as a gangster. The plot is irrelevant, but I couldn't help noticing that at several points in the film, characters stopped the action in order to explain how a Diner's Club card worked. So someone would say "now I'm going to phone Diner's Club to check that this card is valid" and someone else would say "Hey the Diner's Club card comes with a booklet showing you all the places you can use it" or an incredulous supporting player would gasp when told that you could use a Diner's Club card to pay for an air ticket. I assume Diner's Club had sponsored the movie or some provided commercial support in order to introduce the idea of a payment card to a wider audience. The company's website says only that

> *In 1962, Hollywood released a movie by the name "The Man From The Diners Club" followed by the creation of a board game called "The Diners Club Game" by the Ideal Toy Corporation.*

> *[From Diners Club International :: Company History]*

I want that game! The only one I can find on eBay is in the US, but I'm going to see if I can find a copy in time for the Digital Money Forum in London next March.

Tomorrow's Transactions—The 2012 Reader

Listen to the words of the movie's title song! "The man from the Diner's Club is someone who's big with the girls"! You wouldn't be allowed that sort of sexism nowadays, outside of Virgin Airlines adverts anyway.

And now the trivia: the film was written by William Blatty who went on to write "The Exorcist" and features an uncredited Harry Dean Stanton as a New York beatnik.

1995 and all that – 19/12/2011

The newspapers full of their end of year staple, the predictions for the coming year. They're generally wrong, so it's fortunate that no-one pays any attention to them.

> There were things we missed – the financial crisis, the internet and wars – that have had a huge effect on the economy and budgets
>
> [From 2010 predictions from 1989: The Duchess of York never made it to the Moon - Telegraph]

Well, no big ones there. The problem with "futurology" is that it never gets it right about specific events, because it's not about predictions. It's boring to talk about sweeping, general trends - but those are things that are predictable, and the subject of futurology. So futurology is too boring for the end of year newspapers and you get ridiculous astrology-style predictions instead: people read them because they are fun, even though they know they are made up (and essentially random).

This is true in our world too. When it comes to payments and banking, the general trends have been visible for a while. But the pace of change has been surprising. Surprising, I mean, in the sense of glacial. When throwing away some old papers the other day, I came across a curious artefact from the dawn on the modern age (the modern age began with the Netscape IPO on 9th August 1995). It's a booklet from the accountants Deloitte, then known as "Deloitte Touche Tohmatsu International", called "The Future of Retail Banking—A Global Perspective". It has a section entitled "Why has the technological revolution affected banks so mildly?", which was a good question then and an even better one now.

So far as moving money is concerned, the report has a very interesting diagram in the middle of a discussion on "Internet electronic money" pointing out how much cheaper it would be to switch payments across the open Internet outside of the banking system. I wrote about this often at that time. Here's the idea:

- You could pay your gas bill by credit card or bank transfer or whatever at non-zero cost, or:
- You could pay your gas bill via e-purse at zero cost. Here's how I thought it would work, back in the days of Mondex: you log in and see that your gas company needs £32.15, you press a button, £32.15 is downloaded to from your bank account to your e-purse, £32.15 is transferred from your e-purse to the gas company's e-purse (this would have been free using the Mondex e-purse). Job done.

Therefore, I thought, everyone would rush to use e-purses (note: they didn't). But never mind 1995, this idea that money, being nothing more than data, would be switched instantly from person to person around the world goes back to the very dawn of the information age. Writing in the New Scientist magazine in 1963, in an article on "Computers and Money", R. Sayers talks about 1983, forecasting that:

> *Of course, at this stage, transfer of money would be completely automatic; the payment of a birthday fiver from an uncle to a nephew merely a matter of direction and timing of electronic impulses*

Now we all know that this didn't happen in 1983, nor for that matter in 2003, but I have every reason to be believe that it will happen by 2023. Why? Not because of cheques or debit cards or PayPal, not because of government policy or the banking system or social engineering, but because of... yes, you've guessed it, the mobile phone. There's no need to harp on about it here, but the ability of mobile phones to act as terminals as well as "cards" is the key reason why cash replacement is now a possibility, which it wasn't in 1995 no matter how cheap Mondex cards were.

The reason for bringing up this e-purse example is that I still think that e-purse to e-purse, person to person, prepaid balance to prepaid balance payments anchored by tamper-resistant hardware (i.e., SIMs or secure elements) will, eventually, change the shape of the mass market.

> *Peer to Peer payments dis-intermediating most of the links in the current payments value chain are here to stay. They will continue to develop simply because the customer can transact directly with the value producer without any infrastructure provider taking a cut.*
>
> [*From The Future of the Card Payments Industry (& much much more) in the Next 10 Years | Sysparatem*]

I've said a few times, in a few different contexts, that prepaid products haven't done as well as they should have (for a variety of reasons) but that

I think they are set to play a much bigger role in the near-future world of retail payments.

> *Prepaid products, particularly those in general purpose reloadable programs, have begun to transform the lives of millions of consumers. With the full implementation of the Durbin Amendment following the defeat of Tester's Bill, these programs may stand to see broad adoption by millions of consumers.*
>
> *[From Prepaid Programs and the Chance to Change the World - pymnts.com]*

I agree with Tim here, and so do plenty of other people.

> *From the consumer side, prepaid allows consumers to test new opportunities and options without risking a lot of money or putting their bank accounts or credit cards on the line.*
>
> *[From PaymentsJournal - When It Comes to New Payments Technology, Prepaid Will Lead the Way]*

This is a good point, but I feel there's another factor, at least in Europe. You don't need to be a bank to offer prepaid services: the combination of an Electronic Money Institution Licence (ELMI) and a Payment Institution Licence (PI) means that any company can offer a full service: an open-loop prepaid card. I suspect that many of the companies applying for these licences are doing so because they want to use new technology to deliver new services that need payment, if you see what I mean. That is, they don't expect to earn money from the payments themselves, but from the value-added services that need the payments to take place. Therefore, it's reasonable to assume that new entrants using these licenses will mean significant change in the payments world.

The 1995 Deloitte booklet does actually talk about the potential for new entrants, highlighting Microsoft (which was the spirit of the time—today all similar articles talk about Googe), telcos, payment schemes and big outsourcing companies, burt ends up by posing the interesting question as to why this sort of thing had not happened faster. Remember, this was back in 1995. Deloitte says that "one would tend to think that the possibility of a vastly-cheaper and better-specified service would create a tidal wave of change in the banking industry". Indeed, one would. And compared to 1995, we now have a great many more payment choices within the banking industry. Then we had wires, ACH, credit cards and debit cards. Now, in comparison, we have wires, ACH, credit cards and debit cards. Although to be fair in the UK we have the Faster Payment Service (FPS) so that direct credits are now (within limits) immediate. In Kenya they have M-PESA and on the internet we have PayPal, but when you look at the big picture the only really noticeable differences between then and now (in the UK) are the way in which debit cards have replaced credit cards and the decline in cheques.

Deloitte's answer to the question about the pace of change focuses on the conservative nature of consumers and their propensity to become even more conservative as they get older which, across Europe in particular, they are. But I don't think we should deduce from that the payments world in 2012 will be the same as it was in 2011, or 1995, or 1963.

> *Just weeks before the Russian Revolution of February 1917, Lenin suggested that change lay in the distant future and that he himself would not live to see it.*
>
> *[From On the Surprise Element of Revolutions : Why Tunisia and Egypt? | Yue Chim Richard Wong 王于渐]*

Revolutions are like that: they sort of sneak up on you, like the so-called "Arab Spring" or the fall of the Berlin Wall, and I don't suppose the world of banking will be any different. Now that the mobile phone has delivered a platform for change, and new entrants and banks will be competing to work on that platform, I think it's entirely reasonable to say that there will be major changes.

None of which constitutes a prediction. So I suppose I should join in the fun and make the Tomorrow's Transactions predictions for 2012. I'll stick to three of them:

1   The most innovative mass market payment product for the UK in 2012 will come not from a bank or a telco but from a retailer.

2   Mobile e-Identity rather than mobile e-Payment will be the strategic preoccupation of our financial services clients.

3   I will still have to pay for the bus using cash.

OK, that's my neck on the block. Your predictions?

Chapter 9: Payment Systems

Payments systems are integral to transactions, obviously, and right now they are subject to intense pressures, both from the legacy infrastructure and existing businesses and from the new technology and new entrants. There is so much going on it is hard to know where to focus, but I hope this selection of blog posts will help.

Pricing and payment preferences – 15/02/2011

When I was checking in to a hotel the other day, I saw a sign on the counter advising that there would be a £2.50 surcharge for paying by credit card. Naturally, I asked the receptionist about the impact of explicit pricing of payment instruments on customer preferences (remember, I do this so you don't have to). I'm interested in both why retailers do this and what impact it has on their customers.

She told me that it made no difference to business customers, because they aren't paying the bill and they always pay with credit cards anyway, and many of them pay with corporate credit cards and there are no corporate debit cards. For personal customers, most of them paid by debit card anyway, but the surcharge had pushed even more of them in that direction, to the point where probably four-fifths of personal customers paid with debit cards. Of the remainder, most paid with credit cards but some paid with cash. I thought it would be impolite to enquire further as to whether the cash payers were predominantly drug dealers, prostitutes or (given the location of the hotel) politicians.

Are these results typical? To what extent pricing drives payment choices is uncertain. In some cases (remember the case study of IKEA steering customers to debit in the UK) it clearly does, in other cases—such as my favourite case study of the parking at Woking station, where it costs 40p extra to pay by mobile, and half the customers do it—it doesn't. In theory, though, there's nothing wrong with the idea of making the costs explicit and then letting the market choose. Except... A little while back, Deborah Baxley of Capgemini (talking about the US environment) wondered if the appearance of explicit pricing for payment instruments (in itself, a good thing) might lead to a perverse outcome as merchants seek to externalise the cost of payments.

> *Merchants benefit from lower acceptance costs for debit cards. In a surprising twist, incentives and steering could have the perverse result of driving consumers toward cash and checks.*

> *[From Changing the Game in Cards - pymnts.com]*

I think this is a realistic projection, especially given that merchants don't care about the costs they impose on the rest of society by driving up the use of cash and because customers simply do not pay the real cost of cash or checks. I would love for this to change, but it's not going to. It's reasonable to wonder, in response, whether banks can use EMV, NFC, SMS or some other TLA (three letter acronym) to generate added-value around payment transactions and thus stem the shift to cash. In the case of NFC, I think they probably can. Since NFC is now entering the consumer market, it might be time to firm up on some value-adding plans. This has been clear, I think, for some time.

> *Last week Google confirmed that Android 2.3 will support Near Field Communication, as will Nokia and RIM smartphones, starting next year. And judging from Apple's recent hiring of an NFC expert, and patent filings for a probably-NFC-powered iTravel app, the iPhone 5 will boast NFC too.*
>
> *[From I Have Seen The Future, And It Looks A Lot Like Bump (Without The Bump)]*

But just because the idea has been around for some time, that doesn't mean that finding genuinely value-adding applications around technologies such as NFC is easy. But I digress: the clear problem is that when you make the pricing of things explicit, then that pricing appears in the first instance to show an increase. Hence the perverse thinking that emerges.

> *Banks have never lost out because of their gracious generosity in allowing customers to use cheque books, debit cards or cash machines for free.*
>
> *[From The end of free banking would be another slap in the face | Chris Leslie | Comment is free | guardian.co.uk]*

This is what people in the UK genuinely believe. I have no idea who they think pays for all of this stuff (hint: you do) but it does make it very difficult to introduce "real" pricing that allows consumers to make informed choices. This real pricing would take offline prepaid debit as the benchmark and then price everything else from there: debit, then probably cash, then credit, then cheques, that sort of thing. Then the consumer preferences would be meaningful.

Tomorrow's Transactions—The 2012 Reader

More on the debate about whether consumers will pay for m-payments – 21/02/2011

The outsourcing company Accenture conducted a survey to find out if consumers want to use their mobile phones for payments. Unsurprisingly, there is a strong correlation between countries where people have already used their mobile phones for payments (eg, China) and where people wanted to use their mobile phone for payments (eg, China).

> *Overall, 69 percent of survey respondents in Asia indicated they favored using mobile phones for most payments, led by Chinese consumers (76 percent) and India (75 percent), followed by Korea (56 percent) and Japan (47 percent). Outside of Asia, the next highest positive response was in Brazil, where 70 percent of consumers favored using mobile phones for most payments... asked if they had used a mobile phone to make purchases in the past six months, nearly half (47 percent) of tech forward consumers in China indicated they had, followed by Korea (42 percent) and Japan (33 percent).*

[From Interest in Mobile]

Now, the figures cannot represent a desire for mobile out of a lack of alternatives. I'm in China right now, where China UnionPay already has gazillions of cards out there and I've been using my splendid Travelex prepaid Visa card all day without a problem (some shops just wanted signature, some wanted online PIN and signature, I don't know why). Meanwhile, back home, the situation looks rather different.

> *In the U.S. and Europe, combined, however, only 26 percent of respondents favored using mobile phones for most payments.*

[From Interest in Mobile]

Oh well, I guess there's no need to spend much money on m-payment solutions in Europe or the US then, when only a 100 million or so people will want to use them, especially so in the US where another survey shows that few consumers are prepared to pay for m-payments.

> *However, the [Yankee Group] consumer survey results also indicate that less than 10% of respondents would be willing to pay extra for mobile transaction services such as mobile banking, mobile coupons and mobile payments*

[From Less than 10% of US consumers willing to pay for mobile payments • NFC World]

But hold on, I thought. If you asked consumers in the US if they were prepared to pay for debit cards then only 10% would have said yes. Yet everyone has (and uses) a debit card. Hhmmm…

So who does pay for debit cards then? In the US, where the merchant fees are much higher than in Europe, transaction fees are the major source of income. But the economics of debit are different in Europe where the already lower debit interchange and fees mean that in some countries (eg, the Netherlands) the banks lose money on every debit transaction, whereas in some countries (eg, the UK) they make a small but vanishing margin. Yet debit is profitable for banks. Why? It's because the major component of income from debit schemes is not the transaction fee but:

- The interest foregone on current accounts. Consumers who use their debit cards keep money in their current accounts to fund and the bank earns interest on that money.
- The fees earned from unauthorised overdrafts and such like. If you are out spending on your debit card and you see something that you want, you might go into the red to get it. Or you might make a mistake.

This led to an interesting twitter conversation with Forum friend Scott Loftesness. As Scott pointed out, people do, of course, pay for debit cards, but they just don't see explicit pricing. But they might, if the "Durbin debate" ends with issuers being forced to reduce interchange. The National Retail Federation (NRF) in the US has told Congress that delay to debit card swipe fee reform will save banks and their customers more than a billion dollars for every month of delay. Actually, that's not quite what they said…

> *A postponement of the debit card swipe fee reform could cost US retailers and their customers more than $1bn per month, the National Retail Federation (NRF) warned Congress.*

> *[From Debit fees regs delay could cost $1bn]*

I wrote before that if retailers think that they are being so grotesquely overcharged for debit schemes then they should start their own, and I do have to say that I am puzzled that more of them haven't already gone down the decoupled debit route, especially those with strong loyalty databases (eg, Tesco).

> *My wife's visit to Target this week prompted a revisit to the decoupled debit space. Target's value proposition: hand me your check and sign a release form, you will then receive a RedCard linked to your checking account and good for 5% off all future purchases*

Tomorrow's Transactions—The 2012 Reader

[From <u>Decoupled Debit « FinVentures</u>]

Retailers in the US, it seems, prefer a different kind of competition. A little while ago I read a piece in the Financial Times, which I couldn't find given five minutes googling, that said that the regulatory capture of $1 billion a month, most of it going to America's biggest retailers, wouldn't make any difference to the prices that consumers pay. I'm sure that's true, and I don't suppose banks pass on all of that billion to customers any more than retailers would, but let's face it: someone has to pay.

> *Banks have never lost out because of their gracious generosity in allowing customers to use cheque books, debit cards or cash machines for free.*

[From <u>The end of free banking would be another slap in the face | Chris Leslie | Comment is free | guardian.co.uk</u>]

This is what people in the UK genuinely believe. As Scott says, they see debit cards as free. There's no way you can now charge them for them. So why wouldn't mobile payment cost be bundled into the bank account fee just as the debit card cost is? Actually, I suspect that it won't be, for the simple reason that I don't believe that consumers won't pay. Mobility has value. If you had asked me whether I would be happy to pay an 8% transaction fee for using mobile payments a few months ago then I would have told you know. But that's exactly what I did last week when I went and parked at Woking station, cheerfully paying a 40p extra charge for using RingGo (a mobile payment for parking scheme) rather than use cash for a £5 parking charge.

Scott asks how mobile payments can deliver additional value to the merchants. I would say that in my recent dealings with issuer/acquirer/merchants, three general themes have emerged (I stress that these are general: they don't relate to any specific project we are involved in).

- The first is that retailers like mobile wallets. Anticipate lower online abandonment rates with mobile wallets and I suspect they may also anticipate a higher average sale than with cash in physical environments.
- The second is that retailers expect to be able to use these mobile wallets to interact directly with consumers through loyalty products, coupons, special offers and so on.
- The third is that mobile should mean fewer disputes and chargebacks, which cost retailers time and money.

All of which means that the retailers will incentivise customers to use mobile, so customers will use it even if it costs them an explicit fee versus the implicit fee associated with debit. Ultimately, I'm pretty sure, that the fact that only 10% of consumers say they will pay doesn't mean anything.

There's still no end-date for SEPA – 24/03/2011

After sitting in on a few sessions at the International Payments Summit 2011—and in particular the excellent Chatham House session chaired by Forum friend Ruth Wandhofer of Citi—I have to say that in all honesty my professional opinion is that it's a mess. The ECB predicted that SEPA would erode payment margins in Europe by 5-10% (eventually) but that banks and customers would benefit from lower costs in the long run. Yet the cost burden is crushing. According Equens, there are 200 different formats for SEPA Credit Transfer (SCT) and SEPA Direct Debit (SDD) messages. They further estimate that since both the XML message formats and the EPC rulebooks are updated every year, it means 20-30,000 man-days per annum just to maintain the software. And that's for just one processor. What's more, SEPA is reducing competition (and therefore increasing costs) in local markets long before the projected cost savings arrive.

One way to do something to bring on these cost savings might be to enforce and end date. When I had the honour of chairing ECB board member Gertrude Tumpel-Gugerell in Brussels last November, she said that an end-date for SEPA would be her first New Year's resolution for 2011. Well all I can say after IPS 2011, is good luck Gertrude. If there is going to be an agreed end-date this year, I'd lay a pound to a penny that it will be 2019. Frankly, who knows what will have happened to the payments business by then?

Gertrude and others have said that one of the goals of SEPA was to encourage innovation to the payment sector, but has it? Tom Noyes excellent analysis of the current environment ends with three key constraints on innovation.

> *Innovators are dependent on local national relationships to launch a product;*
> *SEPA creates harmonization, but country specific laws and regulatory guidance are unique;*
> *ECB initiatives (ex. See ELMI) create opportunities for non-bank participation in payments, but SEPA has removed all margin from the business.*

> *[From Payments Innovation in Europe « FinVentures]*

I'm not so sure about that last point. SEPA has removed all of the margin if you are bank, but if you are not a bank and are not dependent on their high-cost, highly-regulated infrastructure. All of these issues mean that I can't help but let an evil thought wander in to myconsciousness, a thought-crime of the most serious degree. What is SEPA doesn't happen? What if it ends up defining the standard for pan-European payment infrastructure that is vanishing? Worse still, what if there are sinister forces at work to torpedo the project?

> *The EC will "effectively derail the entire Sepa project" if upcoming regulatory intervention on migration end dates does not include deadlines for phasing out national schemes, says the European Payments Council.*

> *[From Finextra: EC migration plans would 'derail the entire Sepa project' - EPC]*

I don't want to bore foreign readers with the ins and outs of the relationship between the Commission and the EPC, but I will say that it is not good. If the Commission regulatory "intervention" were to be to mandate the EPC rulebooks with a fixed deadline, then banks (I'm pretty sure, having spoken to quite a few bankers about this) would grin and bear it. In some countries (eg, Germany) it might be an unpopular decision, but it would get done. Instead, the Commission seem to want to tinker with what the EPC has been going but without an end date? Why? (Answer: because they are politicians responding to national interests.)

Personally, I think the Commission are derailing the train taking us to lower costs in other ways as well, such as by forcing retailers to accept euro coins and high-value euro banknotes, thus promoting the least efficient and most expensive payment mechanism instead of electronic alternatives that would be better for society.

Making payments is easy, taking payments is hard – 02/04/2011

On "Slate" there was an article entitled "Paying With Your Phone Is Awesome, Because … Because" with a sub-headline:

> *We already have a perfectly fine way to make non-cash payments.*

> *[From Paying by phone is insecure and unnecessary. - By Farhad Manjoo - Slate Magazine]*

Really? That didn't seem to be the case in my household this morning when my wife was hunting for the chequebook because she needed to pay for a school trip and settle a dentist bill. I wanted to pay my son's school £20 on Thursday morning because he was going on a school trip, and I turned the house upside down looking for the chequebook, which I couldn't find. I couldn't pay them with a debit card, or cash (I didn't have £20), or credit card, or bank transfer or any of the other "perfectly fine" ways to make the payment. Which boring tale illustrates the real point, that is, not that...

> *We already have a perfectly fine way to make non-cash payments.*
>
> [*From* Paying by phone is insecure and unnecessary. - By Farhad Manjoo - Slate Magazine]

...but that we don't have a perfectly fine way to take **non-cash** payments. Mobile payments will be a disruptive force because the devices will serve both roles. Richard Johnson of Monitise made this point very well at the Intellect Payments Workstream meeting that I chaired last week. But it isn't only the cheque that is set for extinction because of mobile. Anthony Jenkins, the chief executive of Barclaycard (Britain's biggest card issuer), said that

> *"In 50 or maybe even 10 years' time, we will still be using cash but I don't think we'll have plastic. It is comparable to the move from CDs to MP3 music files," he said. "If I had said 10 years ago that you couldn't pay with a cheque at the supermarket, you wouldn't have believed me. That is now the reality, and we see plastic cards going the same way."*
>
> [*From* End of the road for flexible friend as Barclaycard goes 'contactless']

Now this seems a little far-fetched on first reading. But perhaps, once mobile payments cross the cusp into the mainstream (at, I would guess, around a 25% penetration in the consumer market), the move away from plastic could take place in a generation, much as the move into plastic did from the introduction of the magnetic stripe in the early 1970s.

> *Coins, paper money and plastic cards are going to be the next casualties. Don't believe me? Then visit Korea. The only people who own a plastic credit card there are the ones who travel abroad; everyone else uses their mobile phone.*
>
> [*From* Peter Cochrane's Blog: Near-field tech edges closer | CIO Insights | silicon.com]

The combination of mobile and contactless seems to accelerate the transition: individually they are great, but together they are something special. Mobile payments by themselves have been around forever and have made little impact in the physical world (except for special niches like car parking). I still can't use my mobile to buy a bottle of cold water from a machine in the Tube.

> *The first case of a mobile phone being able to be used to handle a payment was in 1998 as an experiment in Espoo Finland just outside of Helsinki, where two Coca Cola vending machines were installed with a mechanism to accept payment by SMS text messaging*
>
> *[From Communities Dominate Brands: End of Cash? First blog in a series examining the pending doom of minted coins and printed banknotes]*

Adding contactless transforms the proposition from fiddling about sending text messages to a quick tap. As far as I can tell, from the pilots that we have been involved in, customers are not a barrier. They like it. So why doesn't my phone have NFC in it right now, and why doesn't the drinks vending machine on the Tube have a reader?

> *Why is it taking so long? As with Faster Payments, the problem lies with the marketing teams in the major banks.*
>
> *[From The innovative world of UK payments]*

I disagree. I'm no fan of marketing departments, but the problem with mobile payments is different. Banks have never had to deal with payments in this way before: they can control ATMs and POS terminals, EMV cards and FPS. But they don't control mobile, and in particular they don't control the Secure Element (SE), the tamper-resistant hardware that transforms mobile phones from being content devices to transaction devices. There are different ways of dealing with this, but I think it is fair to reflect that the specific tension between banks and mobile operators remains problematic. In some countries they are joining forces, in others they are forging bilateral agreements, in others they are going their own way.

> *While credit card companies might need the carriers to get into mobile payments, they might soon learn that the carriers don't need them.*
>
> *[From In mobile payments, credit]*

Indeed they don't, but that has no relevance to the Isis initiative that is the subject of that post because:

> *Verizon, T-Mobile and AT&T are entering into an agreement to let customers pay for products with their smartphones... they are*

not working with Visa, MasterCard, or American Express on this venture. They're not working alone either, instead partnering with Discover and Barclays on this venture.

[From In mobile payments, credit]

Hhmmm. So in this particular case, the carriers are partnering with a credit card company and a bank. So do they have somewhere to go? Well, let's return to the point. We don't have a perfectly fine way of taking non-cash payments, but soon we will because of mobile phones. And there are some dynamic go-ahead organisations that have already recognised this.

The local Girl Scout group there has teamed up with Intuit to accept credit cards using the company's GoPayment app (and accompanying card reader) for iOS and Android

[From The Gay Geek: GIRL SCOUTS IN OHIO TAKING MOBILE PAYMENTS FOR COOKIES]

Back in the 1980s, there were people who said that mobile phones would never sell because there were payphones everywhere. The POS terminal of 2011 is the payphone of 1981.

Banks and mobile operators are working together on NFC, but will they "win" in the new value network – 13/04/2011

France has been in the forefront of the NFC revolution, with an early commitment to cross-industry co-operation, considerable work on standards and models and an aggressive timetable for getting phones into the market. Remember this?

A dozen French cities plan to launch wide-scale contactless payment and information service on mobile phones with the backing of the ministry of industry, reports Les Echos. The city projects approved under the initiative will receive state assistance for consultancy and engineering, but no other subsidies are planned at this stage.

[From Aid from French Ministry of Industry for mobile contactless]

You will undoubtedly recall that a few months later, the French mobile operators decided to get together with a processor and form a mobile payments proposition to launch a serious assault on the banks' retail payment franchise.

Orange, SFR, Bouygues Telecom et Atos Origin créent une société commune pour proposer une plate-forme unique de paiement en ligne, sécurisée par le mobile.

[From Union sacrée des opérateurs mobiles dans le paiement sur Internet - OPERATEUR DE TELECOMMUNICATIONS SERVICES INFORMATIQUES ATOS ORIGIN FRANCE TELECOM SFR BOUYGUES TELECOM]

Well they've made their first assault on the enemy positions and have been granted a PI licence. Why would they bother, you might wonder, when polls show that the majority of consumers don't want to use mobile payments?

The 59% of consumers who were against the idea, meanwhile, gave their reasons as: Security (79%)

[From Most French consumers not in favour of mobile payments • NFC World]

The answer is, of course, that consumers don't know what they are talking about and it's a waste of time asking them about anything new. Whatever they might say a priori, in all of the pilots and trials that we have been involved in, they really, really, liked mobile proximity.

But there are some real issues, and we need to address them.

Dead phone batteries. Wrong merchant terminals. Terminals turned off. Terminals unrepaired. No terminals at all. These and other, less obvious glitches suggest contactless technology may not be the mobile payments panacea for tattered magnetic stripes and other problems with plastic cards.

[From Mobile]

Well, yes and no. (I am a consultant, after all). Let's have a look at these

Dead phone batteries. NFC is interoperable with the existing contactless payments and ticketing systems. As you may have noticed, your Oyster card doesn't have a battery in it: that's because it is powered through the electromagnetic field of the terminal you touch it to, and the same is true for the NFC interfaces in phones: if the phone has no battery you may not be able to access your m-wallet to check your transactions, redeem coupons and so on, but you will be able to to use it pay in a shop and ride the subway.

Wrong merchant terminals. I don't think this will be an issue. Right now there are some problems with some cards not being accepted in some terminals, but this is the result of standards problems three or four years ago. The contactless EMV standard should interoperate seamlessly. Some of the terminals are certainly "wrong" from the point of view of consumer experience, but that's a different thing.

Terminals turned off. Fair enough, I do see this from time-to-time. But it's a teething problem. There is a problem with terminals being turned off **after** the merchant has rung up the purchase and then having press some more buttons to turn it on, but that's an implementation issue.

Terminals unrepaired. I don't think this is a long term problem. Contactless terminals (since they have no slot or contacts) are considerable more reliable in practice than contact or stripe terminals. Experience from other sectors suggests to me tha tthe cost of maintaining an estate of contactless terminals is less than half the cost of maintaining an estate of conventional terminals.

No terminals at all. This, I think, is the real problem. When I was last in the US, I saw contactless terminals in places where they didn't really have much impact, like in CVS. But in the places where contactless would have really helped and speeded things up—BART machines, airport carts, Coke machines and so on—nothing.

The point is, that those are real issues that do need dealing with, whereas what the public says are their concerns, such as about the security are, in my opinion, not real issues and it should be handled through marketing communications. Oh, wait...

> *85% of users said they considered the protocols for operating with the NFC system to be sufficiently secure.*
>
> *[From Sitges trial results: Consumers pay more often and spend more with NFC phones than with cards • NFC World]*

This must be a translation from Spanish, because I'm not sure that "protocols for operating with the NFC system" translates properly in English, but it's good news all the same. I'm not saying that everything is perfect in the NFC world. Even in France, where progress has been slow despite the commitment of major banks and operators. It's still a new technology.

> *The problems are one of the main reasons bank Crédit Mutuel-CIC has held back on launching its m-payment service, according to Patrice Hertzog, payment systems manager for Crédit Mutuel-CIC. He said it has been difficult for the bank's trusted service*

manager, Gemalto, to set up and manage the bank's PayPass application on SIM cards produced by other vendors, such as Oberthur Technologies.

The problems have occurred despite much standards work by the French Association Française du Sans Contact Mobile, or AFSCM, and prior trials involving multiple French banks, mobile operators and vendors.

[From 'Open' Battles Break Out Among NFC Vendors Over Android]

To be honest, this suggests that vendors are not building TSMs from scratch based on the new standards but are putting wrappers around their existing card personalisation systems. That sort of thing is, to me, more of a real issue than incorrectly worrying about what the public think, but whatever. Things are moving. Even in the US, the new technology is getting a foothold and there will soon be TSMs there too.

The joint venture formed by U.S. mobile carriers to launch NFC-based mobile payment... has selected France-based Gemalto to download and manage payment and other secure applications on NFC phones to be used in pilots expected to be held in three to four cities during the second half of 2011

[From U.S. Carrier Joint Venture Chooses a Trusted Service Manager | NFC Times – Near Field Communication and all contactless]

There's plenty of activity in the US as elsewhere, and since I've been looking at the US for clients recently I was interested to read about the work done by the Federal Reserve Banks of Atlanta and Boston. This work suggests that the success factors for the US will rest on the evolution of an open eco system for NFC.

The mobile infrastructure would likely be based on Near Field Communications (NFC) contactless technology resident in a smart phone and merchant terminals.

Ubiquitous platforms for mobile should leverage existing rails, including the ACH network for non-card payments, and support new payment types that meet emerging needs. Some form of dynamic data authentication would be at the heart of a layered mobile payments security and fraud mitigation program.

...Trusted Service Managers should oversee the provision of interoperable and shared security elements used in the mobile phone.

[From Mobile]

On that final point, things are already moving.

The joint venture formed by U.S. mobile carriers to launch NFC-based mobile payment... has selected France-based Gemalto to download and manage payment and other secure applications on NFC phones to be used in pilots expected to be held in three to four cities during the second half of 2011

[From U.S. Carrier Joint Venture Chooses a Trusted Service Manager | NFC Times – Near Field Communication and all contactless]

So there's plenty of activity in the US as elsewhere and plenty of organisations are looking at how the move to mobile proximity may impact their businesses.

A white paper that outlines the survey findings, including how the most forward-thinking financial institutions are building a business case for mobile payments, is available at www.fiserv.com/mobilestrategy.

[From Forward-Looking Financial Institutions Focused on Mobile]

I couldn't help but think, as I read this, that the very act of building a business case for something like this is fundamentally backward-looking, trying to shoehorn something that is the basis of a new value network into the existing business models. The report says that the factors that the FIs evaluated across these business lines included customer retention and profitability, cost reduction, revenue generation and retention, increased customer engagement and competitive parity. When I looked at the revenue generation part of it, though, it only referred to revenue generation in terms of debit card transactions and keeping the connection to the DDA. This isn't how forward-looking organisations are thinking about revenue generation from mobile payments, they are thinking about delivering entirely new products and services that are simply not possible in conventional (i.e. card) environments, generating revenue from things that banks don't do.

Google is to run tests of mobile payments at stores in New York and San Francisco in the summer, according to anonymous sources cited by Bloomberg. The search engine giant will pay for installation of thousands of NFC cash-register systems from VeriFone Systems at merchant locations, one source told the wire.

[From Finextra: Google]

Well, well. So while financial institutions are agonising over the business case, Google is giving out the terminals for free. It's not hard to see why: they don't care about the miniscule margins on the payment transaction and arguing about how to slide and dice the merchant fee, they care about building new business around knowing who is buying what and where. So leadership in the NFC space is may well shift away from the payment incumbents. Perhaps the answer to the age-old question about whether banks or operators would control the mobile payments space is… neither.

Mobile payments are an important tool for financial inclusion – 15/04/2011

As a chap named Bill Gates wrote recently:

Technology can be a major force to advance financial inclusion, which can help improve the lives of the poor...

He's absolutely right, of course. People who are trapped in the cash economy are the ones who are most vulnerable to theft and extortion, most likely to lose their hard-earned notes and coins or have them destroyed by monetary policies, pay the highest transaction costs, lack credit ratings or references and (in an example I heard from Elizabeth Berthe of Grameen at the Digital Money Forum this year) most likely to have their life savings eaten by rats. So what should be done? Well, having governments take the problem seriously and set targets is a good start.

The RBI target of ensuring 100% financial inclusion in villages of 2,000 plus population in the state by March 2010... banks could adopt the RBI's advice of making use of the business correpondent-BF model, as per the guidelines, to extend the banking services.

This was in keeping with the RBI's decision to launch a renewed drive for opening up of no-frills accounts in respect of families who do not have a bank account, on the basis of the data relating to the public distribution system.

[From Banks urged to take steps to ensure 100% financial inclusion - dnaindia.com]

To continue with this specific case, it has proved very difficult to translate these targets into action in the heavily-regulated Indian market.

> *Adding to their presence, the cost of operating a bank account and the cost of transaction for banking services —which includes deposits, withdrawals, credit and other banking products — is not only high for the consumers but also for the banks.*

[From Financial Inclusion In India]

As far as I can see, banking is a really expensive and really inflexible way to obtain inclusion, and as we all know, there are better ways to obtain inclusion with new technology. In particular, new technology when combined with the business correspondent model mentioned in connection with the RBI guidelines above ought to be delivering more transformation.

> *A Wharton School study pegs the cost of a transaction at a bank branch at around $1 (Rs. 45). At an automated teller machine, it goes down to about $0.40. And done through business correspondents, the cost drops even lower to $0.10.*

[From Banking on technology to bridge financial inclusion gap - Economy and Politics - livemint.com]

Another way forward might be to treat mobile payments as a first step on the ladder to inclusion and try to find a way to bring mobile payments to the mass market and then use the mobile payment platform to deliver other financial services. Naturally, give our work on the project, I can't resist highlight M-PESA in this context.

> *The fact that Vodafone has demonstrated that they can duplicate the success of mPesa in other countries, is of significant importance. This means that the Kenya experience was not a fluke, and that Vodafone has learned what it takes to make these roll-outs work.*

[From Mobile]

I hate to keep going on about M-PESA, but our experiences advising Vodafone in the early days of this project contain a number of useful lessons, in particular about the relationship between new entrants and regulators. But I wanted to make a different point.

A couple of years ago we were doing some work for a client who was thinking of developing something like M-PESA. I won't name them, obviously, but I hope no-one will mind if I mention one of our recommendations. Our Head of Mobile Money, Paul Makin, who worked on M-PESA when it was still whiteboard scribble, was asked what he would have changed in the original specification if he had had the wisdom of hindsights, and his top priority was APIs for MIS access. This is why I wasn't surprised to see this in a report from the front line.

> *Data from M-PESA cannot directly be imported into the management information systems (MIS) at MFIs. For KADET, this means all payments made through M-PESA have to be manually input into their MIS, another opportunity for human error to affect the process.*

[From Mobile]

(I strongly urge you to read this short and fascinating article about real experiences linking to M-PESA in the field, by the way.) Taking the mobile payments transactional data and providing corporate access is, I think, a key plank in the inclusion strategy. In Kenya, financial institutions have already started to use M-PESA transaction data as a substitute for a credit rating when looking at providing loans and I'm sure that new opportunities will arise due course: with the wisdom of hindsight, better corporate interfaces would have accelerated this process.

The disaster in Japan has lessons for payments – 04/05/2011

Someone interrupted one of my rants against cash the other day by pointing out that in the last resort, cash is the only payment mechanism that society can depend on. Their trump card was reference to the aftermath of the recent Japanese cataclysm, where following a magnitude 9 earthquake and a tsunami, the nuclear reactors didn't melt down but the payment system did.

I think this is wrong lesson to draw from it. Yes, there were some temporary problems with the card networks because of the disruption, but it's important to note that this did not impact all cards: Japan has quite a rich retail payment landscape and I saw Nobuhiko Sugiura, Associate Dean of Chuo University Business School, give a good overview of the current situation at last year's *E-Money, Cards and Payments* conference in Moscow. He said that e-money usage in Japan is growing rapidly but still a small fraction of total consumer spending (¥1 trillion out of a total of ¥300 trillion, a 300% increase in the last three years). A third of the population use e-money and half of them (ie, one sixth of the population) use it in their phones. It's a competitive market, centred on non-banks because the Japanese banks have no real interest in handling small payments because of cost. The non-banks, as I've often noted on this blog, have different business models, not based on transaction fees. The railways, for example, don't expect to earn anything from their e-money system, it's about reducing their costs. In comparison, convenience stores want to issue e-money to reduce their cash float. The bottom line is that the use of cash at POS in Japan is "already falling" because of e-money.

After the earthquake and tsunami, the offline electronic money systems (such as Edy and nanoco) carried on working so long as there was power and the backup battery systems or generators were working, so you could still pop round to 7-Eleven and buy your staples. In fact, it was people who kept their money in cash who suffered greatly.

> *In Japan, lots of people—especially older people—keep their life savings in cash in their homes. (The country's banks pay very low interest rates...) This is all well and good, until a tsunami destroys your home and washes your money out to sea.*
>
> *[From Schneier on Security: Unanticipated Security Risk of Keeping Your Money in a Home Safe]*

That's not to say that people didn't **want** cash after the event.

> *The tragedy playing out in Japan this past week highlighted that in times of crisis, there's nothing like cash in hand as the universal method of payment... Mizuho, Japan's second largest bank, reported outages in its payments and ATM networks - coincidentally as demand for cash surged.*
>
> *[From The end of cash for payments? Not so fast! - Microsoft Perspectives on Payments and Core Banking in Financial Services - Site Home - MSDN Blogs]*

So they wanted cash, but did they **need** it? In this kind of catastrophe, where the online POS network goes down but the ATM network stays up and the ATMs remain stocked with notes, you could see people going and withdrawing cash. But suppose there are no ATMs?

Imagine that there was a magnitude 9 earthquake and a tsunami in Woking (unlikely - our last natural disaster was an ice age in 18,000 BCE) and when I go round to Waitrose to buy some bottled water and rice my John Lewis MasterCard proves useless because the acquiring network is down and the ATM proves useless because the ATM has no power. The store manager at Waitrose can leave the food to rot on the shelves or he can accept a signed IOU. He could accept no sale because of flaws in the electronic payments or he could develop a rational fall-back strategy. We discussed this a couple of years ago, with reference to the famous case study of the Irish bank strike.

The owners of shops and pubs knew their customers very well and so were perfectly capable of deciding whether to accept cheques (or just IOUs) from those customers. And since the customers also knew each other very well, they too could make sensible decisions about which paper to accept.

[From <u>Digital Money: Payments without banks</u>]

If I was the manager of Waitrose after the Woking earthquake, I would simply accept payment by writing down card numbers, or photocopying driving licences, or taking pictures of customers, or whatever. The core of the issue is identification and trust, not the payment instruments. As many media commentators noted, society in Japan did not collapse. My conclusion: natural disasters are not a convincing argument for cash.

What should the "mainstream" think about Bitcoin? – 16/06/2011

Anyone in the e-payment space will not have failed to notice the attention that Bitcoin has been attracting over the last few weeks. I have to say that I was surprised by the interest from journalists—I was even interviewed for the Wired podcast and for New Scientist—for what is, after all, pretty small potatoes. Thanks to its open and transparent nature, it's easy to see just how big the Bitcoin economy is. This is how it looked on one of the biggest exchanges on 18th May 2011 when I was talking to a journalist:

Last Price: 7.285; High:7.98; Low: 6.9799; Volume: 34428

[From <u>Mt Gox - Bitcoin</u>]

So a quarter of a million dollars in trades, although you can't tell how much is people shifting bitcoins between their own accounts and how much is new money coming in. That's not a huge business. Yet in some of the more hysterical reporting—the most dangerous idea ever, etc etc—you'd think that China was switching its reserves from dollars to bitcoins.

Because on Friday, the Bitcoin experienced a rather dramatic drop. In the words of one anonymous commenter: "it looks like it lost 1/3 of its value in the last 24 hours. Lots of big sells, complaints of liquidity, and pissed off nerds."

[From <u>FT Alphaville » Bitcoin</u>]

A couple of weeks later, then, the value has fallen and the first bitcoin heist has been reported.

In the first Bitcoin theft of its size, a user has lost 25,000 BTC — or nearly $487,749 at market rates — to an unknown thief.

[From Close to US$500k stolen in first major Bitcoin]

As I somewhat uncharitably posted on Twitter, "help I want my anonymous, untraceable digital cash back!". Now we read that Bitcoin is dead, it's a scam, it's a bubble etc etc. So what's the truth? What strategy, if any, should stakeholders in the e-payments space consider?

> *The only thing that's even kept Bitcoin alive this long is its novelty. Either it will remain a novelty forever or it will transition from novelty status to dead faster than you can blink.*

[From The Underground Economist, Why Bitcoin]

I'd actually started writing something about Bitcoin a while back, when twitter friends pointed me to a paper "Mobile" by Mahil Carr which says that (with no evidence at all to support the assertion) "mobile payments have to be as anonymous as cash transactions" and I'd been involved in a subsequent discussion about whether bitcoin might be suited to this environment. I couldn't help but observe that cash is the wrong benchmark: it isn't as anonymous as some people think.

> *A state police trooper was called to the Subway after the owner said one of her employees found three "obviously counterfeit" $20s in the safe. The owner checked the surveillance video and saw one of her employees, the 17-year-old boy, take bills from his pocket and exchange it for money in the cash register.*

[From subway counterfeit money: subway counterfeit money, teens charged with making fake money on computer scanner - mcall.com]

In a world of mobile phones, twitter and CCTV, anonymity is a high bar to set. In the virtual world, however, anonymity can be an implementation choice, should it be a requirement for a payment system. Personally, I don't think it is. Transactions need to be private, not anonymous, and that means a different set of design principles. In all of my experience, even during my days as a firm proponent of anonymity as a key element of retail transaction schemes, I never saw the slightest demand for this from any of the stakeholders, including consumers. Nevertheless, that doesn't mean that new technology could not, quite easily, lead to entirely new ways of making payments recognising the fact that the underlying technology has changed beyond all recognition in the previous generation.

> *Visa processed 37 billion transactions in FY2008, or an average of 100 million transactions per day. That many transactions would take 100GB of bandwidth, or the size of 12 DVD or 2 HD quality movies, or about $18 worth of bandwidth.*

[From Cryptography, Law and Privacy Blog: Re: Bitcoin P2P e-cash paper]

Will Bitcoin be the new technology to revolutionise money? To answer that, I have to step back a little. Generally speaking, I think there is a problem with language, because people (I mean normal people, not people like us) never think about what money is or how it works. Sterling (the currency) could continue to exist even if there were no notes printed by the Bank of England or coins produced by the Royal Mint. People could sign contracts for Sterling payments, but those payments would be commuted for execution: when the payment falls due, the counterparties agree on a mechanism for exchange (which might be Dollars in a bank account, Euro bank notes or cowrie shells). Why would they, then, sign a contract in Sterling in the first place? Well, it's because they expect the currency to serve as a means for deferred payment in that its value in the future is predictable. I'm not saying that this always works well, because currencies are not as stable as might be hoped, but that's the theory.

Now let's move on to this specific implementation. Bitcoin is a decentralised, peer-to-peer means of exchange. If you have a bitcoin, which is just a string of numbers, you can send that bitcoin (or a subdivision of it) to anyone else on the interweb. If you want to understand how Bitcoin works, a good place to start is the original paper on the topic, "Bitcoin: A Peer-to-Peer Electronic Cash System" by Satoshi Nakamoto. I'm no expert on cryptography but there's no reason I know of to question the basic idea: use a computationally difficult challenge to create strings of bits that it's hard to make but easy to copy, then use digital signatures for transactions. I get my bitcoin (a string of bits) and then in order to transfer them to you I add a digital signature and send them to you. Every time we do a transaction, we tell (essentially) everybody else that the bits now belong to you. The closest analogy is the stone currency of the island of Yap, in the South Pacific. The huge stones that represented money never went anywhere, people just remembered who they belonged to.

Every transfer of ownership is public knowledge, and the physical stone can stay in place.

[From Quezi » How is Yap stone money similar to Bitcoin]

Rather like Bitcoin, in some ways. So far so good. But why would people use Bitcoin? There seem to be three key reasons: one is that they want a cheap, irreversible online means of exchange (cash for the 21st century), another is that they want an anonymous means of exchange (coins for the 21st century) and yet another is that they want to use of non-government currency because they don't trust governments to manage money properly. Let's have a quick look at each of these.

Frictionless low-value payments

Now, having been involved in a previous attempt to create a global, decentralised, peer-to-peer means of exchange that addressed the first two of these issues, Mondex, I'm naturally interested to see how Bitcoin develops. I'm frankly sympathetic to many of its goals, because I too believe that a "frictionless" means of exchange for the online world would stimulate a new era of trade, and therefore prosperity. In an essentially frictionless system, where the transfer of value is simply the transfer of bits, the key problem to overcome is that of "double spending". In other words, if I send you some value (bits), how do you know that I haven't already sent that value (ie, a copy of those bits) to someone else? There are a number of different approaches.

- The usual solution is to have a central register.

- The Mondex solution was to use tamper-resistant hardware (smartcard chips) to store the balances.

- The Bitcoin solution is to distribute the transaction record across the network (every node knows every transaction), which works provided that the timestamps can be co-ordinated properly (otherwise the nodes wouldn't know the order of the transactions). When you get a bitcoin, it takes a few minutes before you can spend it again because the network needs to be updated.

Which is best? It's not really the topic of this post, but I'd say a combination of 1 and 2: a central register plus tamper-resistant hardware so that low-value payments can be handled quickly, offline in some environments.

Anonymity

What the general public want is privacy, not anonymity. If I lose my wallet, I want my money back. This is why I always carry prepaid cards when I travel, rather than carrying cash. In fact I've just been through the very process of getting my money back because I gave my son a prepaid Euro card to use on a school trip in Spain (a Thomson MasterCard) and he lost it when there were still €70 on the card. No-one else can use that card (they don't know the PIN and it has no name on it so they can't pass AVS online) and I am getting the money back. Personally, I think this is closer to the kind of cash that makes sense in the new economy. It's economically infeasible (although not computationally infeasible) to track and research every payment, but when something goes wrong it can be restored. And if I did use the card for some illegal purpose, the police could get a warrant and Thomson would of course point them to me.

I'm not sure that I want to live in a society where unconditional anonymity exists for payments. I don't want the bad guys to be able to operate with impunity. But neither do I want every little transaction I make trawled by corporates, the media, and the government. The solution has to be payment systems with privacy built-in, so that

Private Currency

This may well be the most contentious area for debate. I am a Hayekian, in that I would prefer to see a system of competing private currencies rather than government monopolies, because I think that sound money is an important base for the economy. But this issue is, to my mind, orthogonal to the other two. You could implement competing private currencies in anonymous, pseudonymous or absonymous (note to pedants: this is a word I made up, that's why it fails the spell-check, not because I spelt it wrong) ways and you could implement the mechanism for exchange using all sorts of systems. Whether transactions are reversible or not has nothing to do with the currency.

Trajectory

Is Bitcoin a good currency? I suspect not, but I'm not an economist, so I must defer to the experts. The question that most of our clients are interested in is whether Bitcoin will form a niche parallel economy or whether they will scale into the mainstream economy. I have a suspicion that this won't happen, and that's because the anonymity that is the attractive feature to the early-adopting bitcoiners is not attractive to the mass market.

The best strategy is to learn, and to think about ways that the cryptography at the heart of Bitcoin can be used to deliver new kinds of services in a connected environment. I don't think cash will be one of them.

And another factor is.... – 18/07/2011

There's a super paper in the June 2011 Journal of Payment Systems and Strategy by Paivi Heikkinen and Timo Livarinen from Bank of Finland.

> *This paper highlights the difference between the direct, indirect and social costs of payment fraud and calls for a more holistic approach to security in payment instrument design. The payment industry has done a lot, bit it should do even better and make use of customer-specific parameters and take a stronger role in the whole payment processing chain.*

This really is an important point to make, especially to regulators. I think that payment systems regulation should have explicit goals, and that the most important of these should be to maximise the net welfare, as economists say. In other words, the goal of payment system regulation should be to make payments perform for the whole of society, not any particular subset such as banks or merchants. In particular, the idea of externalising the costs of poor payment system security should be examined. Card fraud provides a simple example:

> *93% of respondents say they are worried about bank card fraud. This fear appears fairly well justified considering that there were over 102,500 cases of bank card fraud identified in 2010, according to Cifas, with many more instances not reported.*

[From Finextra: Card fraud]

Personally, I'm not that bothered about card fraud. I only ever use a credit card, so if the details are used by fraudsters to buy stuff, I don't care (it's the bank's problem, not mine). Actually, the statistic in that quote isn't quite what the source document talks about the:

> *Unwelcome and continued presence of identity fraud, with no sign of any reduction, with over 102,500 cases identified in 2010.*

[From CIFAS - Press Release - 20 Jan 2011]

...but whatever. From the industry perspective, card fraud is a few basis points and falling and entirely manageable in financial terms. But the police would say that this is wrong way to look at it, because card fraud (particularly ATM fraud) is used to fund other criminal enterprises such as drug dealing, so that the social cost is much higher than the cost to the financial sector. This is a general point, by the way, and I'm not picking on financial sector.

> *According to BillingScore, 19.4% of the value of all transactions in the U.K. premium rate sector are fraudulent, or roughly £1 on every £5 spent. "With the premium rate sector in the U.K. mobile industry currently worth in the region of £700 million, this equates to £135.8 million per year being lost to fraud in the U.K. alone," the company said.*

[From UK mobile operators 'hide' £136m annual fraud]

That's an astonishing figure, which tells you more about the margins on digital goods sold by mobile operators than it does about security technologies or techniques! These technologies do work…

Online banking fraud losses totalled £46.7 million in 2010 - a 22% fall on the 2009 figure - as banks installed sophisticated fraud detection software and more consumers equipped their PCs with up-to-date anti-virus protection. The dip in online fraud has occurred despite a continuing rise in phishing attacks, up 21% from 2009.

[From Finextra: UK banking fraud]

I'm sure that one of the major reasons for this fall, and the general containment of this class of fraud in Europe, is the steady migration to two-factor authentication (2FA) for online banking—while there is still no 2FA for online payments, which are general based on knowing a password, not possessing any tamper-resistant hardware. In the US, hardware 2FA is less common but the new FFEIC guidelines may result in more uptake.

It clearly tells financial institutions that the techniques many of them have relied upon, i.e. simple device identification and easily exposed challenge questions, are not good enough anymore given today's threat landscape.

[From FFIEC finally releases new Guidance on Internet Banking Authentication; Better Late than Never]

I'm pretty sure that the dominant 2FA in the US will be mobile rather than the custom devices adopted in Europe a few years ago (such as my splendid Barclays' PIN sentry). This is the kind of thing I'll be talking about at Business and Operational Excellence in Payments in London on 18th/19th October 2011. With the payments industry entering a period of unprecedented challenges, this highly topical two day conference will examine what changes banks need to make in order to maximise efficiencies in payments. From new products for corporate clients to cutting edge solutions in new delivery channels our 40+ distinguished speakers (and me) will explore and debate where the new opportunities to increase revenue really lie.

Signature solution – 06/09/2011

There was a half-written blog post on my laptop that was about the US options for EMV migration, prompted by a discussion I was party to earlier in the year. The discussion was about cutting the cost of US EMV deployment by forgetting about offline transactions.

Let's say for a moment that the US implements EMV and goes the way of on-line PIN verification only.

[From <u>Why US travellers' EMV</u>]

This would be crazy. At the recent Smart Card Alliance conference in Chicago, my colleague Stuart Fiske from Consult Hyperion had a (moderately intemperate) go at a couple of speakers who were saying chip and online PIN was a good idea. He made the point that offline PIN was the only globally interoperable solution and that the US should go with it and he got a big round of applause for doing saying so. I don't see the point of issuing EMV cards and then using them with an online PIN: if the merchant has a PIN pad then why wouldn't you use chip and offline PIN? And I can see a practical problem here: if customers are encouraged to continue to use cards that are chip and online PIN only, then when they get off the plane at Heathrow and try and buy a train ticket in a machine, they won't be able to buy anything because the online PIN won't work (it will only work in ATMs).

Having just got back from a few days in the US, I decided to dust off this piece about the EMV options and tidy it up, because Visa has announced its EMV migration plan for the USA. In our little corner of the payments world, this is officially a big deal.

> *But in a departure from nearly every other global market that has switched to EMV cards, which are commonly called chip-and-PIN for their most prominent security feature, Visa's plan excludes PINs.*

[From <u>Visa</u>]

It would be interesting to understand the reason for this, so I went over to Visa's site to see and I found a rather odd statement.

> *And we continue to believe that long-term static data elements, including PIN, can create an increased risk for fraud. An increase in ATM fraud could occur in cases in which the PIN is stolen along with cardholder account information.*

[From <u>PIN largely unaffected in U.S. migration to EMV</u>]

This is what used to happen in the UK. People would steal card details along with the PIN and then use those details to create counterfeit magnetic stripe cards to use at US ATMs. But they can't do that anymore because the UK issuers have moved to ICVV (which means that the card details on the chip are different from the card details on the stripe, so you can't make a bogus stripe card with chip details). And in any case this only worked because you could copy magnetic stripe cards: you can't use the cardholder data to make chip cards. So once the US ATMs turn off the magnetic stripe fallback for Visa card, counterfeiting isn't a threat at

ATMs and it doesn't matter if someone gets hold of the card details and the PIN. There must be another dynamic.

In the US market there are about six million POS terminals in use and about a quarter of them already have PIN pads. These PIN pads, which are used for online PINs, are already secure enough to use for offline PINs. Hence Visa's point…

> *Visa will continue to support online PIN as a cardholder verification method for debit transactions, and at the same time encourages the move toward future adoption of dynamic cardholder verification methods.*

[From PIN largely unaffected in U.S. migration to EMV]

A digression. If you're getting confused about what's going on here, you need to take a break and go back to EMV basics. The EMV specification allows for a number of different Cardholder Verification Methods (CVMs) and any particular card will have the acceptable CVMs stored on it, in order, by its issuer. These could be (in no particular order):

- Plain-text offline PIN, the default in the UK;

- Enciphered offline PIN—which should be the only option in the UK, but isn't because we started by issuing Static Data Authentication (SDA) cards that couldn't support it. Now we are issuing Dynamic Data Authentication (DDA) cards we really should be moving over to this option to stop PINs from being harvested from terminals that have been tampered with;

- Encrypted online PIN—where there is an offline PIN as well (e.g., my Barclays debit card) then the online and offline PINs are synchronised in the back end.

- Signature.

- Nothing.

You can also have combinations of these, with the most obvious example being signature plus enciphered offline PIN for the paranoid. To illustrate the point with a real case study: one of the UK cards that is in my pocket right now has the following actual CVM list in priority order:

- encrypted online PIN for cash at ATMs;

- plain text offline PIN for purchases;

- enciphered offline PIN for purchases;

- signature for purchases.

This means that if I go into a shop and their PIN pad is broken or my chip is damaged, I can still buy something and sign for it. I could imagine a typical Visa US debit card having a different CVM list:

- encrypted online PIN for cash at ATMs;

- signature;

- encrypted online PIN for purchases.

Please note: this is speculation based on public documentation only. Why does this approach make sense when online PIN only doesn't? Well, the US is never going to get rid of signatures in the timeframe under discussion for EMV this makes for an easy transition. The signature is decoupled from the chip infrastructure as it as anyway so, basically, whatever the chip says the merchant terminal can just ask for a signature anyway and most Americans won't notice any difference.

> *That there are more EMV markets that have implemented chip and signature than chip and PIN.*

> *[From PIN largely unaffected in U.S. migration to EMV]*

There may be another factor here, though. The US is a special case because the interchange on signature transactions is higher than the interchange on PIN transactions (or at least it was: who knows where Durbin will take it) and therefore issuers want to keep signature going for a long as possible despite the large retailers having PIN pads in place.

> *If Wal-Mart had its way, mag-stripe cards would disappear immediately, to be replaced with cards running chip and PIN.*

> *[From Untitled]*

As I said. So why bother with chip and signature? I think the explanation might be that Visa USA, in common with many industry observers, just don't see the current cards and terminals as a long-term technology worth investing in. Hence the reasonable, from their point of view, compromise. You issue chip and signature cards for credit and debit. The debit cards have encrypted online PIN as well for use at POS with the current pin pads. This works fine in the US and at international ATMs. The only place where it causes problems is international unattended terminals that accept offline PIN only (such as Belgian petrol stations) and for international travellers the US banks can issue cards with offline PIN anyway. All sensible from the US perspective. While I was googling for something else on this topic, as an aside, I came across this voice of the customer that confirms this analysis.

I have a Citibank Singapore chip-and-signature EMV card. It caused a lot of confusion in Europe when it was a chip card that wanted a signature, and again in New Zealand as they started their EMV rollout. Only time I recall it failing in Europe was trying to buy rail tickets at AMS, where my mag-only cards also didn't work

[From USA issuers announce EMV]

When I last used my chip and PIN card in Singapore, I was asked for PIN and signature, because of the decoupling mentioned earlier, but that's a digression. At some point in the future, we're going to stop entering PINs in POS terminals. I've said before that in the next generation of consumer payments, we must make a fundamental change in the point-of-sale (POS) user interface by ending the practice of having customer enter a PIN into something that isn't theirs. The cost of providing certified PIN pads is high: making customers buy their own non-certified PIN pad seems like a much better solution all round. Since most customers have already bought a non-certified PIN pad (their mobile phone) that has other security features associated with it, we (the industry) may as well use them. This means using the "PIN" to unlock a handset-based wallet, not to authenticate card transactions.

To see the more interesting future context Visa USA's announcement, then, you have to stop thinking about cards and terminals and start thing about virtual cards and phones. Post 2015 people will be using their chip and signature cards, it's just that those cards will be inside mobile phones and will have all sorts of other security that cards don't so the offline PIN is less relevant. This way, the readers (POS terminals, television, Squares, iPhones and goodness knows what else) will be spared the expense of a certified PIN entry devices and innovative new solutions can come to market exploiting chip-based dynamic authentication. These are, I stress, merely my reflections on the topic based on public statement, but I think they're a reasonable summary of the current situation.

Comments

Dave, very elaborate remarks on the PIN side of the story (unattended POS terminals are still off limits for US chip cards with signature or online PIN, mmh?). I think it is worth pointing out a couple of other aspects that need attention and clarification:

Neither ATMs nor CNP transactions are covered by Visa's announcement, kind of ignoring the fact that these channels become the weakest links in the fraud chain once you have taken care of the POS (see the CNP fraud in the UK and ATM fraud outside of Europe).

As far as I can see the liability shift only covers counterfeit fraud at POS, not lost and stolen fraud (since PIN is not required).

There are no explicit incentives for issuers. If they stick with magstripe, they have the POS transaction liability today as much as tomorrow.

The waiver for PCI DSS annual audit cost is supposed to be the carrot for the merchants. Well, per the small print, they still need to be compliant with PCI DSS and using magnetc stripe cards at chip card terminals does not make the transaction more secure per se.

Finally, as everybody in the industry acknowledges and as the UK and some other markets have so impressively demonstrated, you only reap the benefits of EMV if a market moves as a whole, i.e. you execute a nationwide migration project embraced by all major stakeholders. My guess is that we are still far away from such a project plan. I documented a series of additional inhibitors in my recent paper titled 'Chip in the U.S.- The Facts, Debunking the myths concerning EMV advancement in the United States' published at the SCA website http://www.smartcardalliance.org/resources/pdf/Chip_in_the_US_The _Facts_090611.pdf: Would appreciate everybody's comments.

Posted by: Toni Merschen on 07/09/2011 at 14:06.

Thanks for these thoughtful points Toni. I think the point about PCI DSS as an incentive is that the merchant gets the reduce PCI-DSS requirements (and therefore costs) only if more than three-quarters of their transactions are chip but they will still be able to process magnetic stripe transactions. I know it isn't logical if you think about it (because the magnetic stripe liabilities are still there) but, as they say, I wouldn't get there from here.

Posted by: Consult Hyperion on 09/09/2011 at 17:12.

Dave, it's really worth-while to read the Visa announcement by the letter. Visa 'will eliminate the requirement for eligible merchants to annually validate their compliance with the PCI Data Security Standard for any year in which at least 75 percent of the merchant's Visa transactions originate from chip-enabled terminals. To qualify, terminals must be enabled to support both contact and contactless chip acceptance, including mobile contactless payments based on NFC technology'. So, the transaction does not have to be a full chip transaction, it only has to originate from a chip terminal. And the merchant 'must continue to protect sensitive data in their care by ensuring their systems do not store track data, security codes or PINs, and that they continue to adhere to the PCI DSS standards as applicable'. So, it's not PCI DSS compliance per se that is waived but the annual aufit to prove compliance. Two different things.

Posted by: Toni Merschen on 10/09/2011 at 11:33.

I agree with Stuart that the offline PIN must be the only interoperable standard, there appear to be some European countries that are (actively) issuing cards with the CVM list setup without Offline PIN (they use Online PIN locally falling back to MSR in the UK). However the merchants will do nothing until the other schemes offer a similar PCI-DSS incentive, at the moment merchants will still have to do full compliance audits for MasterCard or Amex. Still it's a big big step in the right direction.

Posted by: Jonathan Vokes on 13/09/2011 at 10:14.

Magnificent analysis Dave, and very useful additions Toni. For what it's worth, I think the debate around US migration to EMV is getting over-complicated, and while Visa are to be congratulated for taking a lead, in some ways they have added to the confusion.

Call me naive, but I don't understand why the US cannot simply migrate to EMV chip with offline PIN as the default but with other CVMs as options, as in the rest of the world. I believe the obsession with mobile payments is a red herring and a distraction. And sorry Dave, but I think your idea of generating PINs on our own mobile phones sounds gruesome, for all sorts of reasons.

By the way, I still think the prediction you forced me to blurt out on our podcast a year ago - that we'd see serious movement on EMV chip in the US by the end of 2011 - was only slightly optimistic

Posted by: Nick Collin on 13/09/2011 at 12:53.

TV's times – 19/09/2011

Earlier in the year I spotted some predictions about payments in 2011 and, since I agreed with all of them, kept a note of them. They were...

Mobile, mobile, mobile. Wallet in the cloud. The digital wallet. Call it what you want, but mobile devices are poised to become a primary form of payment for millions of people around the world... Consider that PayPal saw a 310 percent increase in mobile payment volume on Black Friday 2010 compared to the previous year, and a 292 percent increase in mobile payment volume on Cyber Monday 2010 compared to Cyber Monday

2009. Without a doubt, mobile payments are here to stay and will see significant innovation in the coming year.

[From <u>Five payment trends to watch in 2011 | VentureBeat</u>]

No-one could disagree. Every bullish projection made about mobile is, if anything, an underestimate. The vigour and energy in the sector is building weekly and everyone in retail financial services understands what Eric Schmidt of Google meant when he said that a company without a mobile strategy is without a strategy.

'Appification'. IDC issued a new report that says, among other things, over the past three years the mobile apps space has seen an "appification" of "broad categories of interactions and functions in both the physical and the digital worlds." And this only stands to continue — in fact, the same IDC report projects mobile app revenue to grow from $4.9 billion in 2010 to $35 billion by 2014..

[From <u>Five payment trends to watch in 2011 | VentureBeat</u>]

It's certainly true that I spend a lot of money via apps but with example of the Financial Times live on my iPad right now I don't know how the apps vs. HTML5 thing will pan out in the long run. What I have noticed, though, is that when apps are a couple of quid you buy them to try them out.

A Cashless Society. Now let's not go crazy here, I'm not suggesting that by this time next year we'll be living in a cashless society. Far from it. That said, 2011 will undoubtedly see several significant steps that will take us closer to such a world.

[From <u>Five payment trends to watch in 2011 | VentureBeat</u>]

Given that I bore for England on this topic I don't want to go into it here, except to say that I think I can see two schools of thought emerging about this. The mainstream, if you like, sees cash usage maybe halving over the next decade.

Will these lead to a cashless society?... But it will lead to a less cash society.

[From <u>The Financial Services Club's Blog: Not cashless but less cash</u>]

A more radical prediction, though, might be that while cash usage will continue to fall it will reach a cusp sooner than many might imagine: I think we can already observe this phenomenon in the Netherlands, where some shops are now cash-free.

> *Social shopping is clearly poised for significant growth... Among the key drivers of this trend are micropayments and digital goods. Along the same lines of merging physical world experiences with digital activity, the ability to make quick, small purchases for online content represents a huge opportunity for both content producers and providers.*

[From Five payment trends to watch in 2011 | VentureBeat]

A topic in its own right, but yes it's very clear that connected consumers don't behave in the same way as consumers of old and with Zynga looking for a $20 billion IPO there must be plenty more imaginative and entrepreneurial people looking in that direction. But it's this last prediction that I want to focus on.

> *T-commerce. TV will go from a passive (viewing-only) experience to a highly interactive activity as more and more apps are developed specifically for the platform.*

[From Five payment trends to watch in 2011 | VentureBeat]

Many years ago, I contributed to the Centre for the Study of Financial Innovation's report on "The Internet and Financial Services". I made what I thought at the time was a bold, but reasoned, prediction that the focus on the PC and the web was too narrow and that both mobile and television access to financial services should be part of financial services organisations's strategy (although I underestimated the growth of mobile and overestimated the growth of what we now call "connected TV"). I was reminded of this when I saw a tweet by the always provocative (and accurate) commentator Dean Bubley of Disruptive Analysis. He said...

> *The arrogance of the mobile industry is staggering. "The Internet will be mobile". Really? Tell that to all the companies selling Smart TVs*

Dean's comment stuck in my mind because I'd just purchased a new Panasonic TV and home cinema sound system. Now, the TV and the Blu-ray player both have ethernet ports, as does my Apple TV (which I had been using in wireless mode). So I dug out my Apple Airport Extreme that I used to use to stream music before I got the Apple TV and configured it as a bridge to my home wireless network. Then I got a fast ethernet switch and connected it to the Extreme. Then I plugged the Apple TV, the TV and the Blu-ray player into the switch and, hurrah, they're all online. The first thing my TV did was phone home and download a software upgrade! So perhaps connected TV is finally coming to the mass market after all.

You've hailed connected TVs as the future of television. How will the BBC embrace this?During any one week, we get somewhere between 10m and 13m people in the UK accessing our red button services.. We see a huge potential in migrating those people who are familiar with red button services to being consumers of each of our 10 products in the digital world.

[From INTERVIEW: BBC general manager for news and knowledge on connected TVs :: StrategyEye - Industry Intelligence]

What will you do with your connected TV? I imagine that one of the things you will do is buy stuff, so bringing payments to the channel is vital. Consult Hyperion has done plenty of work on this in the past (we worked on the Sky Barclaycard, for example) and we put forward a number of idea for using one-time password, remote controls and even NFC on different TV-related projects.

Perhaps these aren't radical enough visions though. Some of you may remember that at the Digital Money Forum a few years ago we had a number of students from the Royal College of Art (RCA) in London come along and share their visions for the future of payments with us. We were all knocked about by the super stuff that they produced. I remember one chap who predicted, to universal amusement, that we would soon be paying with gestures. Far fetched? Well, MasterCard demoed that it.

Most impressive — or frightening, depending on how you look at it — was the Xbox Kinect prototype. To purchase a product on TV, users simply wave their hands at an icon in the corner of the screen.

[From In MasterCard]

Life, once again, imitating art. This set me thinking about how difficult it is to imagine how technology might be used in the future. We're all familiar with Arthur C. Clarke's famous observation about advanced technology being indistinguishable from magic, perhaps we should develop a corollary about advanced financial services being indistinguishable from games.

Maps and Road – 23/09/2011

Earlier in the year, I read an excellent report about the future of mobile payments in the US.

> *"Mobile Payments in the United States: Mapping Out the Road Ahead" by Darin Contini and Marianne Crowe, Federal Reserve Bank of Boston; Cynthia Merritt and Richard Oliver, Federal Reserve Bank of Atlanta; Steve Mott, BetterBuyDesign*

[From Mobile]

It's a serious piece of work that sets out to develop a practical roadmap around mobile payments and contains a tremendous.

The foundational components of success suggested by the work group include:

- The proposed environment is best defined by the concept of an "open mobile wallet."

- The mobile infrastructure would likely be based on Near Field Communications (NFC) contactless technology resident in a smart phone and merchant terminals.

- Ubiquitous platforms for mobile should leverage existing rails, including the ACH network for non-card payments, and support new payment types that meet emerging needs.

- Some form of dynamic data authentication would be at the heart of a layered mobile payments security and fraud mitigation program.

- Standards would be designed, adopted, and complied with through an industry certification program to ensure both domestic and global interoperability, including a standard to ensure that devices used to facilitate mobile payments do not create any electronic interference problems.

- A better understanding of a regulatory oversight model should be developed in concert with bank and non-bank regulators early in the effort to clarify compliance responsibilities.

- Trusted Service Managers should oversee the provision of interoperable and shared security elements used in the mobile phone.

[From Mobile]

These components seem to me to be developing rather nicely. The handsets are coming along, there's a nice war developing over control over secure elements (I'm very hopeful that competition will lead to innovation in this area) and non-banks such as Google are active.

> *The digital wallet wars have begun. And credit card giant Visa and search behemoth Google are likely to be among the first to face off in the market as they each try to convince consumers to ditch their real wallets for ones that store credit cards and other information on their cell phones.*

[From <u>Visa</u>]

But the area where there may need to be more concentrated pressure from "the industry" is in the area of regulatory oversight where, to my mind, the start of the separation of banking and payments regulation along European lines would be an excellent step.

The goal should be to put all providers of payment services onto a level playing field where banks and non-banks, technology providers and entrepreneurs can compete to find new ways to exploit the new technologies to deliver the new payment services that we need as the bedrock for the evolution of commerce. It is quite right that providing credit should be a banking business and properly regulated, but that is only one part of the payments business. It's not as if non-banks don't already have a big share of the business.

> *According to the study, more than 25% of all US households are unbanked or underbanked. Most of those households are low-income and/or minority. Unbanked households do not have anyone in the house that has a checking or savings account. Underbanked households may have checking or savings accounts but rely on other financial services such as nonbank money orders, nonbank check-cashing services, payday loans, rent-to-own agreements, or pawn shops at least once or twice a year.*

[From <u>National ACH: 25% of US households Unbanked or Underbanked</u>]

These non-banks might be able to offer innovative services that banks don't, or they might be able to offer the same services as banks but cheaper or faster. Or they might offer the same services but in a better location or more attractive bundle.

The new "Consumer Financial Protection Bureau" will, as I understand things, end up regulating payment entities like PayPal and Amazon. Title X, Section 1002 gives the bureau power to regulate entities that provide "payments or other financial data processing products or services to a consumer by any technological means, including processing or storing financial or banking data for any payment instrument, or through any payments systems or network used for processing payments data, including payments made through an online banking system or mobile telecommunications network". This is getting closer to the European notion of a non-bank payment institution, which I think ought to be the basis for competition. It would be nice for this to happen at the Federal level. Earlier on, for reasons not germane to this post, I happened to be looking at the list of licences that Western Union holds to send money in the US. It would make life so much better, and foster more competition and better services for consumers, if non-banks could obtain the equivalent of a PI licence for the whole US.

NFC is pottering along – 10/10/2011

Last year, PayPal's Patrick Gauthier posted some typically accurate analysis about the US retail payments industry in examining the slow progress on NFC. At that time, Patrick highlighted three key roadblocks.

1. *The economic buyers – i.e. the Mobile Operators and Issuers – have not solved their rivalry: Behind the scene a furious battle has raged on the ownership of the secure element used to secure transactions, a proxy for the question of who will own the customer relationship.*

2. *Consumers have good enough methods of payments as it is: Without prejudice for the vision behind NFC, the need for a new method of payment delivery based on handsets is tenuous... Absent a reason for consumers to want it and a business case for Issuers to support, standalone payments is an unlikely "killer application."*

3. *No good path has been proposed to reach a critical mass of users: If I had a penny for every time I have heard about "the-chicken-and-egg" problem, I would be retired by now.*

   [From NFC: Past, Present and Future - pymnts.com]

Patrick's analysis explains the paralysis in the operator-handset-bank domain that has allowed Google Wallet (and next year, I'll wager, the iPhone, despite the 4GS lull) to steal the agenda. Operators were slow to get behind NFC, but customers liked it and they appear to want more services: hence some observers see the action shifting from a consensual evolution at the interface between the mobile industry and the financial industry to a "screw you" revolution where more aggresive service providers (not only in payments) are using stickers (Albert Hein), microSD (Samsung/Visa) and other technologies (Google Wallet) to simply bypass the bank/operator interface. It's also worth noting that other players are bypassing the banks and operators in other ways, although that's not the main point of this post.

> *We certainly live in very interesting times. The traditional players are zigging – away from mag stripe card technologies (with, perhaps, the exception of Citi and its work with Dynamics) toward a world of NFC/contactless payments. Meanwhile, it seems that PayPal isn't waiting for that world. Instead, it's zagging toward a speedier implementation of, arguably, a new and convenient way to pay that's card-less and avoids the requirements of rebuilding so much of the payments ecosystem.*

[From Zigging and Zagging toward Mobile]

So I'm not saying that the **only** way forward for mobile phone-based retail payments is NFC, although I do think that the convenience of NFC ought to translate into pretty significant market share. For what it's worth, and despite the slow start, the latest forecasts are very bullish about NFC, even in North America.

> *NFCNews also reported that North America will have the biggest chunk of the NFC market by 2016. This will correspond to around $113 billion in mobile transactions. Furthermore, 1 out of every 5 smartphones worldwide will carry NFC technology come 2014, translating to almost 300m NFC-enabled smartphones.*

[From Mobile]

As an aside, I read that one UK operator is especially keen to get NFC out of the labs and into the mass market as soon as possible!

> *Everything Everywhere is doing a big push on Near Field Communications (NFC) devices, aiming to get most of its customers onto the mobile payments service by 2012.*

[From Everything everywhere to push nfc in the uk- The Inquirer]

They'll have to get their skates on to get "most" of their customers onto NFC in the next three months, but it's the spirit of Jason's message that is important: that NFC is going mainstream. Everything in the garden should be rosy then, but there's a gloomy prediction for the operators from ArcChart and Research & Markets in their latest report, which I happened to read on a plane a couple of weeks ago.

The researchers also believe that internet companies such as Apple, Google, and Yahoo are best placed to take advantage of this technology.. Incumbent players in the telecoms market are at risk of being left out.

[From 588 million using NFC payments and services by 2015 NFC (near field communications) news blog]

It's difficult to disagree with this given the current state of things, but it's not a foregone conclusion. It's true, I think, that the operators in developed markets made a mistake 2-3 years ago by not ordering NFC handsets. At the time, as we all remember, the operators found it very difficult to justify the additional cost of NFC because they couldn't see a business case in their spreadsheets and they wanted a more detailed exploitation path. So this is how we've got to this point, where even the people who do have handsets with NFC aren't able to play with it for "serious" applications. Remember this?

Nokia's C7 handset, released some nine months ago, includes NFC hardware but it is currently inactive. This summer, when the phone gets the Symbian Anna operating system upgrade, the NFC chip will be activated and end users will be able to start using their phones to read and write to NFC tags — but won't be able to use them for secure NFC services.

[From Nokia: No mobile wallet support in current NFC phones • NFC World]

It's fair to observe, as I have done before, that there's a lot more to NFC than secure services (such as payments). But one cannot negate a universal affirmative, as they used to say on Monty Python's Flying Circus. A mobile proximity payment service must be secure, but not all secure services are mobile proximity payments. There are plenty of interactive services that will still need to have security. The operators need platforms and interfaces for access to secure NFC services for all sorts of applications, including ones we haven't thought of yet. Yes, this is more complicated than simple interactions, but that's why there is more value in it. Hence you can understand why industry observers are somewhat puzzled by operator strategies.

Vodafone in the U.K. is already blocking the NFC of the BlackBerry Bold 9900.

[From AT&T May Be Blocking NFC On The BlackBerry Bold 9900]

I tried to find out what "blocking" means in this context, but no-one in the office has one of these phones and I didn't want to rely on second hand knowledge. If they mean blocked completely -- as in you can't read or write tags -- that's ridiculous. If they mean blocked as in you can't write apps that access the NFC interface that's ridiculous too, because we need people to get out there and play with this stuff. If they mean blocked as in no access to the UICC SE for SWP, I guess that's tolerable. You can see the argument: the carrier is subsidising, so they want control. But maybe they are wrong. Maybe control isn't the way to shape this market. I doubt that Google will open up their secure element, or Apple will open up theirs, so surely this is a way for operators to regain some ground. Open up the secure elements with standard APIs and let people play with the technology!

I see your 3DS and raise you 4DS – 10/10/2011

I think I may have driven some of our clients to distraction with my constant wittering about digital identity and the need for a more strategic approach to the future of identity and identity management across both the public and private sectors. Specifically, I've been suggesting to some of our clients in the financial services space that they ought to see digital identity as a potential line of business and not merely as technical way to solve a technical problem around single-sign on, authentication and identity theft. Generally speaking, they don't pay much attention to me saying that identity is the new money, but they do pay attention to Facebook.

> Facebook has filed for a trademark on the usage of "Facebook" on business cards and, more curiously, "non-magnetically encoded" ID cards among other things.

> [From Are Facebook]

I'm not particularly interested in the trademark issue, but I pointed this story out to a couple of people in a discussion because I think it illustrates that there are some companies, Facebook among them, who are developing strong long-term strategies around digital identity. Another is PayPal, who made the "Commerce Identity" a centrepiece of their annual innovation event in San Francisco this year.

> EBay today launched PayPal Access, a new identity authentication and log-in technology [that] enables consumers to not only quickly log-in to any website–as they could with Facebook, Twitter or other authentication services–but it makes paying through websites quicker and faster.

[From EBay's PayPal]

Now, if you look under the hood of PayPal Access, you will find that it uses sector-wide standards and not banking or payment standards.

> *PayPal Access provides a way for users to log into your web site using interfaces based on the OpenID 2.0 protoco*

[From Standard OpenID]

As I've said in the past, numerous times, OpenID seems to me to be a reasonable place to begin developing digital identity services and experimenting with digital identity business models. I've gone on and on about this over the years.

> *What with OpenID appearing to gain momentum as a simple, distributed, good-enough single sign-on for the Internet.*

[From Digital Identity: Opening up]

I have discussed the idea of using OpenID with a number of clients, not only in the financial services sector, but I think they thought it was too "techie", or maybe the marketing and business guys just genuinely didn't see "identity" as a bank business. But I have to say that in all honesty I was disappointed, because I thought that a couple of years ago it was a good place to begin experimenting and learning. I'm not arguing the OpenID is perfect.

> *Current OpenID implementation practice is to use non-correlatable identifiers as the URLs that I envisioned for LID, in order to get CardSpace-like privacy features. But then, the first piece of information that is typically pushed to sites, Sxip-style, is the user's e-mail address — a perfectly correlatable identifier if there ever was one. The identity push features in OpenID 2, from their roots in Sxip, are unused beyond a few like name and e-mail address; instead, any meaningful data exchange is performed using OAuth, an (incompatible) branch-off*

[From Johannes Ernst's Blog » The Death Of User-Centric Identity — for now]

This is absolutely valid and correct criticism. But... first of all, I don't have a single OpenID, I have three. There's id.dgwbirch.com which I use for professional stuff, id.davebirch.org which I use for personal stuff and then a third that I use for 95% of my online interaction, a pseudonym unconnected to the other two. From my point of view, this works fine. It's frustrating when I try to log in somewhere and they don't implement OpenID. Perfectly correlatable? No.

But let's stop trying to iterate to a theoretically perfect solution. It's better to start somewhere, otherwise we'll find ourselves sitting around in dreary committees discussing the requirements for identity infrastructure endlessly while that actual identity infrastructure is being defined and built south of San Francisco. It's there, and not in the boardrooms of banks, that identity is seen as a strategic component of future products and services.

> *So I agree with Eric that Google+ is in part an identity service. But "primarily an identity service?" That's notable. Particularly in the context of what he said after that. "If they're going to build future products that leverage that information."*
>
> *[From A VC: Google]*

Meanwhile, my bank is doing... well, nothing so far as I can tell. Which is odd, because my bank has already put me though stringent know-your-customer procedures. And banks remain trusted. And they've spent money giving me a high-security tamper-resistant industry-standard security device, namely a chip and PIN card. There really ought to be some way to reuse this excellent functionality.

> *Why can't the company I work for accept identity assertions or information based on an identity service that has already vetted my existence to an adequate assurance level?*
>
> *[From Burton Group Identity Blog: BYOI – bring your own identity]*

If I could use my home banking dongle as part of a 2FA login to, well, let's call it "Bank Access", then surely I ought to be able use that digital identity in the framework of the Cabinet Office's Identity Assurance infrastructure to log in to DVLA, DWP, British Gas and the World of Warcraft if I want to. I oughtn't to be that hard for the banks to get together (perhaps under the auspices of the The UK Payments Administration) to define the minimum dataset for OpenID sharing (maybe name, address, email and some kind of unique customer id or whatever) and a pilot into place so that people can log into any UK bank— on PC or mobile—using any UK bank identity.

> *I wish Google had sold this to all the banks I cared about rather than just implementing it on its own properties.*
>
> *[From Piaw's Blog: Review: Google]*

I made a few remarks in this direction in my talk at Business and Operational Excellence in Payments in London recently. Ms. Ineke Bussemaker, the Executive VP and Head of Payments Services and Savings at Rabobank kindly referred to my comments and said that I was pointing towards a rethink of 3D-Secure (3DS). This isn't true: I don't think it makes sense to get rid of 3DS given the infrastructure is in place (and, despite the moaning, working). But I do think it makes sense to think of a framework around 3DS, something that I called 4D-Secure a couple of years ago.

> *A direction that might be explored is what you might call "4D-Secure", or 4DS: instead of using bank authentication to log in to something, use bank authentication to log in to an OpenID provider and then use OpenID to log in to things. This has the advantage that service providers site could implement open source standard OpenID solutions rather than interface with 3D Secure.*

[From Digital Identity: 4D Secure]

In 3DS the three domains are the customer, the merchant and the bank. If 3DS is used to authenticate into a wider framework (such as OpenID) then this opens up the fourth domain, which is everyone else who is happy to rely on (and potentially pay for) bank strong identification and authentication services. I think it might be time to dust this off and offer it to financial institutions who, seeing what Facebook, Google and PayPal are doing—are beginning to think that some sort of digital identity and strong authentication strategy might be appropriate to their businesses. After all, I'm sure they don't want to end up having to pay Facebook every time someone logs in to their credit card provider using Facebook Connect, and having no choice but to provide that service because customers simply won't bother to log into anything that doesn't offer Facebook Connect (or PayPal Access, for that matter).

A bit of a show – 22/12/2011

I was genuinely flattered to be invited to speak to the first European Bitcoin in Prague this year especially given that my honest assessment of the project—given in blogs, magazines and even on BBC radio—was not terribly positive. As I wrote earlier in the year in Prospect Magazine

The mass market doesn't want anonymity, it wants privacy. Neither customers nor banks want transactions that are irreversible. And while many of us would like currency management taken away from governments, that doesn't mean an unmanaged solution will be any better.

The conference was therefore an opportunity for me to learn more about Bitcoin and the Bitcoin community as well as to test my arguments with an informed crowd. It was most enjoyable on both counts. My attitude didn't change - I still don't think Bitcoin will crack the mass market - but I did think that there is a lot of valuable learning and experience to be gained from studying it.

I found it particularly valuable to hear from the wider Bitcoin community at first hand. Sergey Kurtsev from IMCEX set the tone in the very first presentation when he said that the central issue is one of trust (I'll come back to this at the end of the post). He suggested that for Bitcoin to obtain widespread adoption they should target "regular people" and forget about banks etc. I'm sure that's true, but it's a mountain to climb. He also said that anonymity is misunderstood and that the public don't need it. I was upset about this, not because he was absolutely correct about it, but because it was going to be the subject of my talk in the afternoon. So it led to some emergency last-minute Keynote acrobatics on my part!

Amir Taaki from the Bitcoin gave a presentation that was quite wide-ranging so I will use his presentation as a peg to hang a few comments on. He is an evangelical proponent of Bitcoin but said, essentially, that there were three problems with Bitcoin: the marketplace, the technology and finance.

1. **Marketplace**. Consumers have no reason to use Bitcoin (which strikes me as a rather important and limiting constraint). The attributes that Bitcoin projects (such as that anonymity) are not valued by consumers and the merchants obviously don't see enough value to drive consumers towards it. And many of the other factors that go to make up a marketplace—everything from help desks and brand adverts to chargeback procedures and dispute resolution—simply don't exist in the Bitcoin space. In an age when the merchants are looking for "ID not IT", this means that either Bitcoin focuses on some pretty thin niches or it has to change in some fundamental ways.

2. **Technology**. There are scale issues, as people much cleverer than me (e.g., Ben Laurie) have pointed out, but the key technology issue is that it's hard to use. It has a heritage of geekdom and it needs a much more user-friendly front end.

The owner calculated the current exchange rate, which has fluctuated wildly in recent months amid rampant hype about Bitcoin. My lunch was $5.51 plus tax: I owed him 0.52 bitcoins. He held up an enormous laminated QR code the size of an entire sheet of paper, which I scanned on my phone yielding: bitcoin:1MTbKpYWnzqmsLvCjdTtwrvuX81g3HCgC. This was the address where I would send the money. Using my laptop, I *opened up my account on the Mt. Gox Bitcoin exchange market, sent 0.52 bitcoins to 1MTbKpYWnzqmsLvCjdTtwrvuX81g3HCgC, and about three minutes later the restaurateur received an e-mail indicating that the coins had arrived.*

[From I Spent a Coin (and I Liked It) — How I Bought Lunch With Bitcoins—Daily Intel]

What could be simpler?

3. **Finance**. I thought Amir's point about "compromising events" was perceptive. If you want people to hold Bitcoins instead of dollars or gold, they have to have real faith. Every time they read about exchanges crashing and money vanishing that becomes more unlikely. I'm not bothered if Barclays computer blows up, because my money is guaranteed (up to a certain level) by the government. If I hold more than that level in a bank deposit instead of storing it in mutual funds, fine wine or real estate that's my problem. Compromising events actually increase people's trust in the current financial system! On the other hand, early compromising events in the Bitcoin space have been undermining.

As I somewhat uncharitably posted on Twitter, "help I want my anonymous, untraceable digital cash back!".

[From Digital Money: Bitcoins and PCs]

I did try to make constructive criticism and when it came to my talk. I tried to highlight some areas of commerce where the existing mass market solutions might be vulnerable to well-crafted alternatives (e.g., social networking, games, kids) or where a significant improvement in security would generate value. I also said that any realistic mass-market solution must be mobile-centric. If there was some way to store keys in a trusted secure element that would make life much easier for the scheme designers.

So, in conclusion, I'm just some guy. But people whose opinion I trust seem to validate my initial responses to Bitcoin. Here's what one of the world's leading cryptographers has to say about it:

Stefan Brands, a former ecash consultant and digital currency pioneer, calls bitcoin "clever" and is loath to bash it out

[From The Rise and Fall of Bitcoin]

Yes. But.

As I have explained previously, Bitcoin is not money. Bitcoin is a protocol.

[From BLOGDIAL » Blog Archive » Why the quoted price of Bitcoin]

Thinking this way does provide a route forward. A couple of the speakers at the event suggested creating a scheme **on top of** Bitcoin rather than use Bitcoin itself. I was involved in a couple of feasibility studies in the 1990s for international financial organisations who were looking at using Modex, DigiCash and the like in a similar way, making them the inexpensive, fast clearing and settlement mechanism within the scheme but not exposing them to the consumers.

> *Bitcoin is the first online currency to solve the so-called "double spending" problem without resorting to a third-party intermediary. The key is distributing the database of transactions across a peer-to-peer network. This allows a record to be kept of all transfers, so the same cash can't be spent twice—because it's distributed (a lot like BitTorrent), there's no central authority.*

[From Online Cash Bitcoin]

If the scale issues can be managed (it's outside my envelope to asses a likelihood) then it is plausible that this low-cost distributed infrastructure could be a way to implement a global P2P solution. As one of the afternoon speakers, who was focusing on marketing, noted it's better to think of Bitcoin as a means of exchange only. You take your money, change it into Bitcoins, send it to the recipient. I saw this idea picked up again recently.

> *While Bitcoin isn't a very good currency, it has the potential to serve as a "metacurrency": a medium of exchange among the world's currencies. In this role, it has the potential to be a powerful competitor to wire transfer services like Western Union.*

[From Bitcoin]

This could be a decent business for some people.

> *He converts some of his income to US dollars, using sites like MtGox.com, which is run by Mark Karpeles in Tokyo, Japan. Karpeles charges a fee of 0.65 per cent, and is earning $2000 per day, along with the equivalent in bitcoins.*

[From Future of money: Virtual cash gets real - 06 June 2011 - New Scientist]

All of this, it has to be said, has almost nothing to do with the pervasive meme of the event, which was wether Bitcoin could form a new gold standard and smash fiat currencies, or the side topic of whether Bitcoins themselves make for a worthwhile speculative investment.

> *Bitcoin enthusiasts have been buying Bitcoins as the price falls, convinced that the price will go back up... But as the hoped-for rally has failed to materialize, more have gotten discouraged or bored and cash out, pushing the price down further*

[*From* The Bitcoin]

That's no to the latter and personally i think it's no to the former as well.

> *Bitcoin is different: It wholly replaces state-backed currencies with a digital version that's tougher to forge*

[*From* Crypto Currency - Forbes.com]

To be honest, this is a little meaningless. Bitcoin may or may not be tougher to forge than US dollars, but that's no why people hold US dollars. By amazing coincidence I'd just finished reading Detlev Schlichter's "Paper Money Collapse" when I found out he was going to be on the programme in Prague and I enjoyed hearing him set out his (compelling, to my mind) case against nation-state fiat currencies.

Detlev, of course, recommends a return to a gold standard rather than the development of a Bitcoin standard but his talk did, I think help, to set out some of the issues and help the audience to disentangle them. During the Q&A session hosted by the incendiary Max Kesier, the "Financial War Reporter" from Russia Today (I'm sure we've all seen it in our hotel rooms by now), I tried to make the point that it might be better to have lots of different kinds of money rather than one, whether gold or euros.

A final point. A number of speakers and delegates made an interesting point about developing trust networks, which is that there are no mechanisms for trust inside the Bitcoin network so some form of co-operation and self-regulation will be needed (sounds awfully like the Visa and MasterCard doesn't it!). This is exactly right: the idea of a decentralised, no-one in charge, payments version of "Occupy Wall Street" sounds great, but in practice you need rules and regulations. Sorry to be dull.

Comments

> Excellent take on Bitcoin. I fully agree. I have a side comment on the 'trust' issue. There have been many recent demonstrations of what happens when the people lose faith in their ability to redeem currency at the value they assume. It is called hyper-inflation! Think of the

collapse of Russia, of Argentina in the 80s, of the Horn of Africa in recent years. When people lose trust in the value of government backed currency, then they start hoarding tangible goods instead of currency. There are runs on banks to withdraw cash that is spent immediately, before the value of the currency goes down even further. Trust does not equate to security.

Posted by: Rene Bastien on 22/12/2011 at 19:33.

If you're interested in reading a bit about bitcoin I would suggest heading to http://newmeraire.blogspot.com/. I don't think the double spend issue has been solved, for the simple fact that some individual or group could own 51% of the network. It's simply a matter of having the money. There are a number of blog posts on the subject by people who are far smarter than I.

Posted by: Keith on 23/12/2011 at 13:25.

Hi Dave, I was also at the conference. You want features, such as privacy, reversibility, NFC and so on. I still think you don't get the point. You can implement them with Bitcoin. What you do not want is to have them to be mandatory. You want them based on context and the needs of the users. Just like you do not want your car or house to suddenly vanish and be replaced by a note by some random guy telling you "transaction has been reversed".

Why should a third party have control over your property? It should not, only if you they offer you a service that you like. Since practically all other monetary systems, apart from physical commodities, require that you depend on a contractual relationship with a particular third party, an issuer or a creditor, Bitcoin has an advantage here. Also, your expectation of having lots of different kinds of money is probably not going to come to existence. Money is subject to the network effect and that limits the number of competitors.

Of course, Bitcoin has a long way to go and cannot succeed unless it satisfies users. But its potential is enormous.

Posted by: Peter Surda on 25/12/2011 at 00:43.

What bitcoin skeptics are really saying when they mention limited privacy over anonymity is that they don't think a digital currency should have the same attributes as physical cash today (namely irreversibility and anonymity). In short, they are promoting a cashless society....and not the good kind.

Tomorrow's Transactions—The 2012 Reader

Posted by: Jon Matonis on 28/12/2011 at 13:07.

Super idea – 03/01/2012

This proves how stupid I am compared to criminals. This had never occurred to me, but as I soon as I read about it I recognised the brilliance of the idea. Banks have tried in a variety of different ways to make it harder for criminals to attach card skimming devices to ATM. So the criminals have looked around for other places where unattended terminals with PIN entry are located and have discovered that the self-checkout machines in supermarkets provide an excellent attack opportunity. Of course!

> *Lucky Supermarkets discovered tampered credit/debit card readers in the self check-lanes of its store in Alameda's Marina Village Shopping Center and 18 other Lucky markets, and is urging those who used the machines to check their credit and debit accounts.*
>
> *[From Warning to Customers of Lucky's Self Check-Out Lanes - Alameda, CA Patch]*

I've actually bought stuff at that Alameda Lucky, although it was last summer so I'm probably safe. I would never, under any circumstances, have used a debit card there anyway. I never use a debit card in supermarkets, or indeed anywhere else. I was forced to use a debit card in Lidl recently because they don't take credit cards, so next time I go there I will use a prepaid card. I buy things at Morrison's in Woking on a more regular basis, and since I won't use my debit card at POS that means no cash back, so that if I want cash I have no option but to use my Barclays debit card in the ATM there. Uh oh.

> *CASH machine users are being told to be on their guard after a cloning device was found at a Woking supermarket. The device was discovered at the Morrisons store in Goldsworth Road.*
>
> *[From Card cloning device found on Morrisons cash machine - News - getsurrey]*

Cards aren't safe anywhere it seems.

> *Susan Grant, director of consumer protection for the Consumer Federation of America, is calling for more security and legal rights for debit card fraud victims. "When unauthorized debits are made, consumers are in a much more troublesome situation ... because the money's been quickly withdrawn from their*

account," she said. "With an unauthorized credit-card charge, you haven't paid it yet."

[*From Thieves Favor Debit Cards*]

Indeed, but this is tackling symptoms, not causes. You can see why this is going on. It's because we still, insanely, put magnetic stripes on the backs of our cards, and those stripes can be copied and used in places where there are no chip readers in the ATMs (i.e., the US). In developed countries, this problem has been recognised and dealt with.

The introduction of chip and pin payment cards has lead to 99 per cent drop in ATM card fraud, says Central Bank of Nigeria (CBN)

[*From ATM*]

I have absolutely no idea why Barclays puts a magnetic stripe on my debit card, I have no idea why John Lewis puts a magnetic stripe on my MasterCard and I have no idea why Barclaycard puts a stripe on the back of my splendid OnePulse Visa card. I have a Travelex US$ prepaid card with a stripe on it that I am quite happy to use in shops in the USA until such time as they install chip and PIN readers. Surely it would make life easier for Barclays and for me if they just declined all stripe transactions on my cards. I can easily transfer money to Travelex US$ prepaid card via FPS, so what's the problem?

Comments

I actually think all these companies like fraud, because it is the reason they can charge 3% or more of each transaction. If it wasn't for this fraud, we'd be more outraged of this cut. The fraud losses probably isn't too bad, and provides the raison d'être for the 3% charge.

Posted by: Mats Henricson on 03/01/2012 at 13:34.

Fallback has long been a sore point in the UK. When the crims steal a valid Chip & PIN card, simply smack the chip with a hammer, or reverse 12volts into it, and hey presto instantly useable mag swipe card.

Pan Key Entry has to be a far safer fallback method than swipe, as you just about guarantee the card number entered is the one on the card, but this is not allowed by the schemes. I think the UK acquirers are generally in agreement that mag swipe is bad and should be removed, but the reason always stated is scheme rules interoperability etc.

Tomorrow's Transactions—The 2012 Reader

Posted by: Gary on 03/01/2012 at 15:10.

If the magnetic stripe on your credit card were accidentally damaged, I suppose you would not need to ask your bank for a replacement in too much of a hurry... Unless you wanted to use it abroad or change your PIN (the motorised reader on ATMs is triggered by the mag stripe, after it has pulled in your card it reads the chip).

Posted by: Michael Kyritsis on 11/01/2012 at 17:46.

I can see clearly now – 19/01/2012

Having observed the mobile money market develop and noted the various types of bank and operator service that have been experimented with around the world, it seems to me that it is the regulatory environment that is the main obstacle to further development. The idea that payments, particularly low-value person-to-person payments, are necessarily part of the banking system and that they must be regulated by banking regulators and they must be regulated as tightly as banking and therefore must be provided by banks has done nothing to help the market to develop and therefore benefit people in a great many countries.

Why is regulation the major obstacle? Well, of the more than 100 mobile money services in action around the globe, still only a handful have scale. Is M-PESA a "black swan" that is a product of a unique combination of cultural, business and technology factors? There are many people who think so, arguing that there Kenyan environment had some very special characteristics, primarily a dominant operator and a large unbanked population with little access to conventional financial services provided through banks. But these characteristics are, frankly, common. They may be necessary, but they simply cannot be sufficient conditions for scale provision of a mobile alternative. Which is why I wonder if regulatory issues aren't really the dominant factors. Without the right regulatory environment, it doesn't matter what the business opportunities are or what new technologies can be exploited. Nothing will happen. This seems to be true in markets where there is a desperate consumer and business demand for these services.

Central Bank of Nigeria is working together with the Nigerian Communications Commission to look at areas where mobile network operators (MNO) come in. But officials of the NCC are intimating that the mobile money operators would still need to come for registration with the telecom regulator. The NCC which is expected to design the regulatory framework on the technology and mode of interoperability to be adopted by the operators for seamless operations, is yet to come out with the guidelines.

[From Obstacles On Mobile]

Nigeria, like India, should be a vigorous and exciting mobile payments marketplace, with innovative and enterprising people creating fantastic new products and services. Nokia is known for innovation, understanding the carriers, global reach, brand recognition and all the good stuff. That's why many people were excited by the Nokia Money launch in India.

> *Registered Nokia stores will act as banking correspondents to Union Bank of India and facilitate service registration, money transfer and cash withdrawal. Nokia will pre-install the Union Bank Money application in its handsets, in addition to offering it as a download to existing handset owners. Customers who sign up for the service will be able to transfer money, withdraw cash from Nokia outlets as well as from UBI ATMs and pay for utility bills and mobile recharges via their mobile phones.*

[From Updated: Nokia]

Yet Nigeria, India and many other countries are seeing very slow progress. And a key reason for this is that payments are regulated, generally speaking, as part of the banking system.

> *Most of the operators we know in this situation would prefer to be directly regulated by their central bank as an e-money issuer or payment services provider. Doing so gives regulators better visibility into and oversight over mobile money services, and makes it more likely that customers will have more services from which to choose in the financial services space. It's a win for everyone involved.*

[From Regulating non-bank mobile money service providers | Mobile]

Now this would have an impact on shape of the market and the structure of the value network evolving within it. Telcos are in many ways being forced into partnerships with banks because of regulation, not because it makes sound business sense. Or they are forced to obtain banking licences (like Rogers in Canada). Better regulation would make for a wider spectrum of alternatives. Telcos could obtain payment services or electronic money licences themselves, or they could partner with specialist organisations or (as should happen) bank subsidiaries that operate under the new licences but with a lower cost base and more flexibility than they could inside a bank. Although I have to say that it is by no means obvious that banks would respond to the innovation challenge (in this area).

Half of banks will still lack a formal innovation programme and budget in three years time, severely restricting their growth potential, according to research from Gartner.

[From Finextra: Cost-cutting banks wide open to disruptive IT innovation - Gartner]

I was thinking about this when reflecting on the discussion panel that I chaired at Management World Americas last year, noting that we are still in the very early days of this new mobile money world and the partnership discussions underway right now are really only exploring the "shallows". The idea of digital money as an element of "smart pipe" infrastructure (I'll write more about this tomorrow) that is delivered to customers through banks, specialist electronic money services, payment institutions, retailers, transit companies and, yes, mobile operators is key to setting the right regulatory framework and I hope the regulators will do more in 2012 to remove this significant obstacle to a vibrant, and socially-beneficial, ecosystem than they have been prepared to do up to now.

Did you celebrate D (+1) Day? – 06/02/2012

You may have missed D-Day (or D+1 day, as it was more properly labelled). From 1st January 2012 electronic payments are officially D+1 (instead of the previous D+3ish). So electronic payments from one UK bank account to another have to be completed in a day.

From January 1, when the changes come into effect, more than 15m payments a month are expected to be rerouted through faster payments, reaching the recipient's account in one working day. The new timescale, known as D+1, is part of European wide legislation introduced more than two years ago to harmonise payment services across the region, making cross-border payments easier.

[From Bank transfers cut to one day - FT.com]

In the UK, these D+1 payments are executed through the Faster Payments Service (FPS). FPS has actually been around for a while, and it was successful from the very beginning. After only six months or so,

Two thirds of all phone and internet payments are now processed through the FPS

[From The Paypers. Insights in payments.]

It spread steadily and, although there were issues, soon began to dominate volume. For a typical consumer, such as myself, being able to log in and send money - effectively instantly - to (to pick a few examples from the last month) tennis coaches, nieces, sons and builders is a terrific boon. And, in practical use, easily more convenient than finding a cheque book and writing a cheque. I had to send one of my friends £25 at the weekend. Since I'd logged in to internet banking to pay a couple of bills, I just texted him for his sort code and account number and then it took two minutes to add him as a payee and send him the money.

> *Most big British banks already allow current account customers to use the UK 'Faster Payments' system, in which transfers are completed in seconds... At present, just over 80 per cent of payments in the UK are made this way, the Payments Council says.*
>
> *[From Banks forced to guarantee 'next-day' internet and phone cash transfers from 2012 | This is Money]*

Rather spookily, I remember reading that specific article in a waiting room at the Payments Council before a meeting and I remember noting how FPS was continuing to grow. Never mind the last couple of weeks. I've used it goodness knows how many times over the last couple of years and as far as I can tell most payments get there within a few minutes let alone a day. This is why the idea of a mobile "front-end" to FPS -- whereby FPS transfers are instructed through a mobile "layer" that links bank accounts numbers to mobile phone numbers -- is seen by many people as being an extremely attractive alternative to cheques in the UK.

> *Where are the mobile macro payments? I am talking about the payments with a higher amount than the ones that are defined as micropayments.*
>
> *[From Where are the mobile macro payments? | in2payments]*

This is a question many people have been asking in the UK. So I thought it would be useful just flag up what has been happening. Consult Hyperion are one of the associate members of the Payments Council and we have a great, shared interest in seeing new technologies exploited by the Council's members in effective and efficient ways.

> *The Payments Council today announced that Allied Irish Bank Group (UK), ING Direct and G4S Cash Services are to become full members of the Council, along with Consult Hyperion... This now brings total membership to 28 members and 11 associate members.*

Tomorrow's Transactions—The 2012 Reader

[From <u>Payments Council - Payments Council welcomes three new members</u>]

The Council has been looking at the issue of mobile payments for some years, and last year it decided to set up a project to move the industry along.

In May 2011, the Payments Council announced an industry-wide project to help participating banks and building societies deliver mobile payments in the UK. Within as little as a couple of years customers may be able to send money using only their mobile phone: either by using text, an app, or their phone's internet browser.

[From <u>Payments Council - Mobile</u>]

This is what they are talking about in the just released UK Cards Association annual report for 2012 where they say that over the last year they have sought to

Facilitate the development of technological platforms to support the deployment of contactless and mobile contactless payments and create dialogue between the payments industry, retailers and other technology companies with an interest in these developments;

Last year, the UK Cards Association (UKCA) commissioned Consult Hyperion to assist them in establishing the Mobile Contactless Steering Group and we have been working with UKCA since then to help the members get together and work out the best way forward. I don't want to comment on what products and services might be coming to the market soon, but what i will say is that FPS gives UK players and excellent base to build on. While D+1 rather than mobile was the original motivation, I would not be at all surprised to see that in a relatively short time, a few years from now, mobile-instruction credit transfers will dominate the FPS volume and will be taken for granted by consumers. A quick NFC tap or barcode scan will acquire the destination bank details (with a proper implementation of digital signatures, naturally) and a couple of buttons will send the money. Easy.

Chapter 10: Cash replacement

This is pretty much the sharp end of the electronic transaction revolution, the "last mile" for the technology revolution and the dematerialisation of transactions. When it comes down to it, can we get rid of cash?

US currency reform would save money– 28/03/2011

What would a rational US policy on the circulating medium of exchange look like? What notes and coins should be in circulation? I think it's time to start thinking about narrowing the range in order to reduce costs (and increase convenience).

One obvious way to reduce costs would be to follow countries including Australia and Canada and in replacing paper banknotes with plastic (polymer) banknotes. In a paper on this called "Production Costs, Seigniorage and Counterfeiting: Central Banks' Incentives for Improving their Banknote Technology" from October last year, Forum friend Leo van Hove, together with co-authors Bouhdaoui and Bounie, calculates that the adoption of such notes would entail a drop in seigniorage revenue of roughly 0.1% (because of higher initial production costs) but would halve the annual replacement costs for banknotes, resulting in net savings of $374m per annum.

Using data from 1998, they find that the biggest cost saving would come from moving to a plastic $20, whereas the replacement of the $100 bill only becomes profitable after accounting for counterfeiting because without the reduction in counterfeiting the decrease in seigniorage revenue exceeds the savings in replacement costs. It's easy to see why: $100 bills are not used to support commerce, so they don't circulate in the US (I'm sure the majority are outside the US and will never be repatriated) and therefore don't get worn and returned for replacement, whereas $20s are still used in retail.

In fact, I've noticed that more and more places in the US will no longer accept bills greater than $20 anyway, so if the US government could be persuaded to give up the seigniorage income from the $100 (in return for much reduced tax evasion and such like) then it would surely be sensible to move the $5, $10 and $20 to plastic and abolish the $50 and $100.

The $1 is another case entirely. The US is crazy to continue producing $1 bills as well as pennies that cost nearly two cents to make. I say scrap both. Give up on the penny and make the $1 coin work (which it would do if there were a deadline for withdrawing the bills). Leo and the chaps note that the "golden dollar" coin costs six times more to produce than the $1 bill (but lasts 14 times longer). If the government were to completely replace the $1 bill with the coin then it would save $116m per annum. This is interestingly slightly less than the estimate of $119m per annum it would save by going to plastic $1 bills.

Maybe we need a new, technology-neutral Durbin-like amendment to reduce the cost of payments in the US, but this time one that doesn't discriminate in favour of cash at the expense of more efficient alternatives and imposes cost-reduction targets on the currency. Incidentally, just to show how up-to-date I am with my finger on the pulse of money, after typing in the above, I settled down and found myself reading this...

> *In American, the questions are still more pressing, involving the return to specie payments, the future regulation of paper currency, its partial replacement by coin, and the exact size and character of the American dollar.*

What hip and trendy blog did I find this on? Actually, it's from "Money and the Mechanism of Exchange" by William Stanley Jevons, published in 1875. Money's a conservative topic.

Tax pressures could boost e-payments in Europe– 11/04/2011

They called April 6th "Black Wednesday" in the UK. Well, I heard someone say that on the BBC. It's because it was the start of the new tax year, and since the government maxed out the credit card, the payments are going up. There's going to be some pressure to collect to more tax, because there's a limit to how much you can put the rates up before avoidance (and emigration) reduces the total amount collected. I wonder if we will soon be going down the Greek route.

> *The Greek government announced Thursday it is shutting down bars and nightclubs... that fail to offer receipts. So far, six bars and clubs have been shut down as par of a broader sweep where two-thirds of all inspected businesses were fined. The absence of receipts allows businesses to avoid value added tax, or consumption tax, the Ministry of Finance said in a press release.*

> [From Euro Debt Crisis - Cash-Strapped Greece Cracks Down on Fun - CNBC]

Now this could be good for the e-payments industry, because the easiest away to avoid receipts and therefore evade tax is to pay in cash. Here, in the birthplace of income tax, the government are apparently going to have something of a crackdown on tax evasion.

HMRC has targeted so-called 'ash cash' or payments to doctors for signing death certificates before bodies can be cremated and also undeclared cash payments to dentists.

[From HMRC targets middle class tax evaders – Telegraph Blogs]

This seems on the margin to me: I shouldn't think the amount of tax being evaded by doctors writing death certificates will amount to one payoff of a local government and I have to say that none of my dentists has ever asked me for a cash payment for anything.

It could even be argued that agreeing to pay your builder in cash might be seen as a conspiracy to defraud the Revenue

[From HMRC targets middle class tax evaders – Telegraph Blogs]

Now you're talking! Agreeing to pay your builder in cash is precisely engaging in a conspiracy to evade tax, and people who do it should be prosecuted. If they paid their share, mine wouldn't be so much.

And it's not just that carrying around cash is inconvenient and time consuming. These days, one of its main functions is to finance the black economy: drug deals, counterfeiting, under-the-table employment and other nefarious activities. Because cash is anonymous, people can easily opt out of the taxable economy – leaving the rest of us to pick up the tab for their use of public services.

[From I'm dreaming of a cashless Christmas - Telegraph]

Getting rid of cash won't eradicate tax evasion, but it will make it more difficult, and hopefully more expensive, thus shifting otherwise black commerce back into the formal economy. And since the scale of tax evasion in Europe is so colossal, small improvements will deliver significant sums to the treasuries. I couldn't find a reasonable estimate for this in the most recent tax year, but I did find this estimate for VAT alone.

The current collection model brings with it a VAT Gap due to e.g. VAT fraud, insolvencies, mistakes by the taxable persons in the VAT return and VAT avoidance schemes. Desk research shows that the VAT Gap for 2009 can be cautiously estimated at 6,9% of GDP and 12% of total VAT liability in the EU-27. This means that, in the EU-27, a total of EUR 118,8 billion has according to those estimates not been collected by the tax authorities in 2009.

Tomorrow's Transactions—The 2012 Reader

[From 118,8bn euros lost in 2009]

Let's say that 20 billion of this is in the UK, and that getting rid of cash would cut it by a quarter. That's an instant five billion bonus to the exchequer. I look forward to my rebate.

Art for art's sake – 19/11/2011

I happened to be watching a mildly diverting TV drama called "Mad Dogs and Englishmen" on a plane the other day. It's about some English guys in Spain. I won't spoil it for you by telling you what it's about, but at one point the chaps are in a bar and they try to pay with a €500 note. The waiter refuses saying that he doesn't have enough change in the till and that, anyway, only drug dealers try to pay with €500 notes. It's meant to be a humorous reference, because (for complicated plot reasons that are not relevant to this post) the note actually does come from drug dealers stash as, I imagine, most of them do. While I was watching it, the cabin crew came around asking if anyone wanted to buy any duty free shopping. I glanced at the in-flight catalogue and noticed that it said that British Airways will accept cash (which I was surprised about) but will not accept "high value notes", specifically mentioning the $100 and €500 notes.

> *A MAN who brought a lawsuit against Continental Airlines for refusing to accept cash for an in-flight transaction has had his case dismissed by a state Superior Court judge.*

> *[From Continental Airlines: Taken to court over a cashless cabin | The Economist]*

I should think so too. What a pointless, expensive and time-consuming hassle it must be to deal with cash on the plane: not just taking it and making change, but counting up and reconciling at the end of the flight then depositing the proceeds, managing and distributing float and so on. But back to the €500 notes. What is the point of them? Am I exaggerating to say that the majority are used for drug dealing? Probably. The majority are undoubtedly used for tax evasion. Look at what's happening in Southern Europe at the moment. Michael Lewis' wonderful, astonishing and frightening report from Greece is a typical must-read. He mentions in passing that:

> *The easiest way to cheat on one's taxes was to insist on being paid in cash, and fail to provide a receipt for services. The easiest way to launder cash was to buy real estate. Conveniently for the black market—and alone among European countries—Greece has no working national land registry*

[From <u>Beware of Greeks Bearing Bonds | Business | Vanity Fair</u>]

I've heard it said before that the predominant use of €500 notes is to evade Spanish property taxes. Tax evasion is endemic in large parts of Europe. Greek doctors apparently earn so little that they are entitled to draw welfare, yet many of them mysteriously live in villas and own yachts. I'm not being nationalistic here, incidentally. It looks as if some British doctors have been careless with their record keeping too.

> *The taxman's amnesty, the Offshore Disclosure Facility and New Disclosure Opportunity, has resulted in over 50,000 voluntary disclosures. In addition, the Tax Health Plan, which was aimed at medical professionals, produced a further 1,500 voluntary disclosures.*
>
> *[From <u>HMRC opens 16 criminal cases over tax evasion - Telegraph</u>]*

As the Deputy Governor of the Bank of Sweden put it:

> *We use more cash than is optimal for society, so what should we do about it?*

Well, use less of it might be a good starting point. Why is it so hard to get going? I'm beginning to wonder if the extensive use of cash to avoid tax is one of reasons why it's proving so hard to get rid of it. Too many people benefit (at the expense of the poor and honest, obviously) from the black economy.

> *With 76% of Capitec customers believed to use taxis as their primary mode of transport, the bank expected them to adopt a smart card technology in preference to carrying around cash [but] Capitec has had limited success with this initiative: taxi drivers are wary of implementing it owing to a lack of trust in "virtual currency", but also because it would be better not to create a paper trail for the taxman to follow.*
>
> *[From <u>Fin24.com>>Money Clinic>>Can South Africans ditch cash?</u>]*

So there's an obvious resistance to cashlessness coming from people who evade taxes. On the other hand, in the case of taxi drivers, the experiences in New York suggest that revenues go up when customers can use cards instead of cash. If people could see that having everyone else pay their fair share of taxes would make them better off, they'd maybe give it a go.

I suppose the other people who might be sad are artists, like the chap who made the room full of $1 bills at the Guggenheim. I went to see it earlier in the year.

> German artist Hans-Peter Feldmann is breaking the museum's Hugo Boss award into $1s to line it with $100,000 worth of currency.
>
> [From Artist to Cover Guggenheim in 100,000 Dollar Bills — ANIMAL]

Bank notes might also have some ceremonial functions, but they are no longer needed to support commerce and industry. I was in a discussion with someone yesterday who mentioned the wedding tradition in some countries of pinning banknotes to the bride. In these cases, I'm sure that enterprising entrepreneurs will produce special "money" that is not actually legal tender, much like the Chinese "Bank of Heaven" notes that you see at New Year. But I have to say that there are some uses of cash that I simply cannot envisage an electronic replacement for.

> The Feminist Initiative (Feministisk Initiativ - Fi) carried out its promise to burn 100,000 kronor ($13,000) on Tuesday morning, claiming that a half-page ad would never have had the same impact in the fight for equal pay between the sexes.
>
> [From Schyman burns 100,000 kronor in wage protest - The Local]

This shows an outstanding appreciation of the art of PR. People have such an emotional connection to cash. People other than me, I mean.

Comments

> Dave - I was speaking to a flight attendant about their shift to only accepting cards the other day. She said one of the main reasons that the airline had done it was because of fraud...but not the fraud I expected. Apparently the flight attendants were caught taking the little booze bottles home, refilling them from their own stash, and selling the refilled bottles on the next flight (but pocketing the cash as no sales of airline inventory were taking place). Shifting to card payment only has the benefits of removing float, etc., but it may have also boosted the official on-board sales of alcohol significantly!
>
> *Posted by: Aran on 21/11/2011 at 18:56.*

> That's what the receipt and the cashtill was invented for: to engage the consumer in the protocol to document the transaction. If the consumer

suspected the sales person of pocketing the money or misdocumenting the transaction, the consumer would alert the store owner. This works because the consumer has an interest in lower prices and honest trading.

Posted by: Aran on 26/11/2011 at 15:13.

Dave: There is another use for the supernote: facilitating the run on the banks. Recent numbers put substantial upticks in supernote withdrawals when Lehman Brothers crashed. It seems inevitable that we're going to see some more of this real soon now... It might not be a good time for banks to try and shift more transactions to themselves, given their tendency to wobble as soon as the markets say boo.

http://financialcryptography.com/mt/archives/001344.html
http://www.economist.com/node/21538195

Posted by: Iang on 26/11/2011 at 15:19.

Render unto Monti – 30/11/2011

The new Italian Prime Minister Mario Monti said, in his initial address to the Senate, that he is declaring a war on cash. Now that the technocrats are in charge, I expect to see more of this kind of fighting talk. Monti is apparently proposing to reduce the maximum cash transaction (i.e., the biggest transaction you can make without reporting it) from the current €2,500 to €300. This would, at a stroke, render all transactions made with €500 notes reportable, just as I was suggesting last week.

Some might argue that you shouldn't be allowed to purchase anything for more than €450 in cash. I would certainly vote for this

[From Scrap it]

Then the police would be able to stop people in the street and prosecute them for having a €500 note, which would certainly raise the cost of criminal activities! The reason for this drastic announcement is the parlous state of the Italian government, made worse by the enormous scale of tax evasion there.

However, companies deal in cash to evade tax, especially in the south where organized crime is endemic. Untaxed transactions in Italy translate into a loss of about 100 billion euro of revenue annually, or 22 percent of the gross domestic product.

[From The Florentine - article » War on cash]

Tax evasion is pervasive and powered by a cash-based economy. The Italian economy and the British economy are of comparable size, but in the UK last year people spent €356 billion on debit cards (the greatest share, by value, of retail transactions) whereas in Italy they spent only €63 billion, or around a sixth as much.

> *With a bright blue apron, lip stud and cheerful smile, she is known to all except the Italian taxman — for whom the Neapolitan waitress has never existed and probably never will. Paid 100 euros a week in cash, the high school dropout is one of hundreds of thousands toiling away in a parallel Italian economy where cash is king, contracts or receipts do not exist and the taxman is cut out of the equation altogether.*

[From Italy's shadow economy moves into political spotlight]

Reducing tax evasion by lowering the threshold for the use of cash will both raise revenues for the state and reduce the tax rates, since if everyone pays their share, the shares will be less (all other things, such as government fiscal incompetence, being equal). It really bugs me that I have to pay such high taxes in the UK when so many people evade them completely, and I'm sure a great many Italians feel the same: they would pay their share if they thought other people were.

> *The reason for such high taxes is mainly because the government has to collect as much as it can from the poor devils who actually do pay taxes – namely those who are paid above-the-board salaries.*

[From Clamping Down on Tax Evasion in Italy]

The squeezed middle, as we call them in the UK. But this isn't really about waitresses hiding tips or childminders working off the books.

> *Fiorio of the University of Milan says wealthy Italians are adept at shielding income from taxes. And a lot of rich people look poor on paper. "Less than 1 percent of the people earn, say, more than $120,000," Fiorio says. "At the same time in the last years you had an increase in luxury cars bought, you had an increase in yachts bought. And so clearly this is hiding something."*

[From Avoiding The Tax Man Could Cost Italians Dearly : NPR]

This may well prove to be a real barrier to change. If it were only the poor evading tax on a grand scale, then you might get a crackdown. But when it's the rich, including members of Parliament (I'm sure), then it's going to be much harder to take action.

A much bigger chunk of the shadow economy is the "richer" part seen in the country's north — one of professionals like dentists and doctors who evade tax, and companies that violate rules by paying overtime off the books or failing to issues receipts for some transactions.

[*From Italy's shadow economy moves into political spotlight*]

I'm certainly not saying that this is a specifically Italian problem, although the scale of the problem in Italy is certainly significant, but it will be interesting to see how the new technocrats decide to approach the issue of cash and electronic payments, the balance between carrots and sticks.

While the Greek economy has the largest underground estimated at 25.2 percent of GDP, the PIGS countries (Portugal, Italy, Greece, and Spain) average 21.7 percent of their economic activity hidden from the official statistics. For comparison, 14.7 percent of German, and 7.8 percent of American output is estimated to be confined to the underground.

[*From Can the Underground Economy Save Europe? - David Howden - Mises Daily*]

Now, obviously, I don't understand the cultural background in Italy, so it's hard for me to comment on why it is (other than tax evasion, criminal enterprises and bribery) that cash usage is so high there, but it's not because Italy lacks infrastructure. There are cards and terminals, it's just that they are used way less than in other European countries. There are 36m debit cards in Italy used for that €63 billion in annual charges, but Italians make 24 card payments each per annum compared to 8 in Greece and 132 in the UK. Carlo Sangalli, head of the retailer's federation in Italy, blames this firmly on the merchant service charges (MSCs) levied by Italian banks. That may be the case, but even if merchants accept cards, Italian consumers will take some convincing to use them. It will be very interesting to see the balance between carrot and stick that will be needed to change this.

This preference for paper in Italy can be attributed to 52% of Italians not really wanting to use plastic money. The fear of fraud and credit card cloning accounts for 14% of Italians not wanting to use plastic. 10% of Italians simply object to paying a fee for having a credit card, or so research by Alter Ego discovered.

[*From Clamping Down on Tax Evasion in Italy*]

Perhaps it's time to go back to my plan of making an interchange-free debit card a condition of having a banking licence, or go down the Dutch route of bundling the MSC for small transactions into the monthly terminal rental or the Brazilian route of offering tax breaks for merchants accepting less cash. If none of these work, then there are still more options. You don't have to get rid of cash to cut down on tax evasion. Mr. Monti has some other alternatives: he could steal data, for example.

> *Herve Falciani stole account data for around 79,000 clients three years ago and fled to France while under investigation before eventually handing it over to authorities. In April, French prosecutor Eric de Montgolfier revealed that the stolen files have been decrypted and launched a tax investigation based on over 8000 accounts related to French customers. The following month Italian police launched their own investigation after being given a list of around 7000 account holders by French counterparts.*

[From Finextra: Spain uses stolen HSBC data for tax probe]

Hhhmmm… tempting. But with cash accounting for 88% of retail transactions in Italy (second only to Greece in the EU) there's no doubt that it's the low hanging fruit.

Electronic legal tender – 27/12/2011

Some time ago, in what seems like a distant, almost mythical age, the European commission published a bonkers recommendation concerning the legal tender status of the euro and setting out a number of principles to, essentially, force unwilling consumers and retailers to use high denomination euro notes and low denomination euro coins. At the time, I said:

> *I think this recommendation is plain wrong, but it doesn't take economics into account. Part of the EU's goal for payment systems should be economic efficiency and forcing your average tabac to take 500 euro notes does not contribute to that goal in any way.*

[From Digital Money: Tender moments]

As Norbert Bielefeld of the European Central bank noted in his excellent article "Dare to be bold: electronic legal tender is an option" in the EPC newsletter back in May 2011, the recommendation flatly contradicts the European Union's strategic objective to switch to electronic payment methods in order to reduce the total social cost of payments across the member states. I don't suppose the Commission's incoherent agenda about payments should be any more surprising than its incoherent agendas about anything else, but surely there's less excuse. Who can be against the desire to reduce the cost to society? That's something of a rhetorical question, but if it does have an answer, then the answer can be found in the parable of the candle makers as set down by the noted French economist and Tomorrow's Transaction blog hall of famer Frederic Bastiat a great many years ago.

> *When the beneficiary of a regulatory change is the net welfare, that means each and every one of us consumers is a little bit better off. But a few people will be worse off. And these are the people (retailers, car manufacturers, farmers or whoever) who set the media agenda and lobby the regulators.*

[From Digital Money: Ad valorem, add value]

Thus, in an economic situation where there are a few big losers but the net welfare is increased because of the large number of small winners, then the lobbying ability of the big losers can force a sub-optimal conclusion to economic negotiations. (This is what you might call the "Cliff Richard effect" as seen in the war between Big Content and the rest of society over copyright.)

This may seem like an esoteric discussion, but it isn't for two very real reasons. First of all, there seems to be general agreement that the euro cannot continue in its current form, in which case new currencies will arise whether at the regional national or subnational level. I was thinking about this because I read that the new Wolfson Prize for Economics (£250,000!) is for someone who can suggest how a country might make an orderly exit from the euro. I've already suggested how this might be done and how the e-payments sector might support social and economic change much to the benefit of the general populace.

> *Greece could pull out of the Euro and create a "hard e-drachma".*

[From What's a Grecian e-urn?]

The second reason why the discussion is not esoteric is that the new technology platforms coming into place in payments will make the creation and distribution of alternative and complementary currencies almost trivial. For a consumer in London to choose between the British pound and the Brixton pound will be no more taxing than choosing a different ring tone on their mobile phone. In both cases the issue of electronic legal tender is real and immediate. Norbert is optimistic.

> *A forward looking solution could however be rather close. Europe's payment systems have proven that they are secure and reliable and they are certainly well overseen. The Payment*

Services Directive has provided for much enhanced consumer protection for non-cash payment instruments and both this Directive as well as the e-Money Directive (now being transposed) allow for quality competition.

[From EPC | Article]

This is the kind of discussion I'm sure we'll see at the 5th London bar camp bank un-conference on 6 February 2012 at Nesta. This event, supported by consult Hyperion, will be (as it was last year) a sell-out, I'm sure, so don't delay! Pop over to Meetup and register for the event today. Note that we have chosen this date as it is the day before Finovate Europe 2012 and we hope that our friends from overseas who are coming to London for Finovate will take advantage and stay over.

Why bother? – 06/01/2012

I saw a picture of one of the new £50 notes in the fish-and-chip shop today. It was on a poster on the wall, advising passers-by on how to tell real from counterfeit £50 notes. It should be easy, because apparently the notes have all sorts of security features. You can read about them here to prepare for the unlikely contingency of someone proffering a £50 in a non-criminal transaction.

New-style £50 Note (Boulton & Watt) - Security Features

[From Bank of England]

I didn't ask, but I doubt that the fish-and-chip shop will take them. It has a chip-and-PIN machine already, and the risk of accepting a phoney £50 must be quite high. Why bother? According to the Bank of England, of the £52 billion of Sterling banknotes "in circulation", about £10 billion are in the form of £50 notes. So £50 notes account for about a fifth of the cash in the UK, but I've not seen one, not even one, for at least a year. ATMs don't dispense them, shops don't want them and apart from money launderers and corrupt politicians, no-one wants them as a store of value (or, at least, no-one who understands rudimentary arithmetic).

Although I live in quite a deprived area of Surrey (Woking), I shouldn't think many people popping in to buy cod and chips twice don't have a debit card, and if they don't then it probably won't be a hardship to limit them to £20s. Obviously, being Woking, we are near some very rich parts of the county and bankers may well come by with wads of £50s to buy cocaine from time to time, but even so, the impact of not accepting £50s is rather limited. This made me wonder why there was a new £50 note at all, since we clearly don't need them. I can't even remember the last time I ever had one. In fact, I can't remember ever having one.

The Bank of England wanted to introduce a new-look £50 note with enhanced security features.

[*From* Design space: £50 banknote - FT.com]

Why? Surely the most-enhancing security feature would be to stop printing them. There must be some other reason why the central bank persists with high-denomination notes. This is not simply a UK phenomenon. When I was last in Canada, I noticed that many shops were refusing to accept $100 bills. None of these shops, as far as I can see, were going bankrupt because of this so the $100 bills are clearly, therefore, not needed for commerce. So why is the Bank of Canada wasting time and money (three hundred million of their Canadian dollars) on creating notes that will only be used for tax evasion and various criminal enterprises?

It is a revamp of Canadian money that begins now and will last for the next two years, as the country's first polymer banknotes – made of thin pieces of plastic rather than paper – are put into circulation. The first denomination to get the makeover is the $100 bill, which began circulating a few weeks ago, followed by the $50 note in March and smaller denominations in 2013.

[*From* Funny money: How counterfeiting led to a major overhaul of Canada's money - The Globe and Mail]

In Europe, governments have begun to realise that the internal struggle between the seigniorage income form issuing notes and the tax losses caused from their circulation must finally be settled in the public interest. Look at what happened in Greece as soon as the technocrats were in control.

Under the new rules all payments in cash will be forbidden above a €1,000 threshold. The threshold was previously fixed at €2,500, surely a bit too high for a country struggling with endemic tax evasion like Italy.

[*From* Open Europe Blog]

The European Central Bank's insane policy of printing €200 and €500 notes will surely undermine the efforts of Greece in this regard. No sane retailer in Europe accepts these notes (largely because of the risk of counterfeits) so they are only used for tax evasion and similar nefarious purposes. The mention of counterfeits reminds me of another recent story.

"India faces an increasing inflow of high-quality counterfeit currency, which is produced primarily in Pakistan but smuggled to India through multiple international routes," said the 2011 International Narcotics Control Strategy Report of the State Department.

[From India faces increasing inflow of counterfeit money: Report - Economic Times]

This is surely another good reason for getting rid of £50 notes: they are an obvious attack vector for our enemies! I couldn't tell a real £50 from a fake sent in by Kim Jong-un to devastate our economy through a pandemic of unauthorised, freelance quantitative easing and I doubt that you could either.

Glossary

2FA (Two Factor Authentication) – Authentication that uses two different mechanisms to verify identity for security purposes. An example of 2FA might require both a password and a smart card thus determining both what the user knows and what the user has.

API (Application Programme Interface) – A set of rules (code) and specifications that software programmes can follow to communicate with each other

ATM (Automated Teller Machine) – An electronic device that allows consumers with accounts to perform financial transactions including the withdrawal of cash; generally known as a "hole in the wall" in the UK.

Card Not Present (CNP) – A card payment via mail order, telephone or online where the retailer cannot see the physical card.

CSP (Communication Services Provider)

DDOS (Distributed Denial-of-Service) – An attempt to make a computer resource unavailable to its intended users.

DNS (Domain Name System) – a hierarchical distributed naming system for computers, services or any resource to the internet or a private network.

ELMI (Electonic Money Institution Licence)

EMV (Europay, MasterCard and Visa) – A standard for Integrated Circuit Cards and their interaction with POS terminals.

eID (Electronic Identity Card)

EPC (Electronic Product Code) – A universal identifier that provides a unique identity for every physical object anywhere in the world.

FIPPs (Fair Information Practice Principles)

GSM (Global System for Mobile communications) – The dominant international standard for digital mobile telephony.

IPS (Identity & Passport Service)

ISP (Internet Service Provider)

KYC (Know Your Customer) – Requirements in the form of due diligence and banking regulation applicable to companies dealing with financial transactions. The goal is for them to identify their customer correctly in order to help prevent identity theft fraud, money laundering and terrorist financing.

MiFare – Contactless smart card technology based on the ISO/IEC 14443 Type A standards developed by Phillips.

MNO (Mobile Network Operator)

M-PESA – A mobile phone-based payment scheme in use in Kenya and now a number of other companies.

NFC (Near-Field Communication) – Wireless communication technology which allows data to be exchanged between two devices within a few centimetres each other.

NSTIC – National Strategy for Trusted Identities in Cyberspace.

Oyster – A contactless payment card used for train and bus tickets in the Greater London area of the UK.

P2P (Person-to-Person) – A financial transaction occurring directly between two people.

P2M (Person-to-Merchant)

PayPal – An online payment service.

PayPass (MasterCard) – The MasterCard brand for the contactless interface to their payment products.

PI (Payment Institution) – A new category of regulated financial institution created by the PSD

PIN (Personal Identification Number) – Usually a four digit number chosen by the user for authorization purposes when they try to access their account. The PIN is known only to the user and the system to allow a way for a machine to identify a valid account/card holder.

PKI (Public Key Infrastructure) -A set of hardware, software, people, policies and procedures needed to create, manage, distribute, use, store and revoke digital certificates.

POS (Point-of-sale or Point-of-service) – It can refer to a variety of definitions including the location of the retail establishment, or the specific counter, however it also could mean the hardware and software of the device used for the money transfer or (most often in this book) the terminal where the transaction occurred.

PSD (Payment Services Directive) – the legal foundation for the creation of an EU-wide single market for payments.

QES (Qualified Electronic Signature)

RFID (Radio Frequency Identification) – A family of technologies, which includes NFC, for zero-configuration data exchange between devices in proximity.

SCT (SEPA Credit Transfer) – The pan-European standard for "push" payments between bank accounts.

SE (Secure Element)

SEPA (Single European Payment Area) – A self-regulatory harmonisation project being introduced across the European payments market by banks with support from the European Commission (EC) and the European Central Bank (ECB). The SEPA initiative encompasses new, standard business and technical frameworks to make cross-border payments with the eurozone the same as domestic payments.

SIM (Subscriber Identity Module) – Is part of a removable integrated circuit card for mobile phones, the SIM cards securely store the keys necessary to identify the subscriber.

SMS (Short Message Service) – The mobile telecommunications network service used for text messaging.

SWP (Single Wire Protocol)

UID (Unique Identity Number)

USIM (Universal Subscriber Identity Module) – A software application for UMTS mobile telephony, which runs on a UICC (an analog of a SIM card) which is inserted in a 3G mobile phone)

VRM (Vendor Relationship Management) - A category of business activity made possible by software tools that provide customers with both independence from vendors and better means for engaging with vendors.

Index

2

2FA, 10, 78, 110, 174, 237, 254, 282

3

3D-Secure, 111, 254

A

All, 2, 5, 16, 39, 46, 55, 77, 80, 84, 86, 90, 104, 107, 121, 130, 146, 172, 183, 195, 200, 217, 219, 240, 258
Amazon, 26, 73, 179, 198, 248
Android, 125, 138, 149, 184, 214, 222, 225
Apple, 9, 11, 17, 42, 48, 70, 127, 135, 185, 214, 245, 250, 252
ATM, 37, 58, 59, 82, 83, 90, 101, 102, 103, 131, 132, 148, 155, 162, 230, 236, 238, 241, 260, 261, 262, 282

B

Bank of America, 91, 114, 137, 143, 199
Bank of England, 133, 233, 279, 280
Barclays, 14, 36, 37, 38, 42, 59, 61, 72, 78, 81, 118, 126, 166, 170, 194, 222, 237, 239, 257, 261, 262
Bitcoin, 231, 232, 233, 234, 235, 255, 256, 257, 258, 259, 260

C

card, 282, 283, 284
CCTV, 49, 51, 232
Centre for the Study of Financial Innovation, 27, 121, 194, 196, 245

cheques, 64, 84, 85, 86, 93, 94, 95, 106, 107, 108, 165, 210, 212, 214, 231, 266
chip and PIN, 26, 60, 65, 67, 109, 110, 150, 155, 240, 241, 254, 262
Consult Hyperion, 2, 5, 50, 84, 85, 91, 103, 106, 139, 145, 153, 154, 157, 159, 172, 202, 238, 242, 246, 266, 267
contactless, 10, 48, 59, 71, 79, 81, 91, 97, 98, 109, 110, 120, 126, 127, 128, 129, 130, 131, 136, 137, 138, 139, 140, 141, 142, 143, 144, 147, 148, 149, 150, 151, 152, 153, 154, 158, 159, 160, 161, 162, 163, 165, 168, 169, 170, 175, 187, 220, 221, 222, 223, 224, 225, 226, 242, 247, 250, 267, 283
credit, 11, 23, 25, 36, 38, 39, 40, 53, 55, 60, 61, 62, 64, 65, 66, 71, 72, 74, 76, 79, 81, 82, 92, 97, 99, 106, 108, 114, 118, 120, 121, 123, 125, 127, 130, 135, 140, 141, 143, 144, 146, 149, 152, 155, 156, 157, 158, 163, 164, 165, 166, 173, 176, 181, 188, 198,절204, 208, 210, 211, 213, 214, 220, 221, 222, 227, 228, 229, 236, 240, 247, 248, 255, 261, 262, 267, 269, 276
cybersecurity, 177

D

debit cards, 59, 92, 106, 119, 128, 141, 143, 144, 146, 159, 160, 165, 166, 186, 210, 211, 213, 214, 216, 217, 240, 275, 276
Deutsche Bank, 55, 124, 186
Digital Money Forum, 111, 128, 129, 148, 202, 208, 227, 246
DMV, 28, 29

E

eBay, 9, 33, 42, 113, 159, 208
electronic pickpocketing, 149, 150, 151
EMV, 65, 108, 109, 110, 111, 143, 144, 145, 146, 147, 153, 154, 173, 184, 214, 221, 224, 237, 238, 239, 240, 241, 242, 243, 282

F

Facebook, 18, 19, 20, 21, 22, 23, 26, 28, 34, 35, 36, 37, 38, 39, 40, 41, 42, 43, 44, 45, 46, 47, 49, 72, 73, 74, 75, 76, 77, 78, 83, 96, 110, 117, 139, 157, 180, 181, 182, 183, 202, 204, 252, 255
FBI, 8
fraud, 10, 16, 33, 38, 58, 59, 60, 61, 65, 67, 68, 74, 110, 114, 125, 145, 146, 155, 156, 161, 162, 167, 178, 225, 235, 236, 237, 238, 241, 247, 261, 262, 270, 273, 276, 283
FTP. *See* Future Ticketing Project
Future Ticketing Project, 151

G

Google, 18, 25, 26, 27, 28, 29, 41, 42, 45, 49, 68, 73, 74, 78, 79, 91, 117, 118, 125, 138, 149, 150, 156, 158, 168, 183, 184, 185, 214, 226, 227, 244, 247, 249, 250, 252, 254, 255
government, 7, 16, 21, 22, 24, 27, 28, 29, 30, 35, 43, 45, 52, 53, 68, 74, 84, 85, 86, 88, 98, 108, 113, 141, 162, 163, 164, 165, 171, 172, 173, 175, 177, 187, 202, 207, 210, 233, 235, 257, 259, 268, 269, 270, 274, 275
GSMA, 90

I

Identification, 29, 283, 284
identity, 7, 10, 11, 12, 14, 15, 16, 17, 18, 19, 20, 22, 23, 25, 26, 27, 28, 29, 33, 34, 35, 43, 44, 45, 46, 47, 51, 52, 53, 60, 61, 65, 79, 82, 89, 96, 98, 110, 111, 112, 149, 155, 162, 170, 171, 172, 173, 174, 175, 176, 178, 180, 181, 182, 183, 194, 195, 203, 204, 236, 252, 253, 254, 255, 282, 283
online identity, 174
theft, 19, 26, 33, 60, 61, 125, 149, 161, 227, 231, 252, 283
IMPF, 110
iPad, 133, 134, 136, 192, 208, 244
iPhone, 9, 16, 17, 59, 80, 118, 126, 136, 143, 147, 170, 192, 214, 249

K

KYC, 15, 52, 82, 87, 132, 166, 283

L

Legal Entity Identifiers, 13, 81
LEIs. *See* Legal Entity Identifiers
LinkedIn, 79, 113, 140, 181

M

MasterCard, 15, 37, 42, 122, 140, 142, 143, 144, 147, 153, 154, 155, 156, 165, 168, 170, 184, 222, 230, 234, 243, 246, 259, 262, 282, 283
MBNA, 37, 38
Mobile, 10, 11, 15, 29, 39, 53, 54, 56, 61, 62, 63, 69, 72, 83, 85, 87, 92, 96, 109, 112, 118, 123, 124, 125, 130, 135, 137, 138, 139, 158, 159, 184, 188, 192, 193, 194, 195, 206, 207, 212, 215, 220, 221, 223, 225, 226, 227, 228, 229, 232, 243, 247, 249, 250, 263, 264, 267, 282, 283
mobile phones, 284
Monitise, 85, 111, 220
Mpass, 55, 188
M-PESA, 15, 39, 41, 61, 62, 65, 70, 91, 94, 114, 115, 122, 184, 185, 189, 190, 207, 211, 228, 229, 263, 283

N

Nokia, 134, 161, 214, 251, 263, 264
NSTIC, 20, 28, 29, 32, 35, 110, 111, 113, 171, 173, 174, 175, 176, 178, 283

O

O2, 16, 36, 48, 62, 63, 80, 141, 161, 170, 184
OpenID, 253, 254, 255
Orange, 17, 54, 59, 63, 80, 91, 184, 185, 223
Oyster, 64, 124, 127, 152, 153, 154, 223, 283

P

P2P, 114, 258, 283
PAYG, 152
Payment Institutions, 123
PayPal, 9, 10, 15, 19, 39, 63, 69, 73, 76, 78, 83, 94, 96, 114, 118, 139, 159, 160, 185, 210, 211, 243, 248, 249, 250, 252, 253, 255, 283
PayPass, 143, 168, 184, 225, 283
personal data, 25, 176, 182, 200
PIs. *See* Payment Institutions
POS, 49, 54, 65, 71, 97, 98, 105, 109, 110, 119, 127, 132, 135, 137, 138, 144, 146, 155, 159, 168, 170, 186, 221, 222, 230, 239, 240, 241, 261, 282, 283
Post Office, 93, 94
prepaid, 13, 15, 16, 17, 49, 55, 63, 65, 68, 73, 83, 87, 88, 122, 124, 125, 128, 129, 130, 140, 143, 144, 147, 158, 160, 163, 165, 166, 170, 210, 211, 214, 215, 234, 261, 262
privacy, 7, 8, 22, 23, 24, 49, 50, 51, 60, 171, 177, 179, 180, 181, 182, 234, 235, 253, 255, 260

Q

QR codes, 30, 96, 139

R

RFID, 30, 49, 59, 96, 129, 161, 284

S

Samsung Tocco, 142
SEPA, 83, 108, 109, 111, 141, 186, 218, 284
SIM, 13, 15, 16, 35, 68, 69, 80, 184, 225, 284
Smart Card Alliance, 65, 108, 144, 173, 238
smartphones, 214, 221, 250
Social Media, 33
social media strategy, 35, 37
Sony, 47
Square, 71, 72, 97, 98, 118, 119, 120, 133, 135, 136, 137, 149
SWIFT, 13, 14, 82

T

taxes, 96, 108, 147, 148, 271, 272, 275
terrorist, 283
terrorists, 8, 15, 88
TfL, 148, 149, 150, 151, 152, 153, 154
transactions, 10, 12, 13, 14, 34, 35, 38, 40, 49, 54, 62, 67, 71, 72, 76, 86, 87, 88, 89, 105, 107, 110, 111, 112, 113, 115, 118, 119, 122, 125, 129, 130, 136, 139, 145, 146, 149, 151, 153, 157, 162, 164, 165, 171, 176, 186, 187, 188, 193, 194, 198, 208, 214, 223, 226, 232, 233, 234, 235, 236, 237, 239, 240, 241, 242, 249, 250, 255, 258, 262, 274, 275, 276, 277, 282, 283
transit, 15, 48, 65, 98, 132, 151, 153, 154, 157, 166, 167, 168, 265
Twitter, 9, 15, 25, 37, 43, 72, 118, 150, 204, 232, 252, 257
two-factor authentication, 78, 110, 174, 237

U

UK Cards Association, 169, 267

V

Verifone, 118
Visa, 23, 42, 52, 53, 63, 75, 97, 98,
    109, 110, 111, 120, 121, 126,
    134, 135, 136, 141, 143, 145,
    148, 153, 154, 155, 156, 165,
    166, 168, 184, 201, 215, 222,
    232, 238, 239, 240, 241, 242,
    243, 247, 248, 249, 259, 262,
    282

Vodafone, 35, 55, 62, 91, 228, 251
VPN, 9, 23

W

Wallet, 28, 29, 117, 118, 150, 156,
    158, 159, 168, 184, 243, 249
web, 10, 12, 18, 19, 20, 23, 25, 27,
    44, 45, 72, 73, 76, 86, 90, 119,
    136, 160, 162, 164, 166, 172,
    180, 181, 186, 195, 200, 204,
    245, 253
WebMoney, 15
World of Warcraft, 35, 72, 75, 182,
    254